Livestock and Equality
in East Africa

Livestock and Equality in East Africa

The Economic Basis for Social Structure

Harold K. Schneider

INDIANA UNIVERSITY PRESS   BLOOMINGTON AND LONDON

Dedicated to the four
pastoral people of East Africa who
did most to help me understand
their way of life:
Amatung and Ezikiel, Lisu and Simon

Manufactured in the United States of America

Library of Congress Cataloging in Publication Data

Schneider, Harold K.
  Livestock and equality in East Africa.

  Bibliography: p.
  Includes index.
    1. Ethnology—Africa, East. 2. Equality.
  3. Herders—Africa, East. 4. Africa, East—Economic
  conditions.   5. Africa, East—Social conditions.
  I. Title.
  GN658.S36   301.29'67   78-20400
  ISBN 0-253-19565-9   1 2 3 4 5 83 82 81 80 79

Contents

MAPS

TABLES

FIGURES

ILLUSTRATIONS

Preface

Although East Africa has probably been the most popular area of Africa for American readers, producing a large number of usually romanticized books, like the animal series by Osa Johnson and her husband in the 30s, the beautiful poetic volumes on settler life by Karen Blixen, the true adventure stories such as Miller's *Lunatic Express* on the building of the Uganda railroad, or the much earlier exploration volumes such as Thompson's *Through Masailand*, there have not been many ethnological introductions to the area, books that do justice to the indigenous people and their way of life. There have been many good volumes on individual societies, some mentioned in the first chapter, but few that sought an overview. Mair's *Primitive Government*, despite its title, is really about political organization in East Africa and is a useful introduction to that aspect of East African life. Huntingford, himself a settler before leaving to go to the School of Oriental and African Studies in London, attempted such an introduction in his *East African Background*, but the book, written during the Second World War, now seems severely dated by its then-fashionable tendency to patronize the Africans, a point of view Huntingford has since outgrown. More recently, Shorter's *East African Societies* is a much more up-to-date and adequate volume but very brief and somewhat ideological.

This book, which began as a general introduction to East Africa, a purpose for which it should still serve, is based on my research experience with the Pokot in 1951–52 and the Turu in 1959–60, as well as more than 25 years' contemplation of the East African ethnological situation. However, the structure of the book took a sharp turn as I studied the relationship between economy and society and certain unexpected but striking correlations emerged, correlations that will be fully explored in this book. These, throwing new light on the causes of state formation and the reasons for egalitarianism in heavily pastoral societies, captured the book, turning it into a treatise on hierarchy and equality as they relate to economy, a subject which seemed more important than a mere, possibly rather miscellaneous, introduction to East Africa.

But because of the change of focus, the book necessarily ignores many aspects of East African life that might otherwise have been treated. A major case in point is religion. I have no doubt that religion, like some of the other ignored topics, will eventually be brought within the scope of the thesis of the book, but I have contented myself, at least for the time being, with sticking to the area of most obvious causality and leaving religion for another time. Some aspects of social life which might otherwise have been inspected are also ignored or only partially treated. For example, the role of women and the way they respond to being treated as subordinate to the politics of men receives little attention. And I have treated East African societies pretty much as static, although the transformations in social structure implicit in the thesis suggest the obvious fact that these societies are not static.

Several people deserve special thanks for making it possible for me to get some kind of control of the East African literature, voluminous as it is. Especially important in this respect is Peter Little, who, despite the fact that he is still a graduate student, has the most impressive control of ethnographic literature of East Africa I have ever seen. Ivan Karp deserves thanks for introducing me to much of the most current literature over which he gained control through his recent studies of the Teso of Kenya, and also for his intimate knowledge of research and researchers in East Africa. Other than these, I owe a profound debt to those East African pastoralists with whom I lived who were gracious enough to take me seriously in my quest for understanding of the role of cattle in East African life, who revealed themselves to me as men and women rather than merely romantic figures. Of these I owe the greatest debt to those to whom the book is specifically dedicated.

Livestock and Equality
in East Africa

CHAPTER I

Ethnological East Africa

THIS BOOK BEGAN nearly thirty years ago with my introduction to Melville Herskovits, the great American Africanist, and his idea of the "cattle complex," which he published in 1926. Subsequently, after spending almost a year living with the egalitarian Pokot of northwest Kenya, among whom the cattle complex was dominant, I began puzzling in earnest over the question of why these people had no chiefs and what connection there might be between this and their disposition to place so much value on cattle.

In the perspective of time it is easy to see that a solution to my question was delayed by the dominant social and cultural anthropological paradigms of the era. On the one hand, cultural anthropology, as represented in Herskovits' cattle complex, was essentially noneconomic in its orientation (which is ironic considering that Herskovits is one of the foremost names in economic anthropology), focusing on the learned, exotic cultural aspects of cattle and society, even refusing to admit that the way cattle are utilized, as in the failure to make production of livestock for food central to animal husbandry, might have an economic interpretation. The explanation for how cattle and other livestock were handled, and for society in general, was to be found in idiosyncratic, divergent historical tendencies that were responsible for creating this charming African anomaly.

STRUCTURAL-FUNCTIONAL THEORY

More significant in delaying a solution to the question was the dominant social anthropological paradigm of the time, the structural-functional theory of Radcliffe-Brown. By 1952 the cultural theory of Franz Boas, as translated to me through Herskovits, was on the decline as the ideas of structural-functionalism, which had been dominant in Britain for some time, penetrated American thought. Africa was the research ground extraordinary of Radcliffe-Brownian theorists. By 1950 this school had already published the classic *African Systems of Kinship and Marriage*, edited by Radcliffe-Brown and Daryll Forde, containing brilliant papers by many of the leading structural-functional thinkers up to that time: Kuper, Wilson, Schapera, Gluckman, Richards, Fortes, Nadel and Evans-Pritchard. The book opened with a long introduction by the master himself, detailing some of the fundamentals of the theory of kinship and marriage as he understood them, illustrated from the papers presented in the book. All of these contributors had done significant field work in Africa, often long before 1950. Schapera had worked with the Tswana of southern Africa since the early 1930s, Evans-Pritchard had commenced his famous research with the Nuer of southern Sudan before the war, and Gluckman likewise had explored Lozi society of eastern Zambia since before the war.

Structural-functional attention to East Africa was slower to develop but was in full swing by 1950. Gulliver was beginning work on the Turkana, leading eventually to further research among the Jie of northeast Uganda and the Arush of northern Tanzania. Others whose work had been begun or completed included Aidan Southall on the Alur of western Uganda, Fallers on the Soga of northeast Lake Victoria, the Harrises on the Taita of northeast Tanzania, Reining on the Haya of southwest Lake Victoria in Uganda, Winter on the Bwamba of western Uganda, Beattie on the great kingdom of Bunyoro, and Middleton on the Lugbara of northeast Zaire, to name only a few.

Seen from my perspective, the thing characterizing almost all of these works was the insignificant attention given to economic facts. Structural-functional theory, as a kind of primitive system theory, was concerned with establishing the relationship of the various parts of society to each other, as in the claim, for example, that the rate of divorce in a society is a "function" of the structure of the domestic household such that where there is no house-property complex, in which each wife possesses her own house, fields, and other productive assets, the rate of divorce is higher because the wife is less thoroughly integrated into her husband's establishment. Such assertions did not require much quantification, although there was more attention to quantification of such things as rates of divorce, percentage of polygyny, and the like than to more mundane questions such as how much was exchanged in bridewealth payments or the rate of production of crops and livestock. The particular orientation of structural-functional thinkers is best illustrated by reference to bridewealth. Seldom were statistics on bridewealth given and when given they were usually superficial. Marriage, in the eyes of these theorists, was a "rearrangement of the social structure," not an economic event, and the amount of wealth passed over was less important than the structure assumed by the rearrangement.

RISE OF
ECONOMIC INTERPRETATIONS

Increasingly since the 1960s there has been a move to abandon structural-functional modes of thought. Jacques Maquet, whose research in Rwanda is well known, probably signaled the turn in the early part of the decade in a paper on "Objectivity in Anthropology" accusing structural-functionalists, with their representation of African and other societies as static, of imperialist bias because, as he saw it, this served colonial interests. Instead, he introduced, elsewhere (1972), a Marxian economic dimension to his analysis, in which he explained the rise of kingdoms in the savannah of Central Africa as due to the control of surplus crops by powerful individuals. But economic anthropology in Africa, especially in East

Africa, has never reached the level of sophistication to be found in other areas of the world, contenting itself, it seems, with the pseudoeconomics of cultural ecology, a kind of variant of structural-functional analysis. In other areas of the world social anthropologists have gone much further. Perhaps the most developed area is New Guinea, where anthropologists have been entertaining economic analysis in the context of study of social structure since after the war, notably in the writings of Richard Salisbury (1962) on the Siane, who explored the effects on social structure of the introduction of steel axes, which with their higher input/output ratios allow a reduction in the amount of time given to material production, leading to some increase in hierarchicization.

Sahlins' classic paper on "Poor Man, Rich Man, Big-Man, Chiefs," although (unlike Salisbury) fundamentally a Marxist argument, also deserves mention. His thesis will be explored in greater detail at the end of the book; but, simply put, Sahlins found the rise of hierarchy in Polynesia generally to be caused by variations in the ability to generate the resources necessary to sustain states, and this, in his view, kept many New Guinea people at an inferior, egalitarian, level, able to produce only big men and not chiefs. Sahlins' work is most illustrative of an often subtle bias in favor of hierarchy and of states that pervades African literature as well as the literature of anthropology in general, a bias which I shall discuss more fully later.

Leach's classic works on the people of Highland Burma had an economic slant from the start, which has recently been emphasized by the brilliant reanalysis of the Kachin material by Jonathan Friedman (1975), who argues that the rise and fall of states, oscillating between egalitarian (gumlao) and hierarchical (gumsa), can be explained by the way production of crops in a certain kind of ecological setting leads to positive feedback effects which create epicyclically steadily increasing degradation of the habitat and society.

On the question of states in East Africa, the structural-functionalists did not seem able to do much better than to suggest that they exist because they are functional for order, and on the question of the reason for egalitarianism they had little to say, preferring for the most part to ignore such systems. While Mair's classic study, *Primitive Government*, was an exception (she found the emergence of states to reside in the control of resources by select individuals), even she had little to say about the causes of egalitarian structures, probably because her economics is not a very large part of her thinking, and because she worked with the Baganda, one of the most highly developed states in East Africa, having little familiarity with the diffuse, stateless people to the east.

Thus, achievement of a higher level of analysis, equivalent to those reached in Oceania and southeast Asia and elsewhere, had to wait upon the appearance in African anthropology of researchers who were more willing to take up one type of economic approach or another.

Among the positive values of the structural-functional orientation was the development of sophistication in dealing with kinship terminology and lineage structure and the implicit separation of social structure from culture. American anthropology was inclined to treat society as merely another form of culture and to explain it, therefore, as subject to laws of diffusion and divergence, like language. Murdock, who is less guilty of this than most, was nevertheless prone to claim in works like his pioneering *Africa* that such social features as forms of descent, lineage structure, and states passed from one people to another. Structural-functionalists convincingly established that various social forms must be explained in terms of how they fit other forms in the social system, a point which also implicitly established the idea that such things as the state are situationally, not historically, determined. States rise where the conditions for them are right. A Nilo-Saharan dialect arises only as an offshoot of another Nilo-Saharan dialect and cannot be generated independently of it. Thus, over Africa the distribution of Nilo-Saharan dialects is almost entirely contiguous in pattern, speakers of one dialect living in conjunction with others of the same family. (There are, of course, occasions of isolation, such as the Nilo-Saharan Barabaig of central Tanzania, well removed from other

Nilo-Saharan speakers of their subfamily, but such exceptions are rare.) Over Africa the distribution of such things as kinship terminologies is much more discontinuous, Hawaiian forms being found heavily concentrated in eastern West Africa but also as far afield as in the societies of the Shambaa of northeast Tanzania and the Lozi of western Zambia. Thus, while it is true, as Maquet charged, that structural-functional theory presented African societies as static, and while there may be truth in the charge that the way English theorists saw African societies was in their class interest, it is also true, as in other systemic theories, such as economics, that static theories seem to be a necessary prelude to the development of more complex, dynamic theories, such as Friedman's modern Kachin analysis.

EAST AFRICA:
AGRICULTURAL AND PASTORAL ZONES

The definition of what constitutes East Africa is fuzzy. In its narrowest sense it often refers simply to the countries of Uganda, Kenya, and Tanzania. But in its broadest, and ethnological, sense it also includes the southern half of the Sudan, Ethiopia, Somalia, and Rwanda and Burundi, as well as a piece of the northeast Congo Basin in Zaire, and should exclude much of Tanzania (Map I). This latter definition is oriented not to colonial and modern national political relations but to the area of distribution in appreciable numbers of large domestic livestock, mostly cattle but also camels in the drier regions in north and northeast Kenya, Somalia, Ethiopia, and Sudan. It is one of the paradoxes of East Africa that while the general public thinks of it as the African habitat par excellence of large wild animals—large grazers like kudu, eland, hippos, and rhinos, and their large accompanying predators, lions, leopards, and cheetahs—ethnologically it is distinctive as the African region without parallel for large domestic animals. The paradox dissolves when we realize that both the wild animals and the domestics are sup-

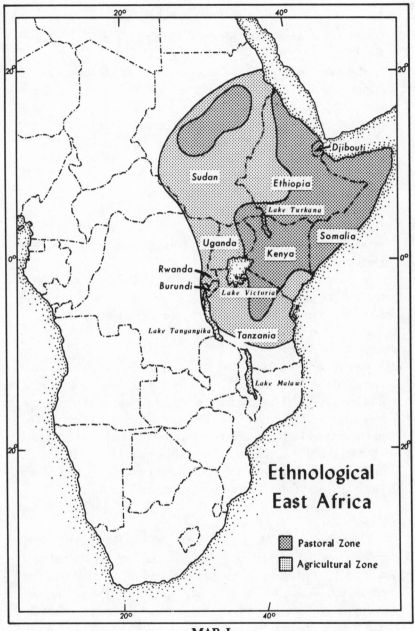

Djibouti

Sudan

Ethiopia

Lake Turkana

Uganda

Kenya

Somalia

Rwanda

Burundi

Lake Victoria

Lake Tanganyika

Tanzania

Lake Malawi

Ethnological
East Africa

Pastoral Zone

Agricultural Zone

MAP I

ported by the same often lush grasslands that characterize much of the region.

Much of Tanzania is in fact excluded from ethnological East Africa because it is infested with tsetse fly to such an intense degree that significant numbers of cattle are excluded. But, in fact, much of the rest of East Africa might also be excluded, as this study will show, because there the number of cattle which can be kept is proportionately too low to alter the fact that the people possessing them must be considered to be primarily agricultural, the impact of these animals on their social structure being minimal. Thus the definition of ethnological East Africa is to some extent arbitrary. But, as the reader will see, including the low-livestock and non-livestock areas in the discussion has advantages for development of my thesis.

Socioeconomically, East Africa may be divided into two regions: the first, predominantly agricultural, may be called the Agricultural Zone; the second, predominantly pastoral, the Pastoral Zone.

Agricultural Zone

This is the portion of East Africa, generally on the west and south, in which the ratio of cattle to people, if there are any cattle, is below 1 to 1 (1:1). Agriculture is the primary form of production for all the people of this zone. The area was characterized in precolonial times by the presence of hierarchical, state governmental systems, the size varying from petty village chiefdoms (as in parts of Ukimbu and Unyamwezi in western Tanzania) to large kingdoms (such as Bunyoro and Buganda in southern Uganda).

Pastoral Zone

This is the portion of East Africa, generally on the east and north, in which cattle, or their equivalents, camels, are maintained at a ratio of 1:1 or better. Agriculture is carried on by most of these people also. Only a few, such as the major part of the Somalis, are able to abandon it altogether. But cattle and camel production, combined with sheep and goat raising to a lesser extent, are the primary focus of production, and agricultural pursuits are subordinate. The people of this area are characteristically egalitarian and non-hierarchical, although those among whom agriculture is still an important secondary activity tend to emphasize lineage as a mode of social organization while the more nomadic pastoralists do not.

Although it is therefore possible to differentiate East Africans into two major blocks in terms of levels of large livestock production as they correlate with the appearance of egalitarian and hierarchical structures, other social features vary from this binary typology although they are not unrelated to the independent variable of large domestic livestock. East Africa may be characterized as having predominantly Iroquois, Omaha, and Descriptive kinship systems, although there are sporadic occurrences of Crow and Hawaiian. Iroquois is coincident with the poorest agricultural populations (generally in the south and west of that block) and Descriptive with the wealthiest of the pastoral populations (generally in the north and east of that block). Omaha is transitional, occurring both among the wealthier cattle-holding Agricultural groups and the southern and generally more agricultural Pastoral groups. As with the division into hierarchical and egalitarian types, it is a subpurpose of this book to try to cast some light on the reason for this kinship terminological distribution.

THE THESIS

The thesis which I shall pursue in this book may be briefly summarized as follows. The two major types of overall organization, hierarchical and egalitarian, depend on the kinds and amounts of resources produced (primarily crops and livestock) and the dynamics of their exchange. Critical to this are the volume of production and volume of exchange which, like the dynamic multiplier effect in economic systems, at some point transform the social structure as a reflex of transformation of the production and exchange activities. If all the constraints on production and exchange characterizing East Africa are held constant (if they are not, high cattle ratios may associate with states, as in Southern Africa), the transformation from hierarchical to egalitarian forms is effected by reaching a ratio of one cow or more per person (and a lesser ratio of camels, since camels are valued more highly). Where pastoralism (as a 1:1 ratio or better) occurs, egalitarianism results from the fluidity of this form of wealth and inability of any persons to monopolize its production. Where the rate of production of large livestock is lower than 1:1, i.e., in the Agricultural Zone, exchanges between people become characterized to one degree or another by submissiveness due to the monopolization of material resources, mainly land, by a few chiefs and aristocrats. Put another way, the egalitarian systems are monetarily inflationary and the hierarchical deflationary.

This outcome is heavily affected by certain ecological constraints of which the major is the distribution of tsetse fly, whose presence may not eliminate cattle production but severely limits it. To an appreciable degree, therefore, it is true that in Africa where there is fly there is hierarchy, or where there are flies there are states. But it should be understood that this holds only because East Africans, sometimes for obscure reasons, all value livestock as repositories of wealth above crops. This outcome is also heavily affected by the widespread availability of good grazing which makes land widely accessible to enterprising livestock entrepreneurs, preventing monopoly by a few.

The distribution of kinship terminologies is explained chiefly by the fact that, where land is essentially the only form of productive wealth of consequence, Iroquois terminology, suitable for arranging cross-cousin marriages, predominates because cross-cousin marriage is a form of political marriage adaptable to a strategy which will provide access to production resources. Where cattle are present in appreciable numbers, even below 1:1, Omaha terminology appears where land and agricultural production continue to be economically important. Omaha terminology defines coalitions of competitors attempting to control mobile wealth among people who are nevertheless anchored to small patches of land. Finally, Descriptive terminology arises among the more extreme pastoralists, reflecting the decline of kinship and expansion of personal mobility, as a rational reflex of the decline of land, through diffuse use, as an important constraint and the rise in cattle and camel ratios.

The need to establish the independent variability of culture and society rests on the need to make manifest the causal bases of East African social structures. Hoe agriculture is known to all East African people. This culture trait, therefore, has no direct causal relationship to the distribution of overall organization or kinship terminology. But variation in the way it is used and the way it is combined with herding, another cultural trait, must be understood in order to understand how social structure emerges as it does. How these culture traits are used depends on relations among people acting within the cultural framework they have inherited, including the way they value livestock compared to crops. These social patterns are therefore analytically distinguishable from culture. By comparing the ethnic groups which I call the Rift Anomaly, in the next chapter, I endeavor to show, by comparing variations in culture and social structure, how the relationship of cultural and social facts work themselves out in complex fashion to produce the types of social structure that characterize East Africa.

CHAPTER II

Culture and Society
in the Rift Anomaly

JUST TO THE north of central Tanzania there lies a cluster of societies which I have termed the Rift Anomaly (Map II) many of whom, like the Isanzu, are in the backwoods, seldom visited. But while they are of small interest to most people other than themselves they are of great interest to ethnologists. They are, in fact, one of the great curiosities of African anthropology. The reason is that unlike any other place in Africa this group of societies has at least one representative of every great African language family: Congo-Kordofanian (the Bantu branch), Nilo-Saharan, Afro-Asiatic, and Click.

The Bantu members are the Turu or Rimi, Iramba, Isanzu, Iambi, Mbugwe or Mbowe, Rangi, and Gogo. Incidentally, the Bantu language is characterized by prefixes denoting person, the prefix *mu-* usually indicating first person singular as in *mu-ntu* or "man," while such prefixes as *a-*, *ba-*, *wa-*, and *aba-*, as in A-rimi, Ba-ntu, Wa-nyaturu and Aba-tutsi, indicate plural, in these cases "the Rimi people," "men," "the Nyaturu or Turu people," and "the Tutsi people." However, it has become conventional in African ethnography to use Bantu prefixes inconsistently and erratically. For all of the Bantu people listed above the prefixes are ordinarily dropped, but under some circumstances one may find them referred to as Wagogo, Wanyaturu, Arimi, and so forth.

12

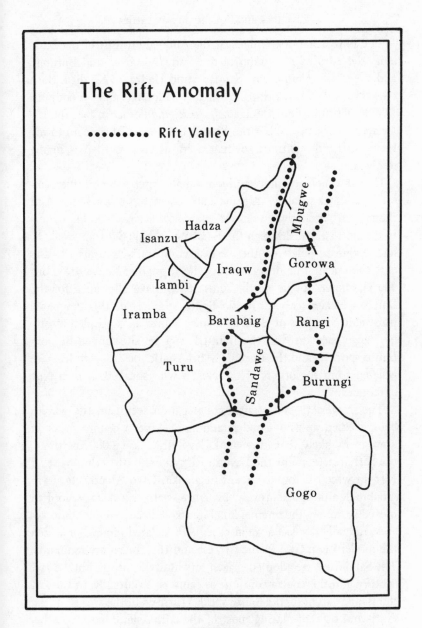

The Rift Anomaly

•••••••• Rift Valley

Mbugwe

Hadza

Isanzu

Iraqw

Gorowa

Iambi

Iramba

Barabaig

Rangi

Turu

Sandawe

Burungi

Gogo

MAP II

The Nilo-Saharan members of the Anomaly consist of the Barabaig, the Afro-Asiatic group of the Iraqw, Gorowa, and Burungi, and the Click group of the Sandawe and Hadza, or Kindiga. Both Newman (1970), writing about the Sandawe, and Woodburn (1970), writing about the Hadza, question whether in fact the latter are Click speakers, but the issue is not of special concern to my thesis so I will continue to treat them as such until it is finally resolved.

How did such an ethnographic anomaly arise? After all, the nearest other Click speakers are some 2,000 kilometers to the south. And the nearest Afro-Asiatic speakers, likewise, are some 800 kilometers to the northwest. Although the Barabaig, as Nilo-Saharan speakers, have linguistic relatives, the Maasai, comparatively nearby to the east, their nearest linguistic cousins, the Kipsigis of Kenya, are about 400 kilometers to the north. Thus, if we make allowance for the Barabaig-Maasai case, only the Bantu speakers of this group are proximate to others of their kind since Tanzania is peopled mostly by Bantu speakers. But the Bantu Rangi are surrounded by non-Bantu speakers and the Burungi, Afro-Asiatic speakers, are likewise isolated from the others of the cluster who speak their own type of tongue.

The mystery of this strange congregation seems on the way to being cleared up as our understanding of African history grows. It now seems likely that in ancient East Africa, say 2,000 years ago, the Rift area (actually the Eastern Rift, in contrast to the Western Rift, in which is found Lake Tanganyika, Lake Albert, etc.) was inhabited almost exclusively by Afro-Asiatic speakers, who had moved in among the original inhabitants—Click-speaking hunters—and gradually displaced them except for isolated groups, of which the modern Sandawe in their forest and the Hadza are remnants. The Sandawe have adopted a sedentary lifestyle only within the last century and the Hadza continue as hunters. Eventually, in the last thousand years or so, the Bantu speakers arrived in the area from the south and east, displacing most of the Afro-Asiatic family. As before, a remnant was left behind in the form of the ancestors of the present Iraqw, Gorowa, and Burungi, as well as a few other small groups in other parts of Tanzania. Then, lastly, Nilo-Saharan speakers pushed down into East Africa from the north, the spearpoint into Tanzania being the Maasai, while the Barabaig later broke off from their linguistic cousins in Kenya and moved to their present location.

Thus the anomaly is perfectly explainable and would be of no further interest to us were it not for the fact that this wide variation in cultural tradition within a small area provides a useful laboratory for developing our understanding of East Africa in general when cultural facts are placed against social. For it is a fact that crosscutting these cultural layers is a set of social characteristics demonstrating the independent variability of the social and cultural.

CULTURE THEORY

There have been two great traditions in modern anthropology to which ethnologists have resorted in explaining the behavior of the people they have studied. The first is the Boasian tradition, developed in America, which used as its central explanatory concept *culture*. Each identifiable society has a culture, a congeries of traditions (what Dawkins [1976] has recently labeled "memes," analogous to genes) handed down from the past and organized into a system. Boasians stressed the supposed systemic nature of culture because they needed to explain why a set of traditions coalesce in a single society. That the coalescence might to a large extent be an epiphenomenon of the formation of society, taken as a different phenomenon from culture, was overlooked due to the unquestioned assumption that society itself was a part of culture.

A feature of this cultural theory, largely unstated but inherent in the concept, was the idea that new bits of culture, also called knowledge or tradition, are sporadically and unpredictably invented. This has to be so in order to explain why new, distinct cultures tended to proliferate, rather like new species of animals which arise from mutations, and why societies that are most isolated from each other are the most culturally varied. The Click speakers are a case in point. The odd (to non-Click speakers) consonants of the Click languages evolved during the long isolation from other Africans of Click speakers and their ancestors. The degree of divergence they represent is a function of the degree of isolation from the Afro-Asiatic, Nilo-Saharan, and Congo-Kordofanian speakers, all of whom are historically less remote from each other. The only reason the members of the Rift Anomaly have not in turn, through convergence based on borrowing, become more alike is that they have been juxtaposed for too short a time.

The theory also explained why none of these people possessed such cultural traits as writing. Writing with a phonemic alphabet is a Middle-Eastern invention passed on to all the Western enclave of cultures after the Bronze Age subsequent to 3,000 B.C. But it never penetrated to the small, isolated enclaves that were African cultures during that time nor up to the great expansion in Africa that occurred after the introduction of agriculture and herding in the second and first millennia B.C.

The fatal flaw in the Boasian theory was its failure to separate culture and society. To put it simply, the theory so laboriously developed by Boas and American anthropology applied only to culture as such—to ideas, knowledge, and any kind of experience that can exist only if transmitted from generation to generation by contact between those who know a thing and those who have to learn it from them. This did not imply that people are largely uninventive, as some Boasians thought, so that new knowledge is rarely invented. But it did imply that most new ideas are relatively worthless and only a few survive the test of time to be cherished and jealously passed from parents to children or from experts to apprentices. Some human behavior, notably the way people group themselves for social action, seems to be situationally caused, arising whenever the circumstances are right. Thus, for example, the Turu organized male relatives according to the system of kinship terminology called Omaha after the Omaha Indians. No one can argue that the Turu got this system from the Omaha or vice versa. Similarly, Turu de-

A water pipe

scent is patrilineal, like the Tiwi of Australia, while Rangi descent is matrilineal, like the Iroquois Indians of North America. And the Mbugwe classify kin according to the Crow system also employed by the Crow Indians.

So, while the Boasians' theory could explain much that is true of this cluster, such as why all their houses are of a type called *tembe* (rectangular with mud roofs and walls) and why they speak related but separate languages, it cannot account for the pattern of social structure.

Like other good ideas, the culture concept was pushed too far. This can be illustrated by referring to what may be described as a chart of levels of behavior:

Animal
Mammalian
Human
Specific Culture
Personal

Some behavior present in all animals may undeniably be ascribed simply to the fact that they are animals. Animals motivate and animate themselves and they are mobile. Flora are normally immobile (or at least non-peripatetic) and have to be stimulated externally. Mammals have certain distinct traits that go along with their taxonomic differences from nonmammals. Perhaps curiosity is one of these. Scratching the ear with the hind foot is common to many of them. Humans, in turn, have some behavioral traits in common, among which are the habits of communicating by vocal symbols and weeping. Then each society or specific culture infuses into its members certain common traits. Americans, for example, are sometimes perceived by foreigners as aggressive, outgoing in some prescribed and unique way. Stereotypes are built on this fact. When we first see a person of another society we first see him at the cultural level, as a reserved Englishman or straightlaced German, and only begin to see him as an individual upon closer acquaintance.

The culture concept was designed to examine and explain the level of specific culture but in the end it came to deny that there are any kinds of behavior that are mammalian, animal, or human, in the behavior of members of specific cultures, just as it came close to denying that individuals have differences. All behavior was treated as cultural, a product of a supposed specific cultural system.

Applying the culture concept to the Rift Anomaly, after shearing it of these imperialistic aspirations, we find that, aside from the languages of its members, there is great difficulty in identifying cultural traits that are genuine local innovations except at the trivial or superficial level. The early German ethnographers, such as Reche (1914), whose commitment to the theory of *Kulturkreis*, which tried to map out the history of cultural invention and diffusion, felt that there was very little in the material culture of this region that was distinctive to it. The important culture of the Rift Anomaly societies, like most of the culture of the rest of the world's people, came from elsewhere.

This is not to say that nothing is original to any of the people. For example, most East African people have distinctive shield styles, arguing that although the idea of the spear and shield may have come from the outside it was everywhere refined and given a local touch. The great ideas, so to speak, are few and so seem everywhere always to have come from the outside. But the little ideas are many and accent the big ideas.

Then there is a further complicating problem. Culture is various, consisting of language, myths, technology, songs, art, and so forth. These are not invented or diffused in the same way. For example, language taken as a system of speech diffuses poorly. Neighboring people may borrow terms from each other, as the Turu may have borrowed the word for God, Mungu, from the Swahili, and then fused it to their own, Matunda, to produce Mungu-Matunda. But they do not ordinarily borrow the whole speech system. This can happen, as when one group thoroughly infiltrates a smaller one, but even then it is a difficult accomplishment.

In contrast, production techniques, such as pot making, spear manufacture, or basket making, perhaps because they are not as complex, can and do pass freely about. The result is that any particular society in the Rift Anomaly cluster displays its origin in its language, but the type of technology it possesses is indistinguishable, except for local accent, from that of other members of the group. All the people of this group, except for the Hadza, have some livestock, goats and sheep if not cattle. And there can be no doubt that these animals were domesticated in the Middle East about the sixth millennium B.C. from whence they diffused to this part of Africa. It seems likely that the Afro-Asiatic or Nilo-Saharan speakers brought them to East Africa and also developed the African breeds, such as the uncommon long-horned Sanga and the common humped Zebu.

A complication for this theory of cultural diffusion appears in the economic aspect of the use of knowledge. Reche, like others who leaned on the culture concept, worked with the assumption that if a people did not have a certain trait it was because they did not know about it. And they ranked culture traits in terms of assumptions about progress, making agriculture more "advanced" than pastoralism, so that possession of a certain supposedly primitive trait, such as a hunting and gathering technology, allowed them to determine the time dimension of diffusionary movements. A case in point is the Turu wooden-tipped hoe. In most parts of Africa, iron technology, which was introduced into the West African area about 500 B.C. and diffused from there, or which may have been diffused into the lower Congo Basin from the east coast, spread rapidly to produce iron-tipped arrows, spears, and hoes. Reche seems never to have considered the possibility that the Turu knew about iron-tipped hoes (as they did) but did not use them because to do so did not make economic sense. They are intensive agriculturalists who plant in sandy ground that can easily be turned with a hardwood-tipped hoe. On the other hand, iron heads were very expensive in precolonial days, when they were, in fact, used as money. To use them simply to appear to be progressive would not have made sense (although it would today when the status of a farmer in the eyes of the powerful might be measured by his degree of progressiveness). Similarly, if Hadza do not raise cattle this is not necessarily because they do not know how.

Whether the culturologist is a follower of Kulturkreis or simply a Boasian, this fact about the economic causes of the appearance or lack of appearance of certain culture traits is discomforting. It means that one has difficulty determining the cultural background of a people outside a resort to language or, perhaps, to some other area of culture, such as art style, which may be poorly known. The fact is that musical and art styles may be one of the most original and distinctive attributes of a society. Certain ethnographers who are skilled in the study of graphic and plastic art, dance, and music can identify the provenience of styles with great exactness. But, as with the culture of a society as a whole, in the end styles are either a composite of elements brought in from the outside or a mere gloss on a basic common form.

Among the cultures of the Rift Anomaly, then, we can identify the historical origins of the various groups by resorting to language, but outside of that there is little to go on. They all either have or know about agriculture and such crops as sorghum, finger millet, bulrush millet, and maize (to name only four of the most important); they all know about or produce pots and baskets (the Turu produce few pots, preferring to import them); they all build tembes (except, perhaps, the roaming Hadza); and they all used to make their clothes of leather.

Agriculture and cattle, sheep, and goat husbandry are techniques derived from the Middle East. On the other hand, banana culture came to East Africa from across the Indian Ocean, from the Far East, and although the people of the Rift Anomaly grow few bananas they probably know about them because they are grown in most places in East Africa where the climate is wet and the soil very fertile. The Portuguese brought maize and tobacco from America after the fourteenth century and now all grow tobacco and many grow maize (excepting, again, the Hadza). Cassava, also from America, has had poorer success.

SOCIAL THEORY

There are also *social* behavioral traits among these people. All of them place a degree of stress on kinship greater than people in most industrial societies. They tend in varying degrees to utilize unilineal concepts of kinship to form groups (clans and lineages); they practice polygyny to one degree or another; and they organize kin in various ways which are strange to Westerners. But in contrast to culture, these various social patterns have a kind of discontinuous distribution, as previously noted. That is to say, the social behavioral features vary independently of the cultural.

In order to show this we may now return to our Rift Anomaly societies and inspect certain correlations between social traits and cultural variation in the group, represented by language, as summarized in Table I. Four social features of these societies are identified: (1) descent: patrilineal, in which kinship is reckoned through the father only; matrilineal, in which it is determined through the

TABLE I

Crosscutting Cultural and
Social Features in the Rift Anomaly*

Society	Descent & Residence	Kinship Terms	Overall Organization	
Barabaig	P1/N or P	Omaha?	E	
Gogo	P1/P	Iroquois	E	ratio of
Mbugwe	Mixed	Crow	S	cattle to people
Iraqw	Mixed	Crow	E	1:1 or more
Turu	P1/P	Omaha	E	↑
Iramba	M1/P	Iroquois	S	↓
Rangi	M1/A	Iroquois	S?	ratio less
Hadza	M1/M	?	E	than 1:1

Key to Symbols:
Descent: P1 =patrilineal; M1 = matrilineal; Mixed =
mixture of patrilineal and matrilineal.
Residence: N = neolocal; P = patrilocal; A = avunculocal;
M = matrilocal.
Overall Organization: E = egalitarian; S = state.

*Sources for this information are: Klima 1970 (Barabaig); Rigby 1969
(Gogo); Gray n.d. (Mbugwe); Winter 1962, 1966, 1968 (Iraqw); Schneider
1970 (Turu); Woodburn 1970 (Hadza); Kesby n.d. (Rangi); and miscellaneous unpublished papers on Iramba.

mother only; and mixed, where both patrilineal descent and matrilineal descent are recognized for different purposes. The latter type is often referred to as double descent, connoting that patrilineality is used to descend one type of property and matrilineal another. But, in fact, the situation is not so clear cut in societies like that of the Wambugwe, where there are matriclans and patrilineages. According to Gray, a man inherits cattle from his father but also gets from his mother's brother the cattle his father paid to that person for the bridewealth of his mother. (2) Residence: neolocal, where the married couple set up residence away from either's parents; patrilocal, where they live with the husband's father; matrilocal, where they live with the wife's mother; and avunculocal, in which they live initially with the husband's parents but the children, when of age, leave to live with mother's brother; (3) kinship terminology, which indexes the way kin and affines (in-laws) are classified; (4) overall organization, whether egalitarian or hierarchical (state).

Inspecting the Table, the following examples of crosscutting will be noticed:

(1) Patrilineality occurs among Barabaig, Turu, and Iraqw (dominantly), each a member of a different language family, as matrilineality occurs among the Iramba and Hadza, also of different families.

(2) Omaha kinship terminology occurs among both Barabaig (by my guess) and Turu, of different language families, as Crow appears among both Iraqw and Mbugwe, also of different language families. Incidentally, that I am guessing that Omaha terms are used by Barabaig has no effect on the demonstration I am engaged in here. When we begin to look at the rest of East Africa we will find ample verification that Omaha crosscuts language family lines.

(3) Egalitarian structures occur among all four language families even though only Bantu speakers have states. But here again, when we look at all of East Africa we will see examples of states among the non-Congo-Kordofanian speakers as well.

Perhaps of even more significance is crosscutting complexes of traits: the Nilo-Saharan-speaking Barabaig are patrilineal, Omaha, and egalitarian, as are the Bantu Turu.

While social and cultural traits therefore crosscut, this should not be taken to imply that each of these has equivalent systemic status. The pattern of cultural features, such as the composition of vocabulary or technology, is a result of chance, there being little systematic relationship between particular word and tool complexes. That a Turu calls God "Matunda" has no necessary relationship to the fact that he builds a tembe house. He could as well build a grass-roofed house and still call God "Matunda." But there *is* systematic relationship between the social traits, the exploration of which is central to this book. This can be illustrated as follows: in Table I, I have arranged these societies in terms of the ratio of cattle to people, the highest at the top and the lowest at the bottom. The Barabaig have somewhere around 10 cows to a person, the Wambugwe about 2:1, the Gogo about 1.5:1, the Turu about 1.2:1, and the Rangi about .5:1. The number possessed by the Iraqw and Iramba is indeterminate, but based on various information I would guess that the Iraqw ratio is about equal to the Mbugwe and the Iramba and just above the Rangi.

What this arrangement murkily illustrates is a transformation in the general structure of society as cattle wealth increases, a transformation which will become much clearer as we look at the whole range of East African societies. The first thing to note is that petty, hierarchical states occur at the lower end of cattle wealth, allowing for the Hadza, whose egalitarianism, if it can even be called that, is based simply on a poverty of resources. And we must allow for the Wambugwe, whose circumstances, as we shall see, are special, producing the rare (for East Africa) combination of cattle wealth above .9:1 along with hierarchy. Otherwise, as cattle wealth rises to 1:1 or above, the systems generally become egalitarian and patrilineal with patrilocal or neolocal residence. The higher level of cattle wealth also generates Omaha terminology, except in the Gogo case (which I will discuss in a later chapter). On the other hand, the poorer cattle people, like Iramba and Rangi, along with chiefs, have Iroquois terms and matrilineality with patrilocal or avunculocal arrangements. The relative poverty of the Hadza accounts for the fact that they utilize matrilocal residence.

Despite the poor clarity of the transformation pattern shown here, that there is a pattern will be clearer from later chapters. It is ironic that in this small sample of societies we find not only the anomalous association of Iroquois terms and great cattle wealth among the Gogo, but also a further anomaly, two Crow societies in a sample of eight, whereas Crow otherwise is very rare in Africa, accounting for less than 3% of all known societies for which we have information. What we know about such societies in general indicates that the strong tendency to egalitarianism generated by cattle wealth is overcome by some strong bias in the distribution of cattle wealth, concentrating it in a few hands and thereby also promoting the appearance of Crow terminology, mixed descent, and hierarchy.

In sum, then, the systematic nature of social features' crosscutting culture is a function of basic economic facts concerned, in East Africa, with the level of large domestic livestock wealth as well as alternative forms of wealth such as land which dominate in the low level systems. In other words, of all the cultural features represented in East African societies, those concerned with production are extremely important for explaining social structure and will therefore receive primary attention, especially in Chapter IV on production and exchange. However, it is well to have an elementary grasp of the general culture form of East Africa in order to be able to maintain adequate separation of cultural and social features. To this task we turn in the next chapter.

CHAPTER III

Cultural Background

RECENT EXPLORATIONS in East Africa, particularly in the Lake Turkana (formerly Lake Rudolph) basin of northern Kenya and southwest Ethiopia, suggest that culture-producing men, probably of the Australopithecine variety, were already present in this area from 3 to 5 million years ago (Coppens et al., 1976). But while these little men were making pebble tools and are therefore part of the cultural history of East Africa, they are so remote from the East Africa of the last 3,000 years as to be irrelevant. They did not know the domestication of plants or animals, how to make and use iron tools, or, probably, even how to speak in ways comparable to modern beings of the type in which we are interested.

Up to the first millennium B.C. East Africa seems to have been chiefly a hunting and gathering ground for San-like (Bushmen), perhaps Click, speakers. About this time the first people with a domestic economy, husbandmen certainly of cattle and probably of sheep and goats as well, who most likely also farmed, appeared (Posnansky 1969; Clark 1970). These stone bowl users were probably the ancestors of the present Cushitic-speaking Afro-Asiatic family, of which the modern Galla and Somali are the main descendants but from whom the present Afro-Asiatic speakers in Tanzania are derived. This group contains our Iraqw, Gorowa, and Burungi of the Rift Anomaly, but also three other scattered groups, the Dahalo of the south Kenya coast, the Ngomwia south of the Sandawe, and the Mbugu of northeast Tanzania. These Cushites lived in the great

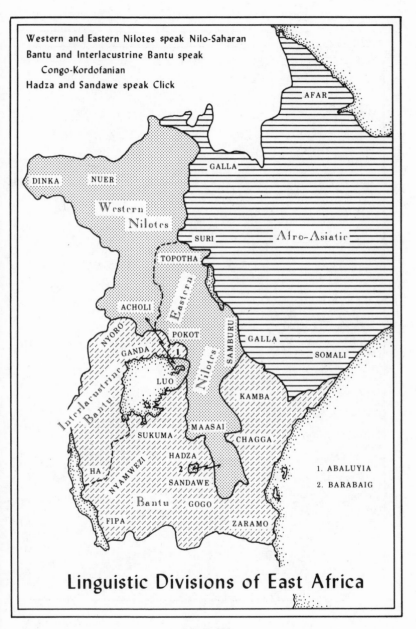

Western and Eastern Nilotes speak Nilo-Saharan
Bantu and Interlacustrine Bantu speak
    Congo-Kordofanian
Hadza and Sandawe speak Click

AFAR

GALLA

DINKA   NUER

Western
Nilotes

SURI   Afro-Asiatic

TOPOTHA

ACHOLI   Eastern

NYORO   POKOT   GALLA

GANDA   1   SOMALI

LUO   Nilotes   SAMBURU

Interlacustrine
Bantu   KAMBA

SUKUMA   MAASAI

HA   CHAGGA

NYAMWEZI   HADZA
                2
            SANDAWE   1. ABALUYIA
Bantu   GOGO   2. BARABAIG
FIPA   ZARAMO

Linguistic Divisions of East Africa

MAP III

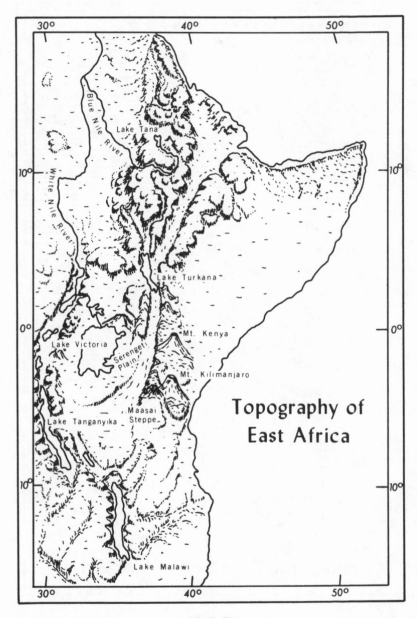

MAP IV

pastoral corrider now occupied mainly by Eastern Nilotes, shown on Map III, which also shows the present distribution of the Afro-Asiatic Cushitic speakers. This corridor can also be seen on Map IV, where it is represented by the eastern Rift Valley, feeding down into East Africa between Mounts Kenya and Elgon out of the Sudd and Kordofan of the Sudan.

These Afro-Asiatic speakers were probably responsible for introducing to the area not only the humped Zebu cattle, as well as goats and sheep, but also sorghum, finger millet, and bulrush millet which later Bantu populations acquired. They also brought in certain other culture traits, an important one of which was circumcision, a Middle-Eastern or Afro-Asiatic-speakers' custom which is still used as part of the initiation ceremony for men entering adult status in many of these societies. Circumcision for men and clitoridectomy for women are not universal in East Africa, but they are widespread.

These Cushites did not have iron, which was introduced into East Africa with the appearance of the ancestors of modern Bantu, coming from the southwest, west, and south. (Sutton [1969] thinks these Bantu did not appear until the first millennium A.D. but J. Desmond Clark [1970] is willing to associate them with the clearing of the Victoria Basin forests in the previous millennium.) The value of iron for production is that it is more efficient for bush clearing and hoeing as well as for warfare so that where it could be acquired it probably led to expansion of agricultural areas as well as to increased military power. However, it should be remembered that right up to modern times the production of iron in East Africa has been difficult, and it was so scarce that it was used as money until contacts with traders from the coast and with colonial governments resulted in the introduction of large quantities of iron.

Along with their iron these Bantu appear also to have brought bananas, which they probably got on the coast opposite Madagascar, an island populated by southeast Asian peoples that had migrated across the Indian Ocean. Finally, they appear also to have acquired cattle from the Proto-Cushites whom they encountered in place, a fact established by Ehret (1967), who shows that the words for cattle which the Bantu all the way from East to South Africa use were borrowed from Afro-Asiatic speakers. With these cultural elements the Bantu were probably able to set up indigenous production systems very much resembling those of modern, precolonial times, except that they lacked maize, which only came with the Portuguese after the fourteenth century. Maize, as we shall see, has important economic effects because it generally leads to increased output relative to labor costs, but its effects in this respect are not so revolutionary as bananas and cassava.

At the present time the distribution of Bantu in East Africa shows relatively recent expansion and fragmentation. For example, Shorter (1973, 41) derives the Nyamwezi, Kimbu, Iramba (and therefore all the other Rift Anomaly Bantu), Bungu, Hehe, Bena, and Nyakyusa from the ancestors of the Sagara on the coast (see Map V). The Gogo, on the other hand, relate to the Eastern Tanzanian matrilineal people such as Kaguru and Luguru. The Kikuyu and probably the Abaluyia Bantu of western Kenya seem also to be related to coastal people like the Giriama near Mombasa.

Sometime after or perhaps simultaneously with the Bantu expansion there began an expansion of early Nilotes from the north. The earliest of these appear to have been ancestors of the present so-called Kalenjin (the Nandi, Kipsigis, Pokot, Barabaig, Sebei, etc.) who also occupied the Rift corridor over a thousand years ago, replacing the previous Cushites who left the remnants I mentioned. Later the ancestors of the present Maasai expanded out of central Kenya and in turn displaced the Kalenjin, leaving the Barabaig and a few other remnants at the southern end while the main mass continued to occupy the western part of Kenya.

NILOTE EXPANSION

Because they are important to the analysis later in this book, we must also take the time to look in some detail at subsequent expansion of Nilo-Saharan speakers other than the Eastern Nilotic Kalenjin and Maasai. The Western Nilotes grew out of the Lwoo, a group in the southern Sudan south of the Nuer and Dinka, who also are members of this general group. Pushing down into East Africa, the Lwoo were responsible for a deep penetration into Eastern Nilotic and northern Bantu groups resulting in the Luo of extreme southwest Kenya and the Padhola of southeastern Uganda, as well as the Lango, Acholi, and Alur further north in Uganda. These latter, so-called River–Lake Nilotes, also enter the story of the rise of the interlacustrine Bantu states, as we shall see.

The rise of the interlacustrine states is complicated by the fact that much is remembered about their origin in myth and legend but the information is tantalizingly insufficient. What appears to have happened is that sometime more than one thousand years ago this interlacustrine corridor between Lake Victoria and the western Rift (see Map IV) was occupied by cattle-keeping Bantu organized as segmentary lineages. Lambrecht (1964) thinks this area must have been free of tsetse fly at that time and so invited penetration by people of the north looking for more grazing room or, as I would put it, seeking to expand production of livestock. These invaders, called Chwezi, and reputed by some to have been Cushitic speakers, probably mingled with the Bantu rather than forcing them out. Subsequently, the rise of population and press for space led the cultivators to cut into the forests, thus creating conditions in the newly-formed open land for the invasion of the area by tsetse flies. As a result, cattle populations would have been reduced, and, by a process explained in detail in later chapters, the groundwork laid for the rise of states and further population expansion. In fact there arose the Bachwezi state, whose symbol was drums. Subsequently, the Lwoo penetration led to the founding of a new state, called Kitara, ruled by the Bito clan. Kitara did not occupy all of Buchwezi (the prefix *bu*, *ru*, or *u*- affixed to the noun base indicates "the country of"); Bunyankole and the states of Rwanda (Ruanda) and Burundi continued to maintain their previous dynasties. But Kitara did contain most of the interlacustrine area including the modern Bunyoro, Bunyankole, Karagwe (in Tanzania), and north Rwanda. Kitara in turn evolved into the pre-modern state of Bunyoro, which in turn

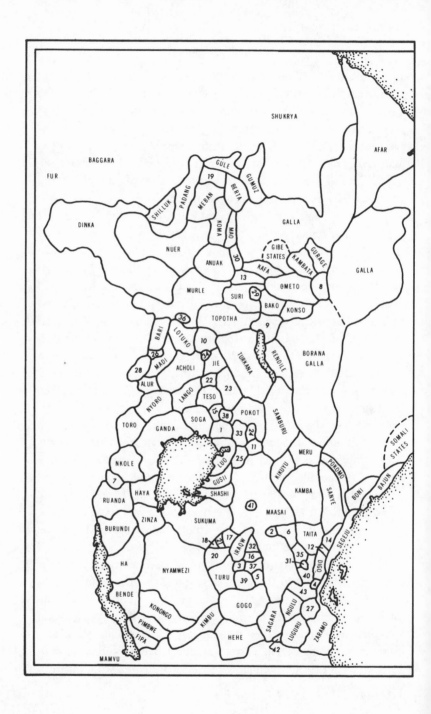

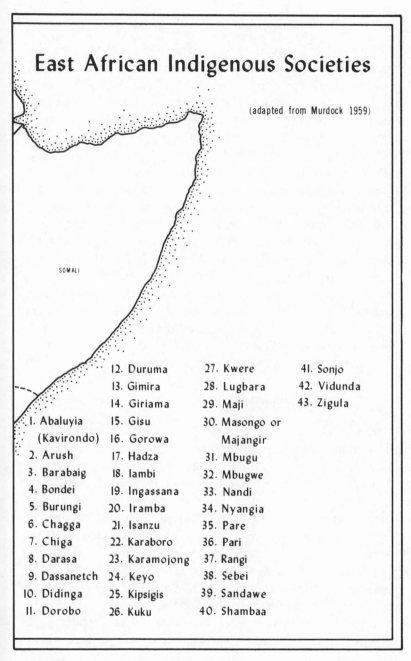

East African Indigenous Societies

(adapted from Murdock 1959)

SOMALI

1. Abaluyia
   (Kavirondo)
2. Arush
3. Barabaig
4. Bondei
5. Burungi
6. Chagga
7. Chiga
8. Darasa
9. Dassanetch
10. Didinga
11. Dorobo

12. Duruma
13. Gimira
14. Giriama
15. Gisu
16. Gorowa
17. Hadza
18. Iambi
19. Ingassana
20. Iramba
21. Isanzu
22. Karaboro
23. Karamojong
24. Keyo
25. Kipsigis
26. Kuku

27. Kwere
28. Lugbara
29. Maji
30. Masongo or
    Majangir
31. Mbugu
32. Mbugwe
33. Nandi
34. Nyangia
35. Pare
36. Pari
37. Rangi
38. Sebei
39. Sandawe
40. Shambaa

41. Sonjo
42. Vidunda
43. Zigula

MAP V

fragmented to give us the collection of interlacustrine states that were there when European colonists arrived.

Most of this prehistory is known from linguistic evidence combined with archaeology and human paleontology, with the exception of the history of the interlacustrine states, which is augmented by oral data in the form of myths and legends. However, our thesis allows us to make some deductions about events for which there is no direct evidence. One such conclusion concerns the rise of the Chwezi state due to reduction in cattle herds by tsetse fly. A more general one is that because all the components of African economy and society which determined their form up to the present period were already present, excepting long-distance trade with Arabs and Europeans, in all probability East Africa for the last 2,000 years has been an area composed of at least petty states and egalitarian societies, the states appearing in the areas dominated by agriculture and the egalitarian in dominantly pastoral regions, most notably the western Rift corridor, the Sudan, and the Horn of Africa. The cultural personnel and tribal designations have changed, but the political and economic facts have remained constant.

THE SOCIETIES OF EAST AFRICA

The societies indicated on Map V are those delineated by Murdock in his volume *Africa, Its Peoples and Their Culture History* (1959). In recent years there has been a good deal of criticism of tribal maps of this type (Shorter 1974) on the grounds that "tribe" is a patronizing term and because there were often no distinct boundaries between these societies anyway. I sympathize with the first criticism and will avoid the term tribe, substituting for it society or ethnic group. The second criticism, I think, is overblown. It is true that the designation of societies on Murdock's map is sometimes arbitrary. For example, the Ometo seem in fact to be a collection of independent societies and the term Maji seems to represent a whole group of societies, like Mursi and Bodi, which might otherwise be thought of as independent. And even the Turu, whom

I know well, could be argued to consist really of three relatively independent societies, the Wahi Wanyaturu, the Wilwana Wanyaturu, and the Anyinganyi Wanyaturu. Information on ethnic groups
has been poorest in the area of Ethiopia, particularly the southwest
where the Ometo, Suri, Maji, and others are located. In recent years
a number of researchers have penetrated this area, giving us much
better ethnographic information. Notable examples are Turton, writing on the Mursi, and Almagor on the Dassanetch or Reshiat. But
it will be a long time before that area is sorted out. Nevertheless,
the societies designated on this map are for the most part established in that form in the literature and will therefore serve for purposes of this book.

The total number of such societies as delineated here is about 105,
depending on how they are counted. The reader newly introduced
to East Africa should be aware that the designation of ethnic units
is complicated not just by the fact that lines between them are often
obscure, but also by the multiple names assigned them, sometimes
for trivial reasons. There is hardly a group of people in East Africa
that is not referred to in the literature by more than one name. For
example, the people now usually designated as Pokot were and sometimes still are called Suk. And the Shambaa are also called Shambala (a normal Bantu alternate pronunciation for words ending in
-aa.) Murdock performed a valuable service in *Africa* (1959) by
attempting to discover and list all cognates. Unfortunately, in the
last twenty years even more alternatives have cropped up. For example, Murdock found it convenient to represent the Somalis in terms
of subtypes including Ogaden, Sab, etc., but I have counted them as
only one unit. If we take 105 as the number then East Africa, ethnologically, represents about one-sixth of the total number of African ethnic groups as Murdock counts them.

EAST AFRICAN LANGUAGES

In East Africa today the distribution of the great African language families (Map IV) is such that the whole of the Horn of

Africa, all of Ethiopia, and much of northeastern Kenya is occupied by Afro-Asiatic speakers, most of them Cushitic speakers, although the dominant Amhara of the Ethiopian plateau speak Semitic. In contrast to Bantu and even, to a great extent, to Nilo-Saharan speech, it sounds very guttural to the English ear. Nilo-Saharan speakers are most particularly represented in the eastern Rift Valley and along its sides in northern Tanzania and all of Kenya, but they are found also in northwestern Kenya and most of northern Uganda. The Bantu speakers occupy most of Tanzania except for the Rift Valley, central and western Kenya, and all the southern and south-western part of Uganda, where they are known as the Interlacustrine Bantu. Bantu is distinct from Afro-Asiatic and Nilo-Saharan be-cause of its general euphoniousness, derived from its almost un-broken consonant-vowel alternation, normally ending, as in Italian, with vowels. All of these languages are tonal to one degree or an-other but tone, used phonemically, never seems as complicated as in some places in West Africa.

The only other thing that needs to be said about East African languages is that due to the nature of Bantu/Arab contact on the coast over the last several centuries, there has arisen a lingua franca called Swahili, fundamentally a Bantu language but heavily infused with Arabic words (Arens 1975). Swahili today is very widely spoken, especially in Tanzania and Kenya, and has been declared the national language of Tanzania. But the extent to which it ac-tually operates as a second language should not be exaggerated. It is most commonly used by indigenous Bantu speakers, like the Kikuyu and coastal Bantu of Tanzania. Non-Bantu speakers are often not comfortable with it and even many upcountry Bantu do not control this lingua franca very well.

TECHNOLOGY

I have already given some indication of the technology of East Africa (or perhaps we should say industry, as Kenyatta [1962, 68] does), that aspect of culture which seems to honor no ethnic boundaries. Kenyatta, as a student in the 1930s, wrote his account of the Kikuyu based on his experiences as a child and young man. In his discussion of Kikuyu technology he lists the following: smelting and working of iron to make spears, swords, digging and clearing knives, ear and finger rings, arrow heads, bracelets, axes, delicate chains, hammers and tongs, tweezers and a few other items; round, thatch-roofed houses with wooden walls; bows and arrows; clubs and knob-kerries of various types; slingshots; shields; pottery; baskets of different shapes and sizes; woven trays; skins for leather clothing (soft and thin for women, heavier for men); and musical instruments of various types. With some variations, all of these things could be found over the whole of East Africa. But to this list we would want to add other things not ordinarily thought of as industries but which nevertheless constitute part of the basic production system of people: livestock, including cattle, sheep, goats, and camels, in some places; chickens (but not pigs, which East Africans generally dislike); crops of great variety of which the most fundamental are sorghum, finger millet (eleusine), bulrush millet (pennisetum), maize, bananas, gourds, and others which will be mentioned in the next chapter. We should even include in this list various kinds of underground habitations designed for protection when under attack, especially the subterranean hideaways of such people as Chagga and Iraqw as described by Clarke (1960, 65); irrigation systems (apparently inherited from the early Cushitic inhabitants of East Africa); deep wells in some arid regions; war organization; and even certain very localized techniques for hunting and gathering, such as the elaborate traps constructed by such people as the Pokot for collecting the colonizing white ants (termites) that spawn at the beginning of the rains and that are considered to be a delicacy. Except for the main and widely spread techniques, there are in fact too many things to be able to mention. Each East African society, to some extent, has a technology of its own, suited to its own particular set of circumstances. To cite a case, the Turu and some other people of central Tanzania have a kind of tool for which there is no English name. They call it a *nyengo*, a combination of axe, machete, and adze,

Bulrush millet

sorghum

finger millet

consisting of a large curved blade hafted on a buttressed handle, which is used for everything from cutting down a tree, to trimming it, to hacking out a desired portion for some objects such as a stool, to the final finishing of the stool.

So widespread are many of these techniques that it is safe for us to work with the assumption, as I said in the last chapter, that any one of them could be used by any East African people if they desired. Their distribution is limited only by choice. This point deserves to be underscored. If we start with the main crops, it seems plain that whether a certain people stress any one of them depends on the conditions under which they must work. Bananas have a very limited distribution because they require lots of moisture and a very fertile soil. Hence, not many East Africans grow bananas, but they can be found growing on most of the mountains, along the sea coasts, on the north and northwest shores of Lake Victoria, and near the other inland bodies of water. Bulrush millet is the most drought resistant of the traditional grain crops so it is found growing in marginal rainfall areas, mainly in the area of the Wembere steppe south of Lake Victoria. Finger millet is scattered all over East Africa, wherever rainfall is comparatively more generous than for bulrush millet. Maize has a narrow distribution simply because it likes a good deal of water in the early stages and this condition is of limited occurrence.

This point can be brought home with more force if we consider the plow. Plows were not used in East Africa before the colonial era (and then only sparsely until the nationalist era) except in the Ethiopian plateau. It is a main tool of cultivation for Amhara peasants and some Somali and Galla. It is tempting to assume that this limited distribution is due to lack of opportunity for diffusion, but this does not seem credible. Although their location on the high plateau, averaging perhaps 8,000 feet, gives the Amhara a certain isolation, there is plenty of opportunity for contact between them and the Afro-Asiatic speakers down below on the south and east and the Nilo-Saharan speakers on the west. Consideration of the economics of plow use by economists (Boserup 1965) and economic historians (Hopkins 1973) have led to the conclusion that where labor is the critical constraint on production relative to land and capital, as it is in the Agricultural Zones of Africa, it is not economical to invest in capital goods like plows unless the marginal productivity of labor falls too low, as apparently it did not in Africa in the usual circumstance. Combined with this we must consider the fact that since the Agricultural Zone was in tsetse area, and since oxen are needed to pull plows, plows were not feasible. In the Pastoral Zone economics dictated that inputs into cattle and camel production are more rational than into capitalizing agriculture. Hence the plow was apparently limited to the Ethiopian plateau, where oxen could be kept but not in large numbers and where high population concentrations may have led to such a decline in the marginal productivity of labor that the plow became feasible.

Cattle, as Map VI indicates, are unevenly distributed over East Africa. The heaviest concentrations are on the northeast and southeast of Lake Victoria. This is explained by two facts. On the one hand, as the map shows, large areas of East Africa are infested by tsetse fly making them essentially uninhabitable for large numbers of cattle, which die of sleeping sickness when bitten by the variety of fly inhabiting these regions. Tsetse fly is limited in its distribution by temperature, relative humidity, and rainfall, as well as by the presence or absence of proper bush cover, but despite these relatively narrow limitations it is able to find habitation, especially in Tanzania. Furthermore, its distribution fluctuates over time. Large areas of Sukumaland southeast of Lake Victoria have been cleared of tsetse in this century, and the consequent increase in cattle population, has had an important influence on social structure. On the other hand, the Haya area of southwest Lake Victoria has been infected in the last century, as has the main interlacustrine area in earlier times. And in some places, such as Dodos County of Uganda, where the Jie live, tsetse infestation has grown and declined from time to time (Deshler 1960), just as present warfare is encouraging its resurgence in parts of Somalia.

The distribution of cattle also reflects varying grazing conditions.

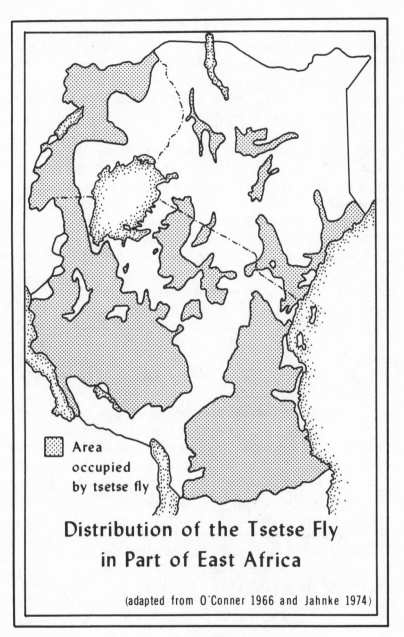

Area
occupied
by tsetse fly

Distribution of the Tsetse Fly
in Part of East Africa

(adapted from O'Conner 1966 and Jahnke 1974)

MAP VI

The Kipsigis, for example, live to the northeast of Lake Victoria and are able to keep over 200,000 head of cattle within a small area. Contrast that situation to the one faced by the Turkana to the west of Lake Turkana, where semidesert conditions severely limit the number of beasts per square mile. This does not mean that the Turkana are poorer than the Kipsigis; merely that they must range over a much wider area to feed their cattle. Thus the Kipsigis traditionally were largely sedentary in their grazing methods while the Turkana were quite nomadic, but the Turkana have a much higher cattle/man ratio.

These East African cattle, according to Payne (1970, 65), are the result of countless cattle migrations and mixings so that attempts to classify them into breeds on the basis of such things as horn types and humps are hopeless. Nevertheless, they are generally humped, with the exception of some humpless types in the interlacustrine area, and they are classified as Zebu, whose characteristics also include their relatively small size (Payne 1970, 146) and variations in color and patterning. Exceptions are the larger Boran of the Borana Galla and the Karamojong cattle. The former, besides their larger size, tend to be white, grey and red, or pied and are humped. The Karamojong are red, roan, or grey and white with larger horns than Zebu, sometimes lyre-shaped, but also humped. Another prominent type is the Sanga, now mostly to be found in the interlacustrine area, particularly among the Ankole and in Rwanda, which tend to long horns and humplessness. Payne feels (1970, 49) these were once dominant and that the present Zebu dominance is relatively modern. Incidentally, the present cattle industry in Kenya is based on bred-up Boran cattle.

As Herskovits understood as far back as 1926, when he published his article on the cattle complex, East Africa is the center of indigenous African livestock production. Some East African societies are enormously rich in cattle and sometimes camels. For example, the Tanzania Maasai in recent years were reported to have 1,100,000 head of cattle for a population of 78,000, the Somali 775,000 camels for a population of 264,000, and the Borana Galla 330,000 cattle and 340,000 camels for a population of 68,000. The ratio of cattle to people among the Tanzania Maasai is therefore 14:1, while the others are also very high. Not all these societies are so rich. As I said earlier, the ratio of cattle to people sufficient to make a significant difference in their social structure is no more than 1:1. Most East African pastoral people, as I earlier defined pastoral, have nearer this figure than that of the Maasai.

Herskovits summarized his view of the cattle complex in these terms (1926, 264–265):

> In East Africa, where currency in any form is absent, cattle con-
> stitute an almost exclusive hall-mark of wealth. The subsistence
> economy of these tribes is based on agriculture; but the number of
> cattle owned by a man correlates highly with his position. That is,
> among these people, as in most societies, position is related to
> wealth and cattle are the sole expression of wealth. It is of no con-
> sequence how much cultivated land or other goods a man possesses,
> for should he not have adequate resources in cattle, he can have no
> place of respect in his society. . . . Notwithstanding this, cattle can
> in no sense be considered money; for nothing can be acquired with
> them except wives, and a long time has elapsed since competent
> students have held to the earlier naive concept that the giving of
> cattle by the family of the suitor to a family of his bride constitutes
> an act of wife-purchase. A cow is eaten only on certain ceremonial
> occasions, or when an animal dies; nor have cattle any other sub-
> sistence utility aside from that of supplying milk, since they are
> never employed as beasts of burden. They are merely possessed and
> esteemed for the prestige their possession brings. But they are not
> money.

This passage, which has been proved wrong in many respects (cattle are money, they are used for subsistence, and they are eaten some-times on other occasions) still conveys a feeling for the special role that large livestock, especially cattle, play in the cultures of these people. Whatever their economic values, they are also often viewed as esthetic objects. Maquet demonstrates this by paraphrasing Andreas Kronenberg's account of the relationship of man and beast in Longarim, one of the Nilotic Murle group of the Sudan (Maquet 1972, 123):

> Among these pastoralists . . . a young boy at the end of his puberty chooses a calf which will become his favorite animal. To tame it, he rubs its back with cow dung every day. Thus begins a long process of identification between the man and animal. The identification will be more or less intense depending on whether or not the calf will one day be castrated. When it gets old, if it has been castrated, the ox is slaughtered and eaten by its "father" at a ritual meal with his age-mates, and is replaced. The favorite bull, which has not been castrated, is never killed, except on the tomb of its "father," and a man may have only one favorite bull in his lifetime. The man is often called by the name of his favorite bull, and in time his own name is forgotten. When a favorite bull fights with another animal, his "father" must kill the latter immediately, and when two favorite bulls fight the "fathers" must also fight. When the bull dies its "father" exposes himself to various dangers in the hunt or in battle; he must wear mourning as for the death of a close relative; he sometimes even commits suicide.

To this may be added that among such people as the Pokot the horns of the cattle may be deformed to enhance the animal's appearance, and a man composes songs about his favorite ox which he sings at public events.

Goats and sheep are important secondary livestock throughout East Africa, but that they are considered distinctly inferior to cattle and camels cannot be overstated. When calculating ratios for exchange of sheep and goats (which look alike because the sheep are hairy, like the goats) the animals usually are aggregated as "goats" and equated to cows (i.e., female adult cattle) at a rate of five or ten "goats" to a cow. Thus a goat is perceived as, at best, worth only one-fifth of a cow or even as little as one-tenth. Although these small livestock are aggregated for purposes of calculation, they are differentiated for some purposes. The sheep is a more sacred animal than the goat and is therefore used rather than the goat in some kinds of rituals such as Pokot purification of adulterers. However, goats may be sacrificed just like cattle on occasion. On the other hand, goats are more likely to be slaughtered for food just for the sake of meat.

Skin or leather clothing, made usually from goat and sheep hides, once very widespread in East Africa, was one of the first traditional industries to go under. Today only a few people still use skins, while cotton cloth has been worn first by the men and then by women for a very long time in some places. Before this new cloth overran East Africa it was produced, apparently, only by the Fipa on the southeast shore of Lake Tanganyika; in all probability they acquired the knowledge of cotton growing and weaving from Arabs who were passing through that area from the coast as early as the eighteenth century. Other than that, the only material for clothing was bark cloth, a kind of manufacture which came with southeast Asian contact and was practiced mostly by the Baganda. Bark cloth is expensive to produce but the Baganda had the labor for it due to the low cost of banana production, and the incentive to produce it since they had comparatively few livestock.

Organized warfare seems to have been confined to only certain East African peoples and reflected special circumstances. The Baganda kingdom is described by Wrigley as having been essentially a war machine (Wrigley 1964) designed to plunder its neighbors in the absence of anything to trade with them for women, cattle, and other goods which they desired. Other than Buganda, the most military of East African societies were probably the egalitarian ones with large cattle or camel populations, and even among them organized warfare (excepting simple raiding) was most common among only the Maasai and Nandi and others of the southerly Eastern Nilotes. Huntingford (1950, 59–60) describes the Nandi war organization, which he knew well:

The tribe was divided into 16 regiments, called *Pororiet*, which was also the name given to the area in which the regiment lived, and this area was divided into parishes, *Koret*, which were sub-divided into sections, *Sirityet*. Each section was in charge of an officer called *Kirkit ap sirityet*, "the bull of the section," or *Kiptaiyat am murenik*, "the leader of the warriors." Thus the regimental area called Tepingot could raise some five hundred fighting men, who came from 27 parishes, and were formed into eight sections (*siriyet*) of about sixty men, each under its Section Leader (*kirkit*). The two senior of these leaders, together with the older men who represented the civilian population, formed the *Pororiet* council, and two of the senior men in the council were called *Kiruogik* or Councillors. These two discussed the details of a raid with the two senior Section Leaders, who as members of the council were called *Kipaiyat*, and met the representatives of the Religious Head of the tribe, the *Orkoiyot*, who was the "sanctioning authority" for any kind of warfare and had two members of his own council (men called *maotik*) in each regimental area. When the *maotik* had talked things over with the regimental officers, they went to the *orkoiyot* to ask for his sanction to carry out the raid, and unless a raid had been sanctioned in this way, it could not succeed. Each *pororiet* acted and raided on its own, unless two or more combined temporarily for a big affair. There was no central unifying authority other than the magico-religious influence of the *orkoiyot* and it should be noted that the magico-religious aspect is prominent. No raid could take place without sanction from the proper authority and this must go through the proper channels. The fighting men formed about 15–20 per cent of the whole tribe, and all the males of the tribe were divided into seven age-sets, one of these sets being composed of the men of military age. Each set was sub-divided into four "fires" or associating groups, two senior and two junior. When warriors were required, either the two senior or the two junior groups were called out, but not usually both, unless a very big raid was under consideration, or it was necessary to have every available man to defend the country against attack by the Maasai.

Contrast this with the Turu who, as far as I could determine, never went out to raid others and were able to organize on a large scale only for defense while at other times each localized group of lineages was in a constant state of semiwarfare with all the others.

Irrigation was mentioned earlier. Irrigation systems of one degree of complexity or another are scattered all over East Africa. The Sonjo, isolated in the middle of Maasai country in northern Tanzania, irrigate, as do the Pokot and Keyo in west central Kenya, and the Shambaa, to name only several cases. Irrigation was possible only in limited areas because the technology of irrigation was based on gravity so only land below mountain streams or in river valleys could be reached. Still, where it was possible and economical it was practiced.

With respect to architecture, the most common structure is the type of house described by Kenyatta, circular with a thatched roof, sometimes lined with mats but more often with clay on the inside walls. The tembe, which I mentioned in the last chapter, is uniquely characteristic of the people of the Rift Anomaly as well as a few others to the south including the Hehe, Kimbu, and Bena. Gluck (1973) believes this is an ancient style derived from an Arab source outside Africa. It is probably, therefore, another remnant of the ancient Cushitic period of East Africa. Other than these two types, a rectangular hut is found in certain areas of the coast and the Tutsi and others of the Interlacustrine Bantu build some houses of reeds in a conical or beehive form. Since the wealth of the interlacustrine state was sometimes great and labor was available, these structures were sometimes very elaborate and skillfully built, even if only of vegetable fiber, providing palaces for royalty. The Maasai build a domed, snail shell-type structure finished with manure spread like plaster, while the Somali and Turkana used rather less substantial structures due to the need for more frequent movement than most East African people. The distribution of these various types of huts cannot be explained simply by technical efficiency, but in part they can. This is a cloudy subject but I suggest that the tembe maintained its popularity where it did in part because the building materials for grass-roofed houses were lacking. Tembes have roofs made of timbers covered with clay. As far as the typical structure—the round hut—goes, it is a physical fact that a circular structure will encompass the most space for the smallest wall area, thus making such a structure most economical to build.

Iron production was also universally known but some regions were more fortunate with respect to this material than others. The Fipa seem to have been large-scale producers of iron lumps which could then be traded as raw material or finished goods to others. On the other hand, some people seem to have considered the manufacture of iron goods to be too expensive, preferring to trade for them. The Turu imported iron goods from the Nyamwezi and, in modern times, utilize immigrant Nyamwezi labor to produce iron goods for them. The Maasai depended on other people to supply them with iron, and the Pokot had itinerant blacksmiths who wandered from place to place taking orders and turning out finished products.

A final item will complete this partial survey of East African technology. Because of the large number of cattle, a large amount of manure is produced, yet few East African people use manure. It is easy to fall into the assumption that in the past they did not know about manuring. Many years ago, I witnessed Pokot housewives each morning gathering up the droppings from the night's confinement in the corral, and throwing it over the corral fence into a huge pile. I had no doubt that these industrious agriculturalists simply did not know what it could do for their crops. When I lived with the Turu some years later and saw them digging out huge quantities of well-rotted manure from their corrals and placing it carefully around their bulrush millet plants I became puzzled over how they had come by such an obviously ancient practice. The solution to the puzzle, of course, is that East Africans know perfectly well that manure has a pronounced effect on productivity, but in most cases where people have enough cattle for the manure to matter, it is not economical to use it. Turu fields and grazing areas are near the house so the cattle can be confined for long periods thus concentrating the manure, and it can be carried with relative ease to the fields. Pokot fields are far from home and transporting sufficient manure to make a difference would be nearly impossible. Furthermore, they must graze the animals over a wide area and so cannot concentrate enough manure for it to make much of a difference.

PHILOSOPHY AND RELIGION

The religious traditions of the three great language groups seem to have an inertia similar to that of the language systems. While we have far less understanding of this than of language, it seems likely that just as Islam is strongly associated with the Arabic-speaking, Roman Catholicism with Romance speakers, and Hinduism with Indians, the Bantu will be found to have a kind of philosophy or theology of their own, and the Nilo-Saharan speakers one of their own. We already have some indication of this in writings of Placide Tempels on *Bantu Philosophy* (1959). Tempels has been accused of projecting certain Western philosophical notions onto Bantu thought but he has nonetheless made a beginning at developing a systematic theory of Bantu philosophy. Apparently distinctive of Bantu thought is the idea that men, living and dead, who are kinsmen in some way, are linked together in such a way that the actions of any one person, whether overt or in thought, can affect others. Ideas of witchcraft, the harming of another person through acts of sorcery or through hateful thoughts, while not uniquely a Bantu concept, are intimately tied to Bantu philosophy. And when harm befalls someone, the source of that harm may be an ancestor, although not necessarily. The idea that the founder of the land maintains an intimate connection with it and must be involved in attempts to bring rain to it or otherwise solve problems connected with its use stems similarly from the notion that ancestors are not gone but merely abiding elsewhere (the Turu place them in a world below the ground) and can bring good or harm to the living. There is a High God, a Creator, like Matunda of the Turu and Kimbu, but the notion of deity is also linked to ancestors. Hence Mungu, a common East African term for the Creator, is in Turu the singular form of *arungu*, ancestors. The fundamental Bantu ritual act is sacrifice to their ancestors of livestock, most importantly cattle where they exist, but also goats or even chickens, as well as offerings of beer or other kinds of food. Thus, the living maintain an exchange relationship with the dead, insuring prosperity and health. In a sense it may be said that a witch is one who does not abide by the obligations inherent in exchange, attempting instead to get something by aggression and bad faith and thereby incurring the wrath of the ancestors.

This fundamental system of belief is, of course, adjusted to the particular circumstances of a people. In some places, where kinship relations extend over a wide area, the interactions of people with ancestors and witches may also be broadly distributed. In a society where relations are narrowly expressed, as among the Turu where they are confined to little clusters of villages, punishment by ancestors or aggression from witches is not believed to extend beyond that little sphere.

Among Nilo-Saharan speakers, whose belief system is even less well systematized by scholars, there is clear indication of a different mode of thought (Nilotic Philosophy?). In the first place, the high, divine force is less substantive and anthropomorphic than in Bantu thought. Whether the Dinka *nhialic*, the Nuer *kwoth*, or the Pokot *tororut*, it is a formless divine "wind." Associated with this are sub-deities or forces represented in natural phenomena: the sun (*tel*) of the Ingassana, or the rain (*ilat*) of the Pokot. In one of the best known of these systems of belief, that of the Shilluk, a culture hero, Nyikang, is the object of sacrifice in order that he may be encouraged to intercede with *juok* who, unlike the Bantu High God, takes a direct interest in people's affairs. In the case of the Pokot, sacrifice is made directly to Tororut and the subdeities— sun, moon, and lightning—through a ritual form called *kerket* in which the men of all the age sets are formally arranged while the open end of the sacrificial semicircle is faced toward Mount Matelo, the home of Ilat. Among the Dinka, Lienhardt (1961) sees cattle sacrifices as symbolic occasions dramatizing men's aim to control their fate by countering events of disorder and death. Cattle are offered as foils for disaster and as substitutes for men who would otherwise be the victims.

An explanation for evil paralleling the Bantu ideas of ancestral and witchly intervention is contained in the view that the normal state of the universe is a precariously balanced order symbolized by "cleanness," which is upset by "unclean" acts, which must therefore be cleansed to restore order. Paradoxically, our best account of this is for the Abaluyia described by Wagner (1954), who are located in western Kenya nearly surrounded by Nilotes. According to Wagner (1954, 44ff) they have:

> ... a very pronounced belief in a dichotomy of good and evil forces. Everything which deviates from the normal order of things, both in the natural and in the social world, is regarded as a manifestation of these evil forces and, hence, as dangerous ... if a person shows abnormal physical characteristics or behaves in a way which is in striking contrast to the norm of custom, he or she is said to "fall *luswa*" (*okugwa luswa*); and if an animal behaves in a way which deviates from its normal behavior or which leads to some unusual happening, it "falls kiragi."

These abnormalities include such things as an infant cutting its upper teeth first; a circumcised man riding an ox; a woman climbing on the roof of a hut; incest; a beard on a woman's chin; a bull calf attempting to mount a person. Among the Pokot such unclean acts are cleansed by various rites depending on their seriousness. In the case of adultery, the parties to the act are made to sit under a tree while a sheep hanging above them is slain to allow its blood to flow over them. They are, in fact, "washed in the blood of the lamb." Furthermore, this association of Nilotic belief with Middle Eastern ideas is probably an index to the close affinity of Nilotic culture in general with the Middle East than is true of the Bantu.

Southall (1970, 31) has made an interesting observation about the Nuer and Dinka, both part of the Western Nilotic group: that they have more religious and moral values in common with the Eastern Nilotics (such as Pokot) than with other Western Nilotics. If the Lugbara can be taken as a measure of this Western Nilotic system (Middleton 1960, 25) it is reminiscent of that of the Bantu:

> The main part of Lugbara ritual is concerned with the relationship between living men and their dead kin. This relationship reflects that between men and groups as they are at the present moment, a relationship which is conceived as controlled and sanctioned by the dead.

And when we turn to the Interlacustrine Bantu, specifically the people of Rwanda (Maquet 1954, 167), if we can believe that this society is a product of a Nilotic invasion, we are not surprised to discover that the creator, Imana, is an underlying force that sustains the universe and with whom are associated the unpersonalized forces of rain, wind, hail, and storms.

The religious system of the Afro-Asiatic speakers seems to be associated with a pre-Islamized form where Islam has not taken hold. Although the Somalis are Sunni Moslems, a faith which nevertheless has affinity with its pre-Islam predecessor, the Galla believe in a High God, Waqu, and his antithesis, Saytan. Among these Afro-Asiatic speakers the Amhara of the Ethiopian highlands are an anomaly. They continue today as Coptic Christians, the form of Christianity which ruled all of Egypt until the Islamic revitalization movement. But even here it is plain that the surface manifestations cover a basic Middle Eastern structure of thought which Islam and Christianity share with these more antique forms.

WORLD VIEWS

This is about as far as we can presently go in attempting to localize beliefs and other cultural phenomena on a wide scale. However, there are certain other known aspects of belief which are worth examining in order further to plumb the depth and flavor of East African culture.

Middleton (1965) tells us of a conceptual system of the Lugbara of western Uganda involving time and space (Fig. 1) in which a distinction is made between near people and far people both in time and space such that near people are normal, so to speak, far people are inverted, and those in between have some superhuman and some inverted aspects. Thus, as the figure shows, people who live beyond the horizon are spacially removed and thus inverted, that is to say, inhuman and evil. Similarly, ancients, including early European colonists, are inverted.

This Lugbara cosmology seems to introduce us to a category of

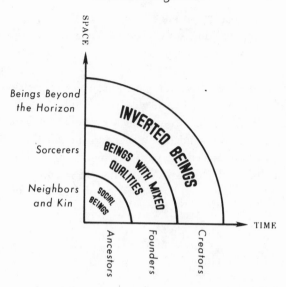

Lugbara Categories of Time and Space
FIG. 1

thought that may be conceived of in some basic respects as human rather than culturally specific, although it has been cloaked in specific Lugbara elements. The scheme, it will be noticed, accords with one in Western thought that makes people who are spacially remote into literal antipodes, such as the people of Australia who were thought to walk on their heads or, in more recent times, extraterrestrial beings with antennae on their heads, etc. And, temporally, it accords with Western notions that as we go back in time our ancestors are more and more savage (that is, the inversion of civilized).

When we discuss revitalization movements later in the book we will see this again when persons who react in violent frustration against society, whether they are Africans or Europeans, express their rejection of normal society by acts of inversion such as "washing" with dirt or engaging in forbidden sexual acts. When we and the Lugbara look back in time or out in space we seem to see the people there as abnormal and when we act out our rejection of society we do so by behaving in ways that are abnormal by usual standards.

A kind of universal cognition which has received a good deal of attention in East Africa has to do with the classification of phenomena in terms of binary opposition, such as the left and right hand where the right is the hand that greets and the left the hand that rejects. Rigby has detailed the particular right/left classification of the Gogo of central Tanzania, a wealthy cattle group, as seen in Table II, which is a partial representation of their total binary sys-

TABLE II
Gogo Binary Classification

Left (hand, side)	*Right* (hand, side)
female	male
hand used after defecation (unclean)	hand used in eating (clean)
weakness	strength
stupid	clever
side on which woman lies in sexual intercourse	side on which man lies
seed planting	bush clearing
winnowing, grinding	threshing
west	east
north	south
down	up
death, sickness	fertility, health
hot (as intemperate)	cool (as calm)
poisonous plants	medicinal plants
red/white	black
young people	old people
junior wives	senior wives
mother (classificatory) and all kin on her left side; affines	father (classificatory) and all kin on his right side
economic cooperation	economic competition

tem (Rigby 1966, 14–15). No clear-cut decision has as yet been reached by social anthropologists concerning how to interpret a scheme like this. Initially one is tempted to associate left with evil and right with good, but this will not stand up because grinding of grain for the staple porridge, which is on the left, cannot be considered to be evil. Nor, for that matter, can these people be said to think of women as evil. As a matter of fact, if the Gogo system is like that of the Turu, as I suspect it is in many respects, men are considered to be hot-tempered and women cool, the former associated with Asis, the sun, and the latter with Mweri, the moon, which is on the right in the Gogo scheme. In a sense it may be said that things on the left are undesirable, but the different horizontal categories do not necessarily have any relationship to each other in any specific sense. That a man is hot-tempered is a binary conception independent of his classification as socially superior to women. There is one possible way to relate the elements on the different sides which is suggested by the opposition of economic cooperation and economic competition. Those things on the left may be conceived of as tension producing and those on the right as unthreatening. At first this may seem ridiculous since to us economic cooperation seems obviously to be less threatening than competition. But if such cooperation is normally viewed as occurring among affinal kin, aimed at oneself, as the left is generally associated with the female side of the family, the interpretation makes sense. This does not explain why red and white are threatening (although red is sometimes associated with blood) nor why north should cause concern, but closer investigation of the meaning of these things might reveal the reason.

Left/right classifications do give some insight into society since each is tailored, at least in some respects, to its specific society. While female is considered to be inferior or threatening to the dominant males in most societies, the classification of mother and her left-hand affinal kin on the left, as opposed to father and his right-hand affinal kin on the right, is specific to Gogo society where circumstances are such (as will be explained in the chapter on marriage and descent) that a man has to depend to an unusual degree on his affines or in-laws rather than treating them as outsiders in contrast to his agnatic or patrilineal kin. Thus those affinal kin on whom he relies are classified on the right with his agnatic kin. This interpretation is confirmed by looking at Beidelman's table of classification for the Kaguru of eastern Tanzania (Beidelman 1961, 156–257) where names associated with the matrilineage are placed on the left and those associated with the patrilateral kin on the right. In other words, there is a clear separation of agnatic kin from affines contrasting with the Gogo case.

Both the Gogo and Kaguru place stress on lineage as an organizing principle, although it is weak among the Gogo. When we look at a society such as the Meru of Mount Kenya, where stress is placed on age as an organizing principle, this shows up in the dual classification with the subordinate age division on the left and dominant age division on the right (Needham 1960, 25). Incidentally, another interesting aspect of Meru classification is the placing of the Mugwe, a "religious dignitary" or shaman, on the left hand. This is an example of revitalization inversion of which I spoke earlier, where the elevation of the left hand, the tension-producing side, to the sacred is a symbol of reform appropriate to a prophet.

VISUAL ART AND MUSIC

When we turn to visual art in East Africa we can only repeat Delange's plaint (1967, 257) that students of African art are in the bad habit of neglecting regions apparently poor in sculpture. One who, like myself, is interested in art in the broader sense is sometimes driven to the opinion that Africanist art experts consider only carved or cast figures and masks as art. By this token, since few East African people carve figures or masks they must have no art. My investigation of Turu esthetics (Schneider 1966) led me to conclude that, at least for them, that which is esthetic is anything which appeals to a person, whether it be an object or an act like a cattle sacrifice, which is given as a gift, a pure altruistic act (*majighana*).

The giver of the sacrifice, if he does it well, is as much a man of majighana as the carver of a well-made stool (an artist). Objects and acts which qualify are *-ja, muja* if singular and referring to a person and the way he or she is dressed, *nja* for anything in the class of *n-* objects, such as cattle, etc. In these circumstances, to single out sculpture as art is pure ethnocentrism.

Over most of East Africa, art is represented in modest form. Among the Pokot a finely polished spear is an object of beauty (*pachigh*). And while not all art is connected to things which have other utility, this is the common practice. Iron goods—spears, axes, machetes or swords, hoes, knives—can be made crudely or with attention to their esthetic appeal. The same may be said of baskets, pots, stools, and even houses. In Unyaturu there was a man known throughout the Kahiu clan area for the beauty of his house. When I examined it I found it to be an ordinary corral with several ordinary tembe-type houses within it, but even I could see that all these structures had been put together with extraordinary attention to detail, giving a general impression of evenness and rhythm.

I think it is safe to say that each ethnic group has a style of its own, a way of shaping spears, doing bead or basketry work, designing pottery, dressing and decorating the body, which is peculiar to them. This is an in-group phenomenon, part of the dynamics of the way groups of people who in some way identify with each other's interests set themselves off from strangers. Thus, for example, the Pokot, like many of the central and southern Eastern Nilotes, dress their hair; in their case, they work a fine clay into it until the hair is lost in the smoothed clay cap, after which the cap is painted with one of two designs. These designs and the general structure of the cap distinguish the Pokot from the Turkana, who have a different style, and from the Karamojong, whose style is like the Pokot's but still different. Such stylistic variation is not confined to headdresses. It shows up, to take the Pokot as example again, in the *ngachar* or *amakuk*, little stool-like objects which men carry on their wrists for decorations but which they also use as temporary props when they are hunkering, or as neck rests to protect their delicate headdresses.

Pokot spears and shields are a distinctive design as are the plugs they wear in their lips and the discs they hang from the septa of their noses.

Huntingford (1953b, 14), who has made one of the few attempts to characterize the styles of whole areas, tells us that among the Eastern Nilotes the northern group (e.g., Bari) are distinctive for carving grave posts, the central group (e.g., Turkana) use small narrow shields, wrist and finger knives, lip plugs and nose discs, headdresses of the Pokot type (even though they are southern Eastern Nilotes), and headrests. The southern group are distinctive for wearing pigtails and ivory arm clamps and carrying spears with a long narrow blade (compared to the Pokot leaflike blade), large oval shields, and long swords. The Maasai variety of this style is much copied by other people on the grounds, no doubt, that imitating those one fears brings admiration to oneself.

If we take the Turu as an example of a non-Nilotic group and compare them to these Nilotes, we would find them quite different. They use rather modest, crude spears, with medium-sized, figure-eight-shaped shields, but augment this with a basketlike shield combined with a staff which, with another staff, were used for stick fighting within the ethnic community. Up to the early part of this century the men went nearly naked, wearing only skin capes, as was true of most of the pastoral people, and let their hair grow long. They had no neck rests but did carve stools.

While on the subject of body decoration it should be noted that certain objects were always prized, usually because they were rare but also esthetically pleasing. The ivory arm bands of the Eastern Nilotes are a case in point, as are beads and coils of copper and brass, usually worn by women, all over East Africa. Where states arose, certain valued objects became attached to chiefs and kings. Shorter (1973), in an attempt to refute the idea that chiefship in western Tanzania was diffused from the interlacustrine area, points out that while it is true that the lion and drums as symbols of chiefship are wide spread, as they are also in the interlacustrine area, toward the south the horn is of equal importance, and the white conus-shell disc emblem was worn by chiefs on their foreheads and sometimes on their wrists and ankles. These shells came from the East African coast and no doubt reflect the general valuing of shells, particularly cowries, before these were displaced as money by the coming of Arabs and Europeans.

In other parts of Africa where sculpture is more common, it is a noteworthy fact that ethnic groups develop styles so particular to them that the provenience of a piece of art is often easily established simply by assessing the style. Similarly, there is no mistaking a Maasai or Tutsi headdress.

With respect to music, Lomax (1970, 195) feels that song styles conform to the general pattern of language distribution so that he identifies Nilotic, Cushitic, and Bantu areas. But Merriam (1978) points out a controversy among ethnomusicologists over whether East Africa should be split musically from West and Central Africa due to distinctive elements in its music. If this should be the case it would argue that music is more diffusable than language and would reflect the great mixing of language families that characterizes this area as a whole.

CHAPTER IV

Production and Exchange

WITH A GIVEN fund of culture people produce goods which, in turn, become part of the cultural milieu that feeds back into the structure of relations, especially in the form of exchanges, which is what we mean by social interaction. In other words, some exchanges have a material component and some do not. The extent to which they do or do not is in part a function of the kind of material production that is possible, and the kind that is possible importantly affects the social structure. This idea is central to Marxist economics, whose "mode of production" is composed of the means of production (or techniques of production along with their special economic characteristics, such as the amount of output which can be accomplished with a certain input of energy) and the relations of production (the social arrangements appropriate to a particular means of production). But, as Smith (1977) has recently pointed out, Marxists do not sufficiently emphasize that the means of exchange are also important, probably more than the means of production, for the structure of society. In this chapter we examine the means of production and exchange in East Africa, saving for subsequent chapters examination of the relations of production and exchange that emerge in conjunction with them.

Even when ethnographers have bothered to explore the production systems of Africans they have usually done so in a way that disguises the amount of planning or choice that must be exercised by the producer by stressing the constraints on choice. The first point that must be established is that even if Africans desire to act mechanically and without thought, the complexity of possibilities in production and the complexity of consequences associated with various combinations of ways of doing things would preclude this. For example, a farmer who ignored how his available labor supply relates to the crops he intends to grow might, as when labor is relatively scarce and the chosen crop maize, find himself so short of labor as to lose his whole crop. The exercise of choice is central to certain aspects of crop production. The particular crops to grow or the mix of crops is a first consideration. Then the factors of production—land, labor, and capital—must be considered. Although labor is usually the element in shortest supply among people of the Agricultural Zone, sometimes it is land, and so economizing must be focused on labor in the first case and land in the second. And where pastoralism is the path of best returns, capital conservation becomes the main focus. Finally, in order to obtain the best factor mix, the farmer is always forced, to some degree, outside the domestic household and into interchanges with other people, near by or remote. Exchange, if only for wives, who constitute the main labor supply, is unavoidable.

ECOLOGICAL DETERMINISM

Why do East Africans produce goods? The conventional, often unquestioned answer is in order to eat or to live. This position, often phrased elliptically, is exemplified by a statement from O'Conner's economic geography of East Africa (1966, 108):

> In much of East Africa the importance of livestock reflects limited opportunities for cultivation. As the 1953–55 Royal Commission stressed, the rainfall over at least one-third of the region is too low and too unreliable to permit any alternative to a pastoral economy.

As most people who are knowledgeable about East Africa realize, livestock, particularly cattle, are raised to an important extent for reasons other than food. But O'Conner's statement seems to imply that if they can, people prefer to raise crops in order to eat.

It is simple to refute such ideas, as simple as refuting the idea that beef raisers in the United States engage in beef production only in order to feed themselves. And it is necessary to make such a refutation in order to establish the idea, central to understanding these economies, that it is better to think of production as focused on utility, just as economists have done for our own economy. Most telling is the recent observation by Dahl and Hjort (1976) that in East Africa the amount of meat consumed by pastoralists is actually quite small. This can be deduced from a few simple facts about cattle raising in this part of Africa. Suppose we have a population of 50,000 people with 100,000 head of cattle, a ratio of cattle to people of 2:1, a high ratio in East Africa. If 10% of those cattle come to maturity for slaughter each year and if the average slaughter weight is 600 lbs., and if the butchered weight is half that, or 300 lbs., this produces 300 x 10,000 head or 3,000,000 lbs. of meat for 50,000 people—only 60 lbs. per person per year.

Fortunately, we have some actual figures pertaining to rates of beef consumption in a study by Aldington and Wilson (1968). Based on deduction from hide sales, their study shows that a take-off rate of 10% is too high in some cases (e.g., West Pokot, where it is 8) or too low in others (Turkana, 12.6, and Laikipia Maasai, 13). But the estimate of butchered weight that I gave is too high for most cases, the weight for Turkana, West Pokot, and Laikipia being 231, 242, and 303 respectively. Nevertheless, the rate of consumption for these three groups given in pounds per person per annum is only 10.6, 27, and 47 respectively. For the 39 groups of people they studied, the average butchered weight was a mere 202.7 lbs., the takeoff rate 13.2% and the consumption rate per annum only 21 lbs. Further, their accompanying study of sheep and goat consumption showed the amount of that meat eaten per person each year was only 3.8 lbs.

Attacking the proposition that livestock are raised for food from another direction, Meyn (1970, 54) has shown that 50% of Kenya's

Ritual slaughter of a steer

cattle population is kept in the high-potential agricultural areas (e.g., 200,000 by 100,000 Kipsigis in the fertile area just northeast of Lake Victoria). It simply cannot be argued that these people keep cattle because this is nutritionally the maximizing course, especially when it is considered that the cost of producing a hundred calories of beef is much higher than an equivalent amount of calories from crops. And, of course, these facts implicitly question the idea that crops are raised exclusively for food; otherwise, one would think, the people would not allow cattle to compete for agricultural land.

Dahl and Hjort's attempt to locate the rationale of cattle raising in milk production was equally futile. Assembling evidence on such variables as rate of calving, calf mortality, death rate of mature animals, rate of milk production, and amount of meat production, among other things, they tried to decide the question of how the structure of a herd (size and composition) relates to food production and the ability to support an average pastoral family. They assume that the main management strategy of pastoralists (by which they seem to mean pure pastoralists or nomads, although this is ambiguous because they draw some of their data from sedentary pastoralists) is to maximize milk production. Furthermore, they stick to this claim despite the fact that their simulations indicate that during the rainy season a "reference family" of six people would require a total herd of 60 animals (milk-producing cows do not produce separately of a total herd system), a number which during the dry season, when fewer cows are producing milk and those that are producing are yielding less, would rise to nearly 600 head. As they point out, Maasai say that during the dry season 10–15 lactating cows are required to provide milk for each person. Very few East African people possess cattle in such numbers and none have animals in that amount for all families. In most places a man possessing such numbers would be considered very well off.

Realizing the impossibility of supporting the claim that herds are managed only to produce milk for subsistence, Dahl and Hjort also consider meat and blood as supplements to milk. But even with this, and allowing for some milk storage in the form of curd and ghee, their simulations indicate the need for a herd of 100 head of cattle per family, which would be impossible.

We must conclude, then, that any close examination of any of East Africa's pastoral people will show that they depend in varying degrees on consumption of grain and other foods, often imported. A survey of East African economies which I did in 1961 (Schneider 1964) showed a clear pattern of intra- and intertribal trade, exchanging livestock for other food (e.g., Maasai trade with Arusha for bananas, or with Kikuyu for grain). P. T. W. Baxter (1975) points out that the highly pastoral Borana Galla have always depended on nonpastoral products in their diet. And Rigby (1968) stresses the value of Gogo cattle for trade for grain, a pattern similar to that which I found among Turu, who actually plan grain production with the idea of marketing it for livestock (Schneider 1970), and Pokot in the mountains who trade grain for cattle to Pokot on the plains. Bates and Lee (1977, 825) base their argument about livestock management on the premise that exchange of live-stock for food is a "well established fact" among pastoralist special-ists.

Thus it is commonly observed that East Africans convert grain into cattle and other livestock when they can. If cattle are con-vertible into most other things of value, giving their producers the kind of economic freedom and multiple options we obtain with money, and if grain is not so easily convertible, then it follows that the prudent farmer, when he can, will convert his grain into live-stock. And it also follows that the farmer, to some extent at least, is not producing grain to feed himself and his family but for the purpose of obtaining livestock, which in turn are not produced for food. The exception to this statement is not, however, a refutation of the main argument. As in modern development situations of uncertainty, farmers will produce grain to feed their families first, holding out what they need, before going into the market. This strategy is overcome when uncertainty is removed so that, as among rural Hausa in West Africa (Hill 1972), all grain may be sold off while the farmer depends on purchasing the grain he needs to feed his family. Thus all crop production is ultimately for the market.

Because production activities are therefore undertaken not only to obtain food, it is better when discussing production to think of the farmer as attempting to obtain utility, this being the combina-tion of all things considered good, whether food, repositories of value, or anything else.

CONSTRAINTS

While it is therefore a mistake to focus only on the constraints to production faced by producers, the decisions they make about production cannot be understood without taking account of the constraints. When we do this we must be clear that what con-stitutes a constraint is relative to the means of production. In East Africa, the most fundamental constraint is the distribution of tsetse fly and, less importantly, deficiencies in grass and water which in

some places make the raising of livestock, particularly cattle, difficult or impossible. Map VI showed, in a general way, the distribution of tsetse fly in the Uganda, Kenya, and Tanzania portion of
East Africa. Map VII, showing the distribution of cattle in the
same area, according to ratios of cattle to people, is the converse
of Map VI, since the ratios of 1:1 or better occur mainly outside the
fly zone.

Glossina, tsetse fly, is a vector for microscopic flagellates of the
genus *Trypanosoma* which causes "sleeping sickness," so called because of the lethargy it produces in later stages of the illness, before
death. Glossina is found within areas possessing these limits (Lambrecht 1964):

Temperature	20°–28° Centigrade (68°–80° F.)
Relative Humidity	50°–80°
Rainfall	25–60 inches (when distributed so the soil does not become waterlogged)

This puts Glossina generally between Lat. 15° N – 29° S, or from
north of Ethiopia's highlands to the southern tip of Botswana.

If East Africans did not prefer to raise livestock wherever and
whenever they can, Glossina might not be so important; but under
the circumstances it dictates to a very large extent the production
life of the people and their social structures insofar as they are dependent on production.

Other than its importance for acting with other variables in determining the distribution of fly, rainfall is critical to both agricultural and pastoral people. As the rainfall map (Map VIII) shows,
the heavier-rainfall areas are also generally the areas of fly. However,
as I pointed out above, some important pastoral people, such as
Kipsigis, Nandi, and Teso, live in high-rainfall areas which are fly-
free because of the operation of some other variable, such as low
temperature.

Within the Pastoral Zone, the lower the rainfall the less dense
the population and the greater the nomadism. People in this area,

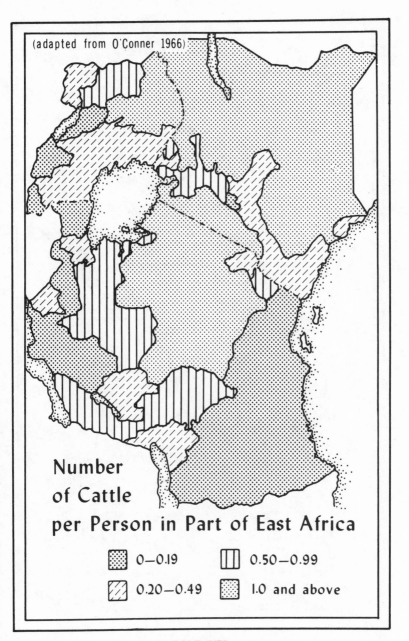

(adapted from O'Conner 1966)

Number
of Cattle
per Person in Part of East Africa

0—0.19   0.50—0.99
0.20—0.49   1.0 and above

MAP VII

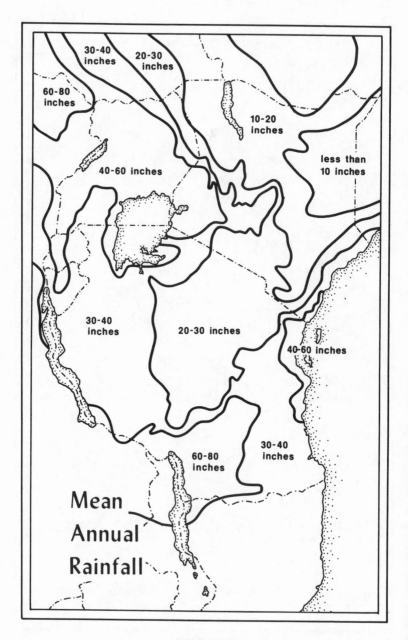

MAP VIII

such as Somalis and Turkana, must move long distances much of the year in order to obtain grazing. This does not mean, however, that their ratios of cattle to people will be lower. In fact, the people in the drier areas tend to have the highest ratios. And this does not mean that people in wetter areas will be less nomadic. One of the prime characteristics of these pastoral economies is individual mobility, literally and socially. Thus while pastoralists in the wetter areas may be able to be more stationary, and some (such as the Turu) are even absolutely sedentary, for many, movement is common for other reasons than finding grazing. Finally, some people, like some of the Maasai, may be nomadic even in more fertile areas if they have so many cattle they can ignore agriculture altogether.

Within the Agricultural Zone the amount of rainfall, and the fact that it is usually crowded into a few months of the year, is a critical constraint on the types of crops that can be grown, it generally being the case that as rainfall increases the type of crop that can be grown requires lower labor inputs for outputs so that the people in the drier areas who have no livestock, such as those in the Wembere steppe south of Lake Victoria, are the real poor people of East Africa, condemned by their means of production to raising low-yield, high-labor-cost crops without any appreciable amount of livestock to back them up.

The next important constraint is the types of crops available. We have already surveyed the range and historical origin of the major African crops: bulrush millet, sorghum, finger millet, maize, cassava, and bananas. Each of these has different nutritional characteristics and growing patterns. With respect to nutritional value, Table III shows Rounce's findings in his study of the crops of the Wembere steppe. There are clear differences in the four main crops with respect to protein content, fat, fibre, and carbohydrates. But there is little clear evidence of how these variations affect the farmers' choices. One suspects that variations in nutritional content are balanced out by crop mixing, which is common and about which I shall say more presently, but there is no hard support for this.

The growing characteristics of these plants also vary markedly

TABLE III
Composition of Various Grains
(Percentage)

Food	Water	Total Protein	Fat	Fibre	Carbo-hydrates
Sorghum, mixed	11.73	10.00	3.06	1.14	72.85
Pennisetum	10.60	12.47	5.00	2.80	67.13
Maize, flint	8.60	11.00	5.00	1.70	72.30
Maize meal, hand ground	15.50	9.00	3.00	—	70.00
Eleusine	10.30	5.40	1.50	3.40	76.90

(Rounce 1949)

and are important for the distribution of the crops in ways that can be seen without difficulty. Thus, for example, both pennisetum (bulrush millet) and sorghum (Table IV) are more drought resistant than maize so that, as one would expect, they are more usually grown in the drier areas. The effect of this on the distribution of these crops is nicely illustrated by the case of the Iraqw, up on the west side of the Rift escarpment in north Tanzania, and the Wambugwe, just to the east of them but down at the bottom. The Iraqw (Winter 1962, 458–459) are primarily maize growers while, down in the dry bottom, the Wambugwe depend mainly on sorghum.

Yields also vary importantly. As Table IV shows, pennisetum is the poorest yielder with maize the next best and sorghum after that. Johnston (1958, 133) lists the crops of western tropical Africa in this descending order of yields:

> Cassava (manioc)
> Plantains (bananas)
> Maize
> Finger millet (eleusine)
> Sorghum
> Bulrush millet (pennisetum)

TABLE IV

Characteristics and Value of Three Grain Crops

	Pennisetum 1	Sorghum 2	Maize 3
Soils	Will produce small yields on worn-out or light soils where others would produce none.	Withstands more water-logging than others. Characteristic of heavy soils.	Ubiquitous where water does not stand. Characteristically planted near to house sites and cattle corrals.
Drought Resistance	Little to choose between 1 and 2. Pennisetum possibly better.	See Pennisetum.	Very susceptible when about two months old.
Period to Maturity	Four and a half to five months.	Varieties vary from three to six months.	As for sorghum.
Yield Range	Up to eight bags per acre.	Up to ten bags per acre.	Up to twelve bags per acre.
Average yield in Average Fields	Two bags per acre.	Four bags per acre.	Three bags per acre.
Length of Storage	One to three years.	According to variety. Six months to three years.	Flint one year, Dent six months.
Striga Susceptibility	Low.	High.	High, but rather tolerant.
Susceptibility to Stalk Borer	Low.	High.	High.

(Rounce 1949)

To this scale I have added finger millet, which he does not consider, and which seems to fall between maize and sorghum. It should also be noted that yield variations between grains and the plantains and cassava are quite marked. For the Congo (Zaire) he has calculated that the yield in metric tons per hectare is .25 and .87 for millets and sorghum on the one hand and maize on the other, while for manioc and plantains it is 11.54 and 9.24.

Incidentally, it should not be assumed from this that the preference for these crops will therefore be in the order indicated. While there is a relationship between labor costs and output such that lower costs are associated with higher output, the relationship is not invariant. While bananas yield somewhat lower than cassava, they are cheaper to produce. And there seems to be a similar inverse relationship between sorghum and maize.

For various reasons, one no doubt being the varying ecological conditions of an ethnic area, the actual staple crops of a people may consist of more than one.

Other than the staple crops, East Africans have a wide variety of supplemental crops which are mixed with the staples in varying amounts and types. The best illustration of the extent to which this may be carried is Knight's study of the Nyika of southwest Tanzania. He lists 43 different crops which they customarily plant, and these are only the most important of a longer list. The total includes all the grains previously discussed plus wheat (obviously a recent introduction), various root crops such as cassava, oil crops such as sesame, legumes including lima beans and groundnuts (peanuts), fruits including oranges, condiments such as red peppers, vegetables of various types, and tobacco. I have the impression that the extent to which crop mixing is carried out varies between agricultural and pastoral people, the latter sticking to a narrower range of crops.

Another constraint on production is soil types. Soils in East Africa generally are not very fertile. The great exception to this generalization is the very rich soils in the banana-growing areas such as on the north shore of Lake Victoria and on the south slopes of the mountains, in well-watered zones. As Rounce's Table (IV) shows, however, there are variations within the less fertile areas, pennisetum being best on the really worn-out soils while maize and sorghum require better soils. One implication of all this which will shortly be considered in more detail is the cost of producing on such soils. It is a common generalization that Africans utilize slash and burn, or swidden, methods of production, which put fertilizer into soils by burning the overgrowth to produce ash, after which the soil is used until it is worn out, after which the farmer shifts to a new site. But such methods are not universal since constraints vary. The banana growers can produce on the same site permanently, for all practical purposes. And some people, like the Turu, are able to utilize the manure from their cattle to maintain fertility on otherwise highly dessicated and worn-out soils. Since they are able to exploit the ubiquitous marshes in their country for reserve grazing, they can keep their cattle near their homes and pen them up for longer periods of time. Other East Africans are not so fortunate, having to abandon manure since it is too expensive to carry to their fields.

An additional constraint that must be considered is the nature of land ownership. It is another conventional assertion that Africans do not own land individually; that it is held by the lineage and parceled out on a usufructuary basis. This idea does not bear close scrutiny, especially in East Africa. In the first place, not all East African societies emphasize the lineage principle as a method of forming groups. The richer pastoralists are most prone to utilize voluntary principles of grouping. But even where lineage is important, as among the Turu, there are not necessarily any leaders who have authority to make such decisions. In the Turu case each man owns his land against all others, inherited legally from his mother's house, and he can transfer such land to others. Lineage intrudes here only in the sense that since members of the same localized lineage have inherent claims against each other for the use of labor or other property, and since exploiting the land requires help from such people at various times, a stranger would have a difficult time utilizing land possessed in the area of another lineage than his own. Nevertheless, sometimes it works out that this can be accomplished.

In places where there are chiefs the situation varies. In some the land may in fact be claimed by the chief and rights to use it must be obtained from him. But even in such areas it is often true that usufructuary rights may border on permanent rights in practical fact. There are two important crosscutting considerations that determine the extent to which rights in land are asserted. One is the fertility of the land and the other has to do with whether it will be used for cropping or grazing. Generally speaking, the more fertile and well watered the land, the more competition to possess it and the greater the expression of individual rights (qualified by the presence or absence of chiefs, who, in effect, assert individual rights also but in a context in which they are able to establish a monopoly condition as opposed to the more egalitarian situations in which no one person can gain control against all others). In the egalitarian condition, as among the Pokot, this principle can be seen operating clearly over three types of land. The least valuable land is swidden in poor rainfall areas, at the foot of the mountains. Such land can be taken freely since there is plenty of it and it has low value, the likelihood of obtaining a good crop from it being poor. The next most valuable is swidden on the mountainsides where rains tend to be good. While individuals do not hold specific plots, such land is hoarded by the voluntary community and parceled out to members in good standing. The most valuable land is irrigated and is situated along mountain streams. Plots within these fields are individually owned and marked by boundaries.

In the Turu case, agricultural plots alongside the homesteads, into which manure is invested, are individually owned by women's houses and marked by boundaries. In addition, grazing plots in the marshes are also individually owned. But land in the forests adjacent to a village is not individually owned although it is controlled by the members of the lineage who would force out anyone from another lineage who tried to use it. Such land is exploited by swidden techniques. And the large grazing areas outside the marshes are individually owned, but grazing lands in the forests, where tsetse fly is liable to be a problem, are open to all.

As to the pastoralists, the richer they are, the less they depend on agriculture and the less valuable to them are small plots of land, no matter how fertile. Thus one finds the Maasai grazing huge herds on some of the most fertile land in Kenya, not bothering to exercise individual rights to the plots. But one also finds Turkana and Somalis ranging over large infertile tracts without any sense of individual control of land, although in the Somali case members of a lineage work together to control water holes.

Finally a word about population density. Shortly I shall say something about Boserup's thesis on the conditions of agricultural growth, in which the question of the effect of population increase on production methods is taken up. This thesis suggests, as do more commonsensical examinations of the problem, that population density ought to be a constraint. But there is some question in my mind about this as far as East Africa goes. East Africans seem somehow to limit population to the mode of production, low density being generally associated with pastoralism and high density with high-yield crops like bananas. It is certain that starvation during severe droughts helps produce this effect in many of the pastoral areas from time to time but this cause is insufficient to explain the pattern in toto, since droughts intense enough to cause widespread starvation occur uncommonly.

Generally speaking, the areas of highest population density are also the areas in which land is most desirable. Allan identifies these areas in Kenya, Tanzania, and Uganda as Kikuyuland, the Nyanza Province of Kenya (where the Abaluyia Bantu and Kipsigis live), Kigezi in southwest Uganda, Rwanda and Burundi, Teso, Sukumaland, the upland regions of Tanzania, the Matengo Highlands in southern Tanzania, and Ukara Island (Allan 1965). To these should probably be added the Ethiopian highlands.

CHOICE

Given these constraints, how have East Africans chosen to operate? In the first place, as I have already noted, wherever they can raise cattle or camels they do so and, apparently, to the fullest extent possible. It was and is a common complaint of colonial and modern governments that such people overgraze the land, an effect of unlimited multiplication of animals. A modern illustration of this propensity to focus on increase in herds comes from Turkanaland where it is reported (Hjort 1976) that Turkana who are engaged in a newly-founded fishing industry are investing their earnings in cattle, heavily increasing the number and aggravating the problem of overgrazing in their area.

Where East Africans are confined to agricultural operations the basic strategy seems to be to increase crop production to the fullest while at the same time conserving on labor which, unlike the pastoral areas, is the chief factor constraint. The importance of a labor shortage relative to other production factors in nonindustrialized societies is a fact that has been increasingly recognized in recent years during which various researchers have suggested that it is at the base of the use of swidden methods, bridewealth customs, slavery, and the importance of lineage as a grouping principle. Boserup (1965) maintains that this labor shortage accounts for the widespread use of swidden, as opposed to intense cultivation. Swidden, which requires plenty of unused land, allows the farmer to get right to the business of cultivating and planting without the laborious expenditure of time spent clearing the land of all obstructions, investing extensively in fertilizer and tools. It is labor rather than capital intensive, the chief cost being labor inputs, not capital inputs. This does not mean there is no cost to preparing the land. Swidden typically requires the trimming of all trees and shrubs on the plot to be used so that the sun can penetrate and so that the ash from these cuttings can fertilize the crop. But the cost of this preparation is far less than would be the case with intensive methods. In Boserup's view, swidden continues until the press of population, with an accompanying loss of labor productivity at the margin (for reasons I shall not go into here), makes intensive agriculture the economical path to follow.

The pattern of cropping in East Africa appears to reflect well the problem of labor shortage and the need to economize labor. A study done by Heyer (1971) of Kamba production will illustrate the point.

Heyer chose to analyze the production problems of Kamba farmers in terms of producing for the cash market but since they were using traditional methods of production the fact that they were cash cropping does not affect the relevance of the analysis to traditional operations. Her technique was to employ linear programming, a method of deciding with precision how various mixes of crops, land, labor, and capital constrain each other so that the precise mix necessary to achieve a precise goal (the greatest amount of food or, in this case, the greatest profit) can be determined. In order to keep the analysis from becoming too massive she concentrated on relating the available labor supply and land to the production of a limited number of crops: maize, beans, peas, finger millet, sorghum, and bulrush millet. As the problem was set up, the farmer was faced with a total of 243 possible combinations of crops, labor, and land of which 35 to 50 courses of action were of types which a farmer would seriously have to consider. The results of her study showed that maize combined with beans is an option open to farmers who have sufficient labor relative to land, but as labor becomes scarcer relative to land, sorghum, as one crop, enters as a rational possibility replacing maize.

Incidentally, this study shows, even with a severely limited number of variables, just how complicated farming can be in an apparently simple system and how unlikely it is that farmers can act simply on the basis of tradition. Miracle (1967) in fact has claimed that while African farming is far less productive than American, it is far more complicated.

Johnston (1958) supports the conclusion that in a labor shortage situation African cereals are preferred. His study of tropical agriculture in Western Africa shows that sorghum is more costly to produce than maize in terms of acre, pound, and 1,000 calories per unit of labor input. That is to say, as in Heyer's conclusion, Africans prefer not to grow sorghum if they can grow maize because the output relative to labor input is better for maize. They will shift to sorghum only when they are forced to do so. Johnston's study (1958, 144) gives us a ranking for crops in terms of cost of production, from highest to lowest: bulrush millet, sorghum, maize, cassava, and plantains. What this suggests, reasoning from Heyer's conclusions, is that if a complicated enough cropping situation could be modeled with linear programming in some East African setting, producers might be seen as trying to move down this scale seeking ultimately to raise plantains and to stay away from bulrush millet.

A study of staple crop production in Uganda by Hyde and Langlands (1974), one of the results of which is illustrated in Map IX, may be interpreted as follows. Bananas, or plantains, which dominate north and east of Lake Victoria and on Mount Elgon on the eastern border, are grown in these places because they *can* be grown, and they would probably be grown in most other places in Uganda if they could be. Cassava dominates the western part of Uganda, which is no doubt well watered enough to support it compared to the east, and would seem to be a substitute for plantains since it is the next cheapest crop to produce. Finger millet, which is not on Johnston's chart, but which I place between sorghum and maize, would be a choice for the central part of Uganda, which is not rich in livestock but which has sufficient rain, in contrast to the east which is dry and dominated by sorghum.

That these conclusions about Uganda are probably not far-fetched is further suggested by Johnston's study of changes in cropping in the northern Congo Basin where, over the centuries since knowledge of New World plants has entered, African cereals and yams were abandoned (yams are the most costly of African crops) for maize, which in turn has been abandoned as the staple in favor of cassava in the last hundred years, except in areas where plantains will grow, just to the west of Uganda.

Crop maps for the rest of East Africa are not available, but the general picture is clear. Plantains, as already noted, are found in well-watered areas of rich soil, but outside Uganda such areas are scarce. Cassava has not achieved wide acceptance outside Uganda, probably because it too requires much moisture and, as the rainfall map (VIII) shows, conditions become progressively drier, on the average, as one moves from west to east. Similarly, maize requires a

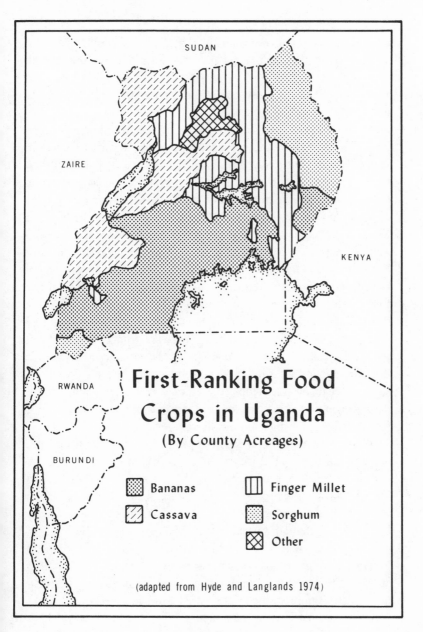

First-Ranking Food Crops in Uganda

(By County Acreages)

Bananas

Cassava

Finger Millet

Sorghum

Other

(adapted from Hyde and Langlands 1974)

MAP IX

good deal more moisture than the African cereals and so is found spottily. Thus the rest of East Africa is dominated by the African cereals, with bulrush millet, the least preferred crop but the one that does best in the driest conditions, dominating the driest crops areas, such as central Tanzania.

A word must be inserted here regarding the Abyssinians of highland Ethiopia who represent a special case as regards production, just as they do culturally. Living on the average at an altitude exceeding that of any other East African people, which has helped preserve their cultural identity, they have developed a unique complex of productive goods. They have cattle, sheep and goats, as other East Africans, although not in large per-capita numbers, but they are also able to keep some horses and donkeys (the latter present all over East Africa and very prominent here). Their main crops—wheat, barley, and teff—are suited to the higher, colder conditions. Of the three, only wheat occurs elsewhere in East Africa: it was relatively recently introduced into some of the highland areas of Kenya and Tanzania. Besides the presence here of very complex hierarchical structures, testifying to the predominantly agricultural nature of this area, agriculture is intensive, dependent on the plow. While on the subject of unusual crops, the Gurage of Ethiopia and certain nearby people depend on a plant called ensete or false banana, about which little is known economically.

Swidden is a common method of production in East Africa, but, as I have already said, it is not universal. It is often possible to engage in intensive operations without huge cost and when this is so East Africans will do so. The Turu system of manuring is a case in point; plantain production is another. It requires comparatively little labor, so that land becomes the chief constraint. Otherwise, irrigation is used wherever possible, as I have also said. In order to irrigate, large dams must sometimes be built but most are small as are the ditch systems and there is no need for large capital investment such as pumps since water is fed through gravity.

Some East African people, such as the Kara and Haya, have turned to very intensive agriculture. The Kara people of Ukara Is-

land in southeast Lake Victoria, described by Allan (1965, 199ff),
excellently exemplify how varied the mix of crops and cropping
methods can be. In many respects the Kara are like the Turu in
that they raise both livestock and bulrush millet. And they use
manure to obtain a crop. However, they have gone much further
than the Turu and actually utilize the resource of the Lake to help
grow fodder to feed the cattle. The digging of fodder pits, harvesting
and transporting of hay, digging of pits to capture manure and
urine, and other practices are very labor intensive. As Allan points
out, the people work very hard to obtain their results. But, he also
notes, the results are not lavish. That the Kara would go to such
lengths seems to suggest that they are indeed stimulated by incen-
tives, in this case the incentive to obtain a living in a sparse habitat
where there is no alternative. All East Africans, no doubt, could
crop as intensively as the Kara if it mattered.

The Haya are banana producers but they do not have naturally
fertile soil, although they have the rainfall and humidity for this
crop. They have evolved a system whereby they set up houses in a
circular fashion and mulch within the circle, depositing everything
that will enrich the soil (Friedrich 1968). In other words, they have
created the soil they need with, no doubt, huge expense in labor,
for reasons that are unclear but which must have compensated for
the investment. The Haya at one time had large herds of cattle
which they lost through the incursions of tsetse, but one presumes
they could have grown cereal crops in the savannah in which they
live.

To summarize, the extent to which labor was the critical factor
of production, and still is in most places, varied from low in the
fertile banana-growing areas to quite high in the dry tsetse areas
such as much of Tanzania. And in some places, like Ukara and Bu-
haya, agriculture became quite intensive, enduring the high labor
costs either because they were unavoidable or because the ultimate
payoff was high. But in all areas of the Agricultural Zone, labor was
normally the most important factor of production although land
may have become the chief constraint in areas of banana production.

This is further reflected in the fact, noted by Goody (1973) in his comparison of production and social organization between Africa and Asia, that bridewealth was nearly universal in Africa, even in the Pastoral Zone, an example of the few exceptions to this being the Barabaig, pastoralists of the nonagricultural variety, who employ dowry, a payment, as Goody says, for taking a woman off one's hands. The low bridewealth paid by Maasai, despite their wealth, may also reflect the fact that they do not engage in agriculture, although the evidence for this conclusion is not conclusive since the nearly nomadic Turkana and nomadic Somali pay high brideprices. Bridewealth is a correlate of the demand for female labor, the main supply of labor in indigenous production systems. Everywhere it is women who are the backbone of agricultural production.

With respect to the question of choice, considering that, unlike in West Africa, women were usually thoroughly subordinated to men and thus unable to establish independent identity as a production force, men were faced with the need to decide how to expend resources on women treated as a malleable work force. The outcome of the process was overwhelmingly unequivocal. Allowing for cases like the Barabaig, or perhaps the Maasai, where women were not important in the production of crops, livestock were invested in acquiring variable rights in women up to the maximum permissible by resources (Schneider 1964). Murdock (1967) and I, in separate research, found that the amount of bridewealth transferred for rights in women correlated with the ratio of livestock to people; the richer the society, the more they paid, and the greater the rights they obtained.

However, it should also be taken into account that investment in women was usually for a dual purpose, to obtain children as well as labor. Thus women were seen as a type of capital, equivalent in many ways to livestock, whose production of children and crops was parallel to the production, by livestock, of offspring and food, such as milk, or manure among people who used it. Female offspring were a source of wealth, through the bridewealth, and male children were a source of wealth since they became members of the father's group and thus a source of power. But while cattle or camels might provide a means of achieving egalitarian status, children did not, simply because the complexity of restrictions on marriage and kinship did not permit a sufficiently high rate of increase of family to accomplish this. For now, no more will be said on this subject, which will be examined more completely in the next chapter.

Communal cooperation in house construction

The presence of lineages, which will also be examined in more detail in the next chapter, seems to relate in good part to the need for male labor in large, dependable amounts at critical points in the production process. One of the chief characteristics of these groups of unilineally related men is that they come together on request (being unable, usually, to refuse such a request) to weed fields, thresh grain, open new swidden fields, build houses, sacrifice to the ancestors (as for rain), and repel enemies. As we shall see later, the importance of lineage declines appreciably in certain heavily pastoral areas.

Hopkins (1973), speaking of West Africa, has associated the rise of slavery there and variability in its intensity to variable degrees of labor shortage. And Douglas (1964) has detailed the apparent situation which existed in Central Africa up to the colonial period with respect to the "pawning" of people. Central Africa, of which southern Tanzania is really a part, depended heavily upon swidden, using *chitemene* or "wide circle slash and burn" and various types of composting (as in Nyiha) for production of crops in the total absence of cattle. The need to conserve labor was severe. But in East Africa in general it seems not to have attained the level of intensity of these last two areas.

The extent of pawning, servitude, or slavery (whatever one chooses to call it) in East Africa before the Arabs created large scale markets for slaves in the eighteenth and nineteenth century is not clear. But it seems to have been confined to the selling or pawning of children. The Turu used to pawn children to Nyamwezi traders in exchange for grain during periods of drought, a practice which seems to have occurred in many other places, as one would suspect.

It is difficult to say why slaving remained so underdeveloped here as compared, for example, to West Africa or Central Africa, but the obvious deduction from the economic approach I am using is that despite the critical importance of labor in the Agricultural Zone, the more favorable production possibilities for crops and the presence of pastoralism on a larger scale worked against it. It is demonstrable (Schneider n.d.) that slaving correlates negatively with pastoralism in East Africa, no doubt due to the fact that pastoralism is a capital-intensive, rather than labor-intensive, process. Slaves, in fact, are seen as a kind of human livestock to which cattle or camels are superior. But, like women, who are also in some respects seen as human livestock (they are often referred to as "cows"), their potential for capital growth is not good compared to cattle and they are abandoned for cattle and camels where possible.

Turning to the question of economic choice among pastoralists, the situation with respect to cropping choice is in many ways less clear than it is for agriculturalists. On the one hand, it is plain that

pastoralists do not ordinarily allow cropping requirements to interfere with cattle and camel production. The Maasai, as we have seen,
occupy good agricultural land (or did in the past), but only the
Uasin Gishu, in the highlands of the Rift in Kenya, and the Arush
or agricultural Maasai engage in agriculture, the main body of
Maasai, including the Samburu, closely related to Maasai, eschew-
ing it altogether. The Turkana engage only desultorily in agriculture,
the dry conditions in their country demanding freedom to move,
and the Somalis, except for some in the south (the Sab), are also
entirely nomadic. No doubt these people could find areas in their
lands in which to engage in agriculture if they chose to do so. The
Pokot exemplify the choice situation facing such pastoralists. In a
land containing both good grazing and good agricultural land, they
choose to grow crops extensively only if their cattle operations fall
below what is economically supportable, at which point individuals move to the mountains and engage in agriculture until they
can recoup their losses by selling grain to pastoralists or by other
means. It is perhaps for this reason that bulrush millet, which probably would do well in the drier areas, is not grown. Rather they
choose for the most part to grow finger millet and some sorghum
in the better growing areas, crops which probably bring a better return for the time expended. And there is at least one area in the
mountains specializing in maize production.

Pastoralists, when they efficiently can combine agricultural operations with cattle or camel production, do so. This occurs where
grazing for large herds can be mixed with cropping, a condition that
occurs where rainfall is high enough, as in Tesoland, Kipsigisland,
or Jieland. The Kipsigis have been maize growers for a long time,
as a result of impetus in the early part of the century from the colonial government. They now keep large numbers of cattle in an
area which also produces large amounts of maize for export. And
the Teso, about whom I shall say more in the last chapter, who
have been enticed into cotton growing since early in the century,
have developed an efficient system which takes advantage of plowing operations for cotton to increase finger millet production while

Herding Zebu cattle

at the same time continuing the production of cattle at a high level.

On the whole, there is a clear tendency for crop production to be inversely correlated with livestock holdings, a fact which may be concluded from Table V on the ratios of cattle to people in a sample of East African pastoral people when it is noted that every society in the Table with 6:1 or better is effectively without agriculture, allowing for the fact that the Uganda Pokot should really be seen as part of the larger Pokot society in which, as noted earlier, pure pastoralism is a strategy open to those who can achieve it but where failure leaves open the option of going back to the mountains to engage in agriculture. The Somalis are not included in the list because they are almost exclusively camel raisers. However, everywhere they are found, camels are considered to be more valuable than cattle by a ratio of about 3 to 1. Thus the Somalis, with 2.9 camels per person, have approximately the equivalent of 9 cattle per person. Similarly, the Rendille, Borana, Samburu, and Turkana have camels in ratios of 9, 5, 8 and .1 per person, which similarly augments their ratios of livestock to people.

TABLE V
Ratios of Cattle to People in a Sample
of East African Pastoral People

Agriculture lacking or insignificant	18 : 1	Barabaig of central Tanzania
	17.5 : 1	Samburu of Kenya
	15 : 1	Maasai of Tanzania
	9 : 1	Rendille of northern Kenya
	8 : 1	Dorobo of Kenya; Uganda Pokot
	6.5 : 1	Borana Galla of northern Kenya
	6 : 1	Kenya Maasai
Agriculture important in varying degrees	4 : 1	Karamojong of Uganda
	3.7 : 1	Jie of Uganda
	3.6 : 1	Dodoth of Uganda
	3 : 1	Kenya Pokot
	2 : 1	Kipsigis of Kenya
	1.7 : 1	Meru of Kenya
	1.4 : 1	Teso of Uganda
	1.3 : 1	Giriama; Kitui Kamba
	1.2 : 1	Taita
	1.1 : 1	Turu of Tanzania
	1.1 : 1	Machakos Kamba

The figures on which these ratios are based were gathered from various sources including Morgan (1969), volumes of the Ethnographic Survey of Africa series of the International African Institute and individual monographs.

The dominant economic fact about cattle production in East Africa is that the cost of producing and maintaining this form of capital is kept to a minimum, making it similar to open-range beef raising in America, contrasted with the intensive feeding and production of milk cows. But East Africans do not raise cattle for beef and so the size of the animals is not a first consideration, although normally all males except the number needed to reproduce the herds are castrated, thereby producing larger, tamer animals. The average weight of full-grown steers, as previously noted, is probably only about 700 pounds or less, compared to a full-grown two-year-old Hereford steer in this country whose weight might be double that. The size varies, of course, with grazing conditions, Maasai, Karamojong, or Borana cattle seeming generally to be larger than those of more agricultural people like the Turu.

Unlike in the western Sudan, livestock must be housed at night to protect them from carnivorous animals. It is therefore generally the case that pastoralists' homesteads are corrals within which the houses of the inhabitants are placed along with the animals, the large animals in the open area and the small ones in the houses. The reason for this is that it would be easy for a lion or leopard to take a calf, sheep, or goat from an open corral at night while it would have more difficulty with a full-grown bovine.

Other than this major cost, no fodder is raised for cattle (the Kara and Chagga being excepted); feeding is accomplished by grazing in the open; there is no shelter from the rain or other elements; and medical care is minimal. For a Turu cattle raiser, for example, keeping cattle consists chiefly of providing a corral to keep them in at night and arranging a deal with an owner of grazing land to graze the cattle in return for herding duties. In Pokotland, grazing land is not owned, so it is merely a matter of taking the herd out each day (when it is one's turn to herd, although Pokot also use their wives as herders at times) wherever some grazing can be found until all the grass is gone. When that situation occurs, the younger men must take them to remote areas, leaving the main part of the family at home—but this does not happen every year. And in places like Turkanaland herds must move constantly to find grazing. Africans will sometimes endure large costs in order to keep cattle. The Chagga of Mount Kilimanjaro are famous for having raised their cattle in underground pens to protect them from Maasai raids, carrying fodder to them that they had cut from the wild savannah. And the Wambugwe, on the other side of Maasailand from Chagga, who were also faced with the problem of frequent Maasai raiding, built very large tembes in which they kept the cattle. According to Gray (1963), the Sonjo, an enclave in the center of north Maasailand in Tanzania, were unable to keep cattle because of the high incidence of raids so they began raising goats instead. Since goats and cattle are equatable, this meant that the Sonjo did not have to abandon animal husbandry as an economic system.

Raiding for cattle was not simply a Maasai preoccupation. It was common to pastoralism as a means of production. Again, the degree to which a society was (or is, because it is still prevalent, as in Karamojongland, Pokotland, Turkanaland, and other remote areas) prone to indulge in raiding seems to have depended on the ratio of cattle to people; the high-ratio people all seem to have been prodigious raiders, including some agricultural pastoralists like the Pokot and Nandi. The reason might be that as ratios rise, dependence on the animals for meat, blood (taken from the live animals), milk, and exchange for grain rises. Thus a paradox: those who had the most were, in a sense, most likely to be short of animals. While raiding has been reduced considerably in East Africa, the remote areas where it still goes on exhibit another paradox. As government pressure to sell animals to the new-style beef markets increases, the pressure to indulge in raiding to recoup the losses increases. Hence such "developed" pastoral societies as the Karamojong, who have even taken to plowing, are notorious raiders.

Finally, we must examine the way droughts affect pastoral operations. Droughts are an important factor to most East African people at all times but in varying degrees. Since annual rainfall usually comes within a few months, leaving the rest of the year dry, the crops chosen must be suited to long dry periods and also to intermittent drought. As already indicated, the African cereals are uniquely suited to such conditions and such crops are still in the majority in the grain-growing areas.

But there are also intermittent droughts over longer periods. Less is understood about this but Dahl and Hjort (1976) have noted that some authors feel that droughts tend to occur in ten to twelve-year intervals, an opinion with which the Turu agree. However, Turu feel that such droughts are minor and should be differentiated from really disastrous droughts, which cause starvation among people, and which happen once in a lifetime. Through simulation Dahl and Hjort have studied the effects on herds of the less-severe droughts. The important conclusion from this study is that because droughts of about two years' length cause calving to cease, oscillations, or wavelike alterations, are generated in the structure of the herd (e.g., at the fourth year the normal new influx of heifers to begin calving is missing) that threaten the herd's future (because, as in any oscillation, a positive feedback effect causing acceleration of change rather than dampening it could be induced in a negative direction, like deflation, causing the demise of the herd). The effects of a two-year drought could cause oscillations over a long period, perhaps ten years, and a three-year drought would have even more severe effects.

With respect to the choice situation faced by the pastoralist, all this suggests that at any time the manager would surely be sensitive to the forces of oscillation in his herd and would have to be making decisions to counter them. For example, he might have to effect exchanges to get his heifer population in balance. After a drought the manager would be even more severely tested and this condition would probably induce an increase in the rate of exchanges among managers to balance their herds. Ultimately, as Dahl and Hjort suggest, a maximizing strategy for any herd manager would be to get as large a herd as possible thereby decreasing, linearly at least, the chances that a drought could induce a deflation of the herd.

Another effect of drought should also be noted. Among the Turu, and therefore very probably over most of East Africa, the threat that drought poses for herd managers is an opportunity for specialists in grain production. Turu farmers who have few cattle store grain against the occurrence of droughts in the expectation of selling the grain to the pastoralists, who have decreased their own grain production at the margin because of the superior profits in animal husbandry. During the drought, grain prices skyrocket and a general redistribution of cattle takes place against the movement of grain. Droughts, therefore, have a positive, egalitarian effect which is often overlooked by outsiders.

Dahl and Hjort note that during a year of "normal" herd growth the rate of increase is about 3.4% with an increase over ten years of 72%. Massell (1963), applying a Cobb-Douglas function to Turu data on the production function, calculated an annual rate of return on investment of about 20%. Although figures like these are subject to criticism, there is ample indirect evidence, including the powerful pastoral propensities of all East Africans, to support the conclusion that pastoralism is seen as very profitable. Thus, the question arises as to how this can be if it is true that every ten years or so herds are subject to disastrous threats like the ones detailed by Dahl and Hjort, and perhaps once in a lifetime, as in the case of the great drought in the Sahel and East Africa in 1973, herds may be almost completely destroyed. The answer is complex and I shall not meet it directly. It seems sufficient to suggest that the pastoralist is not very different from the business speculator in America, particularly the speculator in stocks, who despite a crash like that of 1929 moves back into the market as soon as he can, who sees the short term profit from such investment as superior to other forms of investment despite the chances of great loss over the long haul. As Keynes is reputed to have said, "In the long run we are all dead." In any case such a chance at great profit is better than no chance at all, which is the fate of the total swidden agriculturalist.

EXCHANGE

The traditional view of East African economies, which considered each household as ideally self-sufficient and denied the existence of media of exchange, is linked to another traditional view that there were no markets for goods. By this I mean that it has been conventional not only to assert that no marketplaces existed, but also to deny that there was a market in the technical sense of profitable exchanges going on, whether in a marketplace or not. This amounts to a denial that there were people who went to the market for goods they did not produce, and producers who turned out goods for these demanders. It is probably because of the existence of this tradition that the most obvious market of all, the market for women—the marriage system—was claimed not to be a market and marriage not to be a transaction. Increasingly this view is being discredited along with the recognition of currency, markets, and nonself-sufficiency. There can be no doubt that women perform valuable services, producing goods which have general value and for which other people are willing to pay. And there can be no doubt that valuable commodities are exchanged for them. This is the definition of a market system and essence of an economy. To insist otherwise is to define economics so narrowly as to make the concept useless.

The first thing we must consider when we view the exchange system is the relativity of markets. The volume of trade, the velocity of trade (the speed with which goods move from one person to another against the medium of exchange), and the value of trade (calculated in terms of exchanges with European markets) is usually so low when compared with our market system that it is easy for us to decide that no real economy existed in indigenous systems, in most places. This, of course, is a fallacy. The important consideration for determining whether an economic system exists is not only these elements of volume, velocity, and relative value but whether it is indeed a system. Were people depending on others to produce goods to accomplish their goals? Were people producing goods because there was a demand for them? And were the decisions of one about producing or consuming dependent on the actions of the others to any degree? The answer, of course, is yes. The rule of exogamy, which required men to obtain wives from outside their kin groups, forced them into the market to obtain wives, which in turn forced a circulation of media of exchange, notably livestock. The concentration on production of livestock led producers to grow insufficient grain to feed themselves and forced them into the market for grain. And the exchange of cattle necessitated by such things as marriage and the need to obtain grain would have caused imbalances in some herds, threatening oscillatory effects such as just described and requiring further exchanges with stock associates (which I will describe later) to counter the threat.

The grain producers, in turn, depended on the pastoralists' demand for grain to make their production decisions reasonable, producing grain in excess of household needs in order to obtain livestock. It is no more true to think of East Africans as having no economic system because the volume and other measures of production, consumption, and exchange did not compare with ours than it is to think that an industrial country has less an economy than America if its gross national product is half that of ours.

Exchange occurred in East Africa in three different ranges. First of all, there was intrasocietal exchange. This included, most noticeably, the exchange of women through the marriage system based on the common practice of lineage exogamy. Sometimes women were traded outside the society, as was often the case between Kikuyu and Maasai, but the common exchange of women was intrasocietal, as one would expect considering the general tendency (similar to our own) of ethnic prejudice, but also because the value of an exchange with a foreigner was less than within the society for reasons which will be discussed later. Among many Arabs, including the Bagarra or Cattle Arabs of the Sudan (Cunnison 1966), the consideration of cost led normally to a first marriage with father's brother's daughter, that is, patrilateral parallel cousin marriage, a practice which most East Africans could not engage in because they did not allow lineage endogamy.

In addition to marriage, there is another very important type of internal exchange. It goes under different labels—livestock loaning, stock associateship—and is institutionalized enough so that most East African societies have a word for it: Turu *uriha*, Gogo *kukoza*, Pokot *tilia*, and, perhaps, the Somali *heer*. This practice, which will be discussed more fully later, is as much an exchange as marriage even though, like marriage, it is not a total transfer of rights (quitclaim). That is to say, when the Pokot gives his tilia partner a cow in exchange for a steer but retains a partial right to the cow, he has engaged in an exchange, even though that exchange is not total. One of the peculiar biases in anthropological writings is the idea that the only exchanges which are "economic" are those which are total or quitclaim. The fact is that the most significant part of our own economy is the contract relations which exist between exchanging partners. The same is true in East Africa where, for example, the marriage exchange system is usually a continuing contract relationship rather than a total exchange operation. And, in fact, the impact of the economy on the social structure rests on this fact. The differentiated roles people play in relation to each other are based on the contractual exchanges between them.

An East African cattle raiser customarily sends some of his stock to be held by other men. This practice is often explained as a means of distributing the animals so that not all will be lost in case of a raid or a localized outbreak of disease. In fact, to judge by the Turu case, the reasons can be enormously complex. Just as a sample we may list here some of the reasons a Turu husbandman might send his animals to be taken care of by another man in a different community (which is usually where they are sent): to guard against loss from localized disease; to obtain the goodwill of a respected man; to lessen pressure on grazing resources; to obtain the husbandry skills of the borrower; to favor relatives who need help; to lessen the work burden on oneself; to hide one's wealth; to provide one's daughter with milk for her children when her husband has insufficient cows; to effect an exchange for a steer while keeping partial ownership in the loaned cow; as a response to demands that one be generous with one's wealth; to get rid of small stock which use up grass but produce little manure; to gain the deference of others.

Undoubtedly this list could be extended, because what it amounts to is a partial list of the strategies a man may employ by using his cattle to maintain and increase his wealth while also allying others to him.

The reasons a person may choose to borrow animals are equally complex (and a loaner is also usually a borrower): to get milk for the family (cows give milk only when nursing calves); to obtain manure in order to increase grain production; to establish a tie with a rich man; to put up a good front, since no one knows for sure whether you own the animals or not; to replace the animals one has loaned to others (!); to do a favor for a friend who must, for some reason, disperse his cows; to get a good bull for servicing one's cows; as a favor to a friend who has taken your cow on loan (and, perhaps, wants to balance his herd).

Other than these internal exchanges there are movements of other goods: grain loans and exchanges; exchanges for iron goods, pots, baskets, and other products where specialization is involved. Although it is true that most people can make any of the goods they use, it is not always sensible for everyone to make his own. Thus it is common for certain people to be known as superior pot, basket, stool, or sword makers, just as some women make better beer than others and are therefore able to sell it on occasion. Because of this in some places marketplaces developed: Arush/Maasai, Somaliland, Kikuyuland, Kiga, and in many other places.

The second kind of trade may be called intersocietal direct because it is direct between two groups. Very little attention has been paid to this kind of trade, partly because (as I have said) there has been a tendency to think of East African societies as isolated from each other. But it is also a fact that compared to much of the rest of Africa, marketplaces for intersocietal commerce were rare in East Africa. What trade there was was conducted rather discreetly. Kenyatta and Leakey (1977, 479) tell of how Kikuyu who desired to trade with the Maasai would go to Maasailand and work through a friend who as part of the transaction would provide the man in a strange land with protection. Since standing armies did not exist in East Africa, it was ordinarily feasible for people to travel among strangers so long as they went in groups large enough to pose a challenge for any local citizens who chose to assault them.

There were some marketplaces. Feierman (1974) speaks of internal markets in Shambaai, near the north coast of Tanzania, and also of markets such as Makuyuni at the south tip of Shambaai where regular trade was conducted with the Zigula people to the south. These markets were held every five days and the Shambaa customarily brought bananas and tobacco to exchange for seeds, game meat, salt, and grain during famine times. Interestingly, even though these two people lived side by side, climatic conditions in this area are such that they had different harvest times so that they could trade with each other for grain during their own short seasons as well as buy seeds so that they did not have to hold out all their seed grain for the next planting. This is a good example of why trading occurs, a juxtaposition of shortage and plenty creating alternating demand between the two groups. Makuyuni market also served coast people who thereby moved goods from the isolated areas behind the coast to the coast and thence to the world, so to speak, since the goods could be bought by seagoing Arab traders.

Another example of marketplaces comes from Wagner's account of the Abaluyia. The ethnic complexity of these people, who have only in recent times come under a common designator, indexes the production conditions that would serve to cause the rise of fixed markets. Wagner (1954, 27–28) lists the positions of the various Abaluyia as follows: north of the Nzoia River, in order of proximity to it, are the North Wanga, the Marach, the Hayo, and the Vugusu (or Bugusu, and related Tadjoni). South of the river and nearest to it are the Nyala (or Kabras, or Kakalelwa); then come the Tsotso, Marama, South Wanga (and Mukulu), Holo, Isuxa, Idaxo, Kisa, Nyole, Logoli, and Tiriki. One of the markets serving this complex of ethnic groups, which continued down into colonial times, was at Mbale, in Uganda, even though most of these people are in Kenya. The kinds of indigenous goods traded there when Wagner studied them in the 1940s were probably much the same as in the past. These included pots, pipes, baskets, quail cages, grindstones and grinders, string, maize, sorghum, eleusine, beans, sugar cane, sesame seeds, groundnuts, tobacco, bananas, salt, beads, oranges, lemons, cattle, sheep, goats, chickens, firewood, charcoal, knives, pipestems, bows and arrows, stools, wooden bowls, spoons, peas, honey, snuff, meat, fish, mats, and soda. The participants in the market included Luo and Nandi, as well as such members of the Abaluyia Bantu enclave as Logoli, Nyole, Tiriki, Kisa, Idaxo, and Isuxa.

The agricultural Maasai or Arush on Mount Meru in Tanzania

had a regular market for trading with plains Maasai and later, when the Arush had occupied the lower plains, for trade with their plains fellows. Since the mountains and plains were specialized for different kinds of production, the mountain people bought such things as leather for clothing and goats in exchange for bananas.

Even though marketplaces were rather rare, most ethnographers speak of some kind of regular intersocietal trade, accounts which, when aggregated, suggest a pattern of regular and widespread movement of goods between societies. The Gusii and Luo on the northeast and east coasts of Lake Victoria also had different climates, which promoted the movement of food between them (LeVine 1962). I have spoken of Maasai and Kikuyu exchanges. At other points in Maasailand besides Kikuyuland and Arush there was also trade, such as with the Sonjo, who obtained goats and cow's milk from the Maasai in exchange for gourds (eight gourds for one goat when Gray was there), women, and children. And Shambaa traded tobacco to Maasai for livestock. Other than this, the Meru people on Mount Meru traded with the Arush on the plains; the Lugbara obtained fish from the Madi, iron ore from the Congo, and papyrus mats from the Kakwa in exchange for goats. The Kikuyu traded with the Kamba, another example of trade promoted by differential harvests, in which grain moved against livestock. The Barabaig traded with surrounding people (Turu, Iraqw, and others of the Rift Anomaly group) for grain in exchange for livestock. The Karamojong traded regularly with certain people like the Tobur and Tepes (who lived in highland enclaves in Karamojland) for metal goods, shields, baboon skins, tobacco, and the like. The Shambaa traded with the Pare to the north for iron goods, with Kamba for ivory, and with the Nyika people behind Mombasa. The Turu and Nyamwezi exchanged iron for livestock, the Turu obtained pots from Iramba, and the Turkana traded with the Pokot for grain. This sample list should make it plain that intertribal movements of goods was not exceptional.

A third type of trade may be called intersocietal indirect, which must be distinguished from long distance trade, an innovation of the eighteenth- and nineteenth-century Swahili and Arabs. Inter-societal indirect trade is really only an extension of intersocietal trade. It seems likely that every part of East Africa was in one degree or another linked with every other part by indirect trade. One good piece of inferential evidence for this is the value of cattle. If one attempts to relate the amount of brideprice paid in various societies to rights obtained in wives, as I did several years ago (Schneider 1964), one striking revelation is that from one part of Africa to another the amount of rights gained seems to be about the same for about the same number of cattle. It is as if we are dealing with a rationalized market in which monetary values are equalized over the whole area due to the fact that arbitrage, the playing off of one local economy against another, is eliminated due to the general spread of knowledge, through trade, of values. An Arab trader could obtain a large amount of ivory from a Nyamwezi chief for a few cheap beads only until the chief discovered what only the Arab previously knew, that in the market outside East Africa his ivory was worth a lot more beads.

The equalization of values of cattle might be due to the fact that indirect intersocietal trade, linking most societies, disseminated information about exchange values in the same manner as the chief and the Arab. A good example of how this might happen is contained in a rare illustration of indirect trade from Uganda (Driberg 1925, 29). In Figure 2 we see five groups variously exchanging goats, cattle, and grain: Tirangori, Kokir, Didinga, Dodoth, and Acholi. Driberg describes the movement of these commodities (as indicated in the figure) and from this we can imagine some of the economic reasoning that must have been going on. The basis of this trade system was the fact that each of these groups was ultimately trying to obtain a certain mix of grain, goats, and cattle in the production of which each was differentially successful. The Kokir obtained goats from the Tirangori in return for cattle. They then traded the goats to the Didinga for cattle. The Didinga shipped grain to the south for goats. They then traded the goats to the Acholi in the west for grain. The rationale for this is that the Kokir

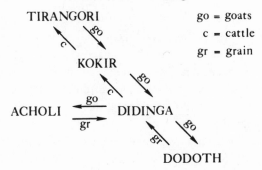

Indirect Trade in Northern Uganda

FIG. 2

are buying cattle from the Didinga to resell to the Tirangori for a profit (the cut of the middleman) and they are buying goats from the Tirangori to sell to the Didinga for a cut. Similarly the Didinga are selling goats to the Acholi for grain in order to resell the grain to Dodoth for a profit. In all this movement of goods, the cattle would have played the chief role of medium of exchange, and because the market was integrated the value of cattle would have become standardized. Thus the value of the grain would have varied as it was handled by middlemen and as it became more and more remote from the place of production while the cattle would have remained constant and served as a means of calculating prices relative to scarcity. That the goats moved against cattle in some places suggests that they would have been treated as a commodity rather than as a lower denomination of cattle.

I do not believe this interpretation of Driberg's data is farfetched because when I worked with the Pokot of Kenya I regularly encountered men who were buying goats in the eastern part of Pokotland and then moving them to the Karamojong area of Uganda to trade them at higher prices for cattle. Furthermore, examples of entrepreneurship within these societies are not hard to come by. When the colonial government began a destocking campaign in Unyaturu in 1956, entrepreneurs took immediate advantage of discrepancies between the internal Turu economy and the external colonial economy in order to make a profit. The chief discrepancy was that in their system the Turu valued cows over steers while in the colonial system steers were valued over cows. Thus, if an entrepreneur could buy a big steer in the internal system for the established exchange rate of 60 shillings (Shs. 60) and sell it in the colonial beef market for Shs. 250, he could then move back into the Turu system and obtain two and a half heifers at the standard exchange rate of Shs. 100 per heifer. Strange as it may seem, this opportunity did at times present itself to the watchful entrepreneur. La Fontaine (1958) records how the Gisu of Mount Elgon trade up to cattle by starting with field rats which are exchanged for a hen, which with her progeny is traded for a female goat, which with her progeny is traded for a cow. In north Gisu at one time twelve field rats bought a hen, six hens a goat, and three or four goats a cow.

CURRENCIES

Which brings us to the subject of currencies. For a very long time, up to recent years, there seemed to be a strong reluctance to accord to any African goods the status of currency, money, media of exchange. This has now changed. Einzig (1966) in his monumental work on "primitive" money includes in his account such items from East Africa as iron, salt, livestock, beads, cowry shells, cloth, and slaves. Similarly, Sundström (1975) lists cloth, copper, brass, pewter, guns and ammunition, iron, salt, cowries, beads, slaves, horses, and cattle. While this breakthrough is significant for understanding African economies, it is insufficient if we merely stop at designating goods as money or non-money. Money in fact is a relative concept, goods that act as money being distinguishable from other goods only by degrees.

The essential feature of money is the demand for it relative to other goods—that is to say, the relative inelasticity of demand for it. This is why livestock can act as money in these economies. There is probably no other good, certainly none as common as livestock, for which demand is so constant. Thus, while grain may be greatly desired just before the harvest, demand for it may fall to zero after a good harvest. Grain, therefore, would not make good money and no one ever lists it as such. The demand for cattle fluctuates, but there is always a strong demand. Thus, the farmer who has a good harvest may not be able to sell his grain, but he can always find a market for his cattle. It is because of this that cattle or other consumption goods are inexorably transformed into something other than what they were designed for in the first place, so to speak. And, as we have seen, once items begin to be used as money, this has an effect on their other uses. Iron tools acting as money are sometimes transformed in such a way that they can no longer function as tools. Cattle used as money are less useful as food or milk producers.

The general inelasticity of demand for cattle over the whole of East Africa is not characteristic of all monies. The demand for salt is localized, appearing as money most notably among the Galla, who keep it in bar form. A people like the Barabaig would not care to treat it as money because they have a huge deposit of salt in Lake Balangida, making salt a free good among them. Historically the demand for certain goods has altered with the result that some old monies have been reduced to a mundane state. Cloth, once a rarity in East Africa, lost its monetary status with the entrance of the colonial powers and the importation of cheap cloth. Beads and cowries are no longer money because they have become very common and cheap. Iron goods no longer have a monetary function because iron is now easy to come by. Slaves have no value because slavery has been abolished. In fact, about the only historical item which still has a monetary function is livestock, although among urbane East Africans this has also changed, with livestock being valued much in the same way that Europeans and Americans do.

Another thing about East African indigenous currencies that must be kept in mind is that those things which attain monetary status are not treated discretely but are amalgamated in the minds of the people into a monetary system. Thus, as pointed out earlier, a certain number of goats will be equated to a heifer or a steer so that calculations may be made in terms of goats as common denominators, and payment may be made with them as well. If a man owes three-fifths of a heifer to another, he may settle his debt with three goats.

These standardized ratios of exchange, similar to our willingness to exchange four quarters for a paper dollar (even though the value of the silver or other metal in the quarter may not be worth the metal behind the dollar), used to extend to other goods before these goods became too depreciated in value. The Turu monetary system had cattle as the big notes, goats and sheep as denominators of those, iron goods as denominators of sheep and goats, and cowries or beads as denominators of iron goods. Today among many rural East Africans these lower-denominator goods have been replaced with European-type money while the livestock remain as media of exchange. In 1960, again among the Turu, a goat was exchangeable for Shs. 20 and, since a heifer was equal to five goats, this made a heifer equal to Shs. 100.

When the idea of money as a good for which demand is relatively inelastic is grasped it is easy to understand why it is that throughout East Africa, wherever the European system has not taken over, all large-scale exchanges are made in livestock. Up to very recent times almost everywhere nothing but cattle, sheep, and goats were acceptable as bridewealth payment.

There is another aspect of the monetary system that is more difficult to explain. But understanding it is essential to getting a grip on the indigenous economies. In our economy, monetary objects obtain a portion of their value from the fact that they can be loaned out at interest. A person who holds money not only attains a superior control position in that he can obtain any mix of goods he desires, but he also has the option, at times when he finds that investing in goods is not convenient, of loaning the money out at interest, thus profiting more directly. It is because the East African can do something similar to this with cattle that cattle are especially valuable. The heifer, as a potential breeder of calves, and the cow as one who is already an established breeder, are the most valuable of large livestock among cattle-oriented people. Bulls and steers are also valuable but less so than cows. The offspring of a cow are equal to full-grown cattle with the result that breeding cows are very profitable. When the cows are not being used in exchanges they are busy reproducing themselves. It seems to be generally true that on the average cows in East Africa have a life of about twelve years and produce about five calves. This, without further consideration, means an annual return of about 41% per annum over the life of the cow. If we allow a 25% failure-to-calve rate over the entire herd, the average cow will produce a total of only 3.75 calves, thus reducing the annual return to 31%. Further, taking into account chances of death by disease and other constraints, the annual return would be even lower. As I mentioned earlier, Massell calculated from the Turu data an annual return of 20%, but the average rate by Dahl and Hjort's calculations would be less, although still appreciable.

The value of considering the return on investment in cattle, even if only approximate, is brought home sharply if we consider what it takes to make an equivalent return by investing in agriculture. Using Turu figures again, in the harvest of 1960 a grain grower could obtain one heifer for 20 *debes* of grain. Since each debe equaled 40 pounds, the heifer was equal to 800 pounds of grain. This, in turn, was equal to about 2 *kius*, a kiu being a grain bin holding about 400 pounds of grain. A man and his wife, putting all their resources and energy to the production of bulrush millet, could not expect to grow much more grain than this in one year. Thus, while a cow, virtually unaided and only lightly guarded (by a young boy, more often than not), can produce a calf, the whole household must be mobilized to produce its equivalent worth in grain. Of course, low productivity is common enough in the drought-prone area so that any grain that can be saved from year to year may increase enormously in value in a bad harvest year. In 1938 one Turu bought heifers for 120 pounds of grain apiece. Nevertheless, it is easy to see why the African would consider resources put into cattle as superior to those put into agriculture, allowing for the fact that prices fluctuate.

CONCLUSION

To summarize, in terms of means of production, as opposed to relations of production, which we treat in the following chapters, East Africa consists of two zones, Agricultural and Pastoral, the former containing ratios of cattle to people of less than 1:1 while the latter contains ratios of 1:1 or more, although all those with the lower ratios among the pastoralists are also engaged in agriculture. Within the Agricultural Zone, whose membership is essentially determined by the prevalence of tsetse fly, making large livestock raising nearly impossible, the chief consideration in the factor mix for production of crops is labor, whose relative scarcity leads to the use of swidden methods, unless more intensive methods without higher costs are possible, women as a labor market and bridewealth to secure them, lineages as a method of mobilizing male labor for short-term, highly developed agricultural operations, and slavery in some instances.

Within the Pastoral Zone, agricultural pursuits become more and more marginal as the cattle/people ratios (or camel/people ratios) increase, until they disappear altogether among the wealthiest pastoralists. This is because the return on investment in animal husbandry is much more profitable than agriculture.

All East African economies are and must be involved in interhomestead and wider exchange networks whose most important elements are exchanges of livestock for women and grain. However, within the Agricultural Zone, since livestock are comparatively rare, exchanges importantly involve service leading to important social structural effects which will be detailed in succeeding chapters. These movements of goods are facilitated by the widespread use of a variety of repositories of value of which the most important are livestock but which in other times also included such commodities as salt, cloth, iron, and guns.

CHAPTER V

Marriage, Descent, and Kinship

ANTHROPOLOGICAL TREATMENT of East African societies has emphasized certain elements of social structure, particularly marriage, descent, and kinship organization and terminology, while avoiding economics, although G. P. Murdock, as long ago as 1949, in his landmark *Social Structure*, argued at length and convincingly for the need to examine the economic base of change of residence at marriage, which he took to be the key cause in determining descent and kinship. In recent years there has been a shift in the direction suggested by Murdock in the work of people like Jack Goody on West Africa (1973) or Peter Rigby on the Gogo (1969), to name only two.

The strongest case for taking economics into account was made by Fredrick Barth's (1967) analysis of production and social structure among the Fur of Darfur (to the north of the Dinka) in the southern Sudan. He identifies two types of households, the first joint, in which husband and wife work cooperatively, and the second conjugal, in which they go largely independent ways, the latter associated with agricultural production and the former with nomadic pastoralism. According to Barth, whether one or the other is favored depends on its advantage for the type of production chosen. Translated into a different context, this is like saying that whether a society has localized lineages or nonlocalized lineages depends on the kind of production activities in which the people are engaged, and whether those activities demand cooperation or

105

not. The kind of descent and marriage systems and kinship terminologies that East Africans have also reflects these considerations.

THE HOUSE-PROPERTY COMPLEX

Throughout East Africa the characteristic form of homestead is based on what Gluckman (1971, 242) calls the house-property complex. In this "a man transmits property to his sons through his wives." This may be contrasted with a kind of system in which the wives and sons are pooled and sons inherit from a general estate.

The house-property complex (which for the sake of brevity may now be referred to as the H-P complex) is not, then, a physical aspect of homesteads but a kind of arrangement of relations in which a man heads a household and allows his wife or wives to conduct their own production operation, passing the proceeds to their sons (daughters ordinarily do not inherit and are, in fact, part of the estate to which their brothers lay claim). Nevertheless, this arrangement takes on a physical dimension which can be illustrated from the Turu system (Fig. 3). This mature Turu homestead, by which I mean that it has more than one house (and therefore more than one wife), is not typical because with three wives the male head of this homestead would exceed the statistical norm, which is 30% duopolygynous and 66% monogamous. Nevertheless, the

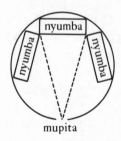

Mature Turu Homestead
(Khaya)
FIG. 3

fundamental pattern generated by the H–P complex is the same for larger or smaller homes. Each house (*nyumba*) within the homestead (*khaya*) contains its own cooking and grain storage facilities, independent fields outside the khaya, and separate and inviolate areas within the corral for the collection of manure, as indicated by the dotted lines. So thoroughly separate are these houses that in cases where disputes between wives of a homestead become very serious, one may move her operations outside the khaya and build a separate homestead for herself. This is an extreme measure since in the usual course of events women are too shy and socially debased to be able to deal with the external world alone. In the affairs of the house, the wife faces in, producing wealth and children, and the husband faces out, exchanging with other homesteads. In order for this to work the husband and wife must have a *modus operandi* which will make it worth his while to deal with the world for his wife and worth hers to cooperate with him. This means in both cases some sacrifice of independence.

Figure 4 exemplifies the modern form of homestead in an Acholi community in northern Uganda. These people have fewer cattle than the Turu and do not use manure for agriculture, with the result that the homestead does not conform to certain Turu characteristics based on large-scale herding. Still, the H–P complex expresses itself in the fact that the house of the head (1) is contained within a single boundary (13) with the houses of his two wives (2) who have their separate kitchens (4).

While the physical structure of these homesteads is not particularly unusual in East Africa, it could be that the H–P complex expresses itself in other ways. The important fact is the way the husband and wife or wives relate to each other.

Gluckman, in accordance with his interest in marriage and divorce, thought that the H–P complex conferred a greater degree of stability than marriage where property is pooled. However, this does not seem to follow. The glue in the H–P complex is the kind and amount of property which a husband can confer on his wife when he marries her (a good or poor piece of land; a small or large num-

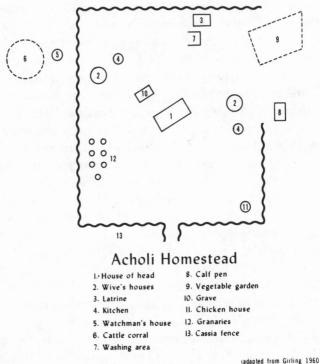

Acholi Homestead

1. House of head	8. Calf pen
2. Wive's houses	9. Vegetable garden
3. Latrine	10. Grave
4. Kitchen	11. Chicken house
5. Watchman's house	12. Granaries
6. Cattle corral	13. Cassia fence
7. Washing area	

(adapted from Girling 1960

FIG. 4

ber of livestock). In those societies where there is generally less wealth it might be predictable that marriages are tenuous, as a wife will frequently decide that there is little future with a certain man and, H–P complex or no, leave him for another. In fact, the evidence from East Africa is that marriage is not particularly stable in most places (Schneider 1964). The Turu, as I have noted, are some of the more successful livestock raisers, yet the rate of divorce is so great that almost no marriages succeed in the early years and men and women shift about frequently.

The question of the rate of divorce and its meaning does not concern us now so much as the question of why the H–P complex arises. Fundamentally it seems to be associated with the appearance of mobile wealth, particularly livestock. The concept of mobile wealth comes from Murdock's earlier mentioned study of social structure (Murdock 1949, 205) where, for example, he associates the rise of polygyny with the appearance of "movable property," which challenges land as the chief form of wealth. It is therefore no surprise that generally patrilineal East Africa, where cattle are widely held, can be characterized by the H–P complex while Central Africa, which Gluckman knew better, cannot be. Matrilineality, in which a man transmits wealth to his sister's sons through his sisters, is much more common and land, an immobile commodity, is the more common form of wealth. But other things than livestock are movable and the high rate of patrilineality in East Africa extends into the areas of relatively low livestock production, indicating that patrilineality does not require high ratios of cattle or only cattle.

UNILINEAL DESCENT

In East Africa the method of calculating descent is nearly uniformly unilineal, one of two methods used in human societies, the other being bilateral, as in America. In the unilineal system descent is traced through only one parent instead of both as in the bilateral method. The content of descent may vary greatly. In perhaps the simplest form it may consist of nothing but a name, so that if descent is traced through the father's side of the family the child takes the father's name, as the father took that of his father. In this sense even Americans practice unilineal descent. But in East Africa the content of descent is usually more significant than this. Normally property inheritance is prescribed by the method of reckoning descent. There are two most common types of unilineal descent, patrilineal and matrilineal. In the patrilineal system, which is the usual in East Africa, property would pass from father to son, in the matrilineal from mother's brother to sister's son. That is to say, women are seldom treated as equal to men and they cannot inherit property, so a man does not inherit from his mother in the

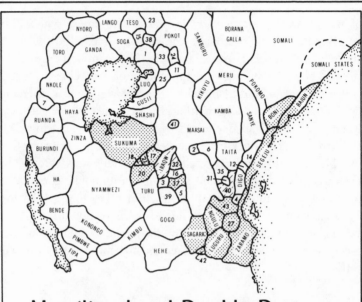

Matrilineal and Double Descent
in East Africa

Matrilineal Descent   Double Descent

1. Abaluyia	11. Dorobo	21. Isanzu	35. Pare
(Kavirondo)	12. Duruma	23. Karamojong	37. Rangi
2. Arush	14. Giriama	24. Keyo	38. Sebei
3. Barabaig	15. Gisu	25. Kipsigis	39. Sandawe
4. Bondei	16. Gorowa	27. Kwere	40. Shambaa
5. Burungi	17. Hadza	31. Mbugu	41. Sonjo
6. Chagga	18. Iambi	32. Mbugwe	42. Vidunda
7. Chiga	20. Iramba	33. Nandi	43. Zigula

Ethnic unit numbers correspond to those on Map V.

CLL·

MAP X

legal sense. But, paradoxically, the wealth which a man inherits comes from his mother's household, the product of her labor and management. In a sense, a man really inherits from his mother in both types of descent so that what he really obtains from his father (patrilineal) or mother's brother (matrilineal) is control of his mother's property. The close ties that often exist between mother and son rest on this fact.

There are a few East African examples of a rarer form of unilineal descent often mistakenly labeled double descent (my reason for saying this will become clear shortly). In this, found among the Wambugwe, the matrilineal method is said to be used for some things—say, descent of movable property— and the patrilineal for other things—such as descent of political office. Double descent is not the same as bilateral descent, since in the latter all property from both parents is aggregated and passed on to the children as a unit rather than being segregated into lines. Finally, double descent should not be confused with mixed unilineal descent such as occurs among the Sukuma, where some lineages (a group of unilineally related people) utilize patrilineal and others matrilineal descent. Nor should it be confused with alternating unilineal descent, as found among the Shambala, where descent may proceed from mother's brother to sister's sons in one generation but from father to son in another, creating a kind of unilineal descent grouping resembling the lineage but which is called ramage because of this fundamental alteration.

The rarity of both matrilineality and double descent (not to mention mixed and alternating unilineal descent) in East Africa can be seen by looking at Map X. The data are insufficient to say with certainty, but it seems likely that in addition to the cluster in eastern Tanzania, which includes such people as the Kaguru and Zaramo, other coastal people such as Segeju, Bajun, Digo, and Boni were also matrilineal. It should be added, however, that by my definition of ethnological East Africa in Chapter I these matrilineal societies should not even be included. If the arbitrary map were to be arbitrarily extended further south, the number of matrilineal societies would increase since the Makonde of southeast Tanzania and their cousins in northern Mozambique are all matrilineal too. The reader will appreciate that the value of including any matrilineal societies on the map is to make possible the inclusion of a division of the economic contrast between matrilineal and patrilineal forms of descent.

It is important to notice that in historic times matrilineality has come under attack, so to speak. Beidelman (1967) says of the eastern Tanzanian matrilineal cluster that they have increasingly turned to patrilineal descent. The Rangi of the Rift Anomaly have shifted in this direction in recent times. The Sukuma have taken to patrilineality in historic times in the places where cattle have been introduced. And in Unyamwezi there seems to have been a shift which, however, has not encompassed the chiefs, probably because gaining control of a chief's daughter would be too expensive for the kind of mobile wealth (which does not include many cattle) which they have. The map, therefore, must be read as only suggestive. Our evidence for matrilineality comes from different times and is confused by the fact, so important to the thesis of this book, that it is not a culture trait or fixed condition, but something that is subject to fluctuation from historic forces. These matrilineal systems tend to be the poorest in East Africa in the production and control of movable property, subject to shift at the first appearance of significant movable wealth. Hence, the map would tend, generally, to show a wider spread of matrilineal systems as one goes back in time to before the colonial period.

Probably the majority of East Africans use unilineal descent to determine group membership. Such groups are called lineages. A patrilineage is a group of persons who cooperate in some way and who often live together (although not necessarily), whose membership is determined by patrilineal descent. In order for such a grouping to be possible a method must be used to segregate one segment of unilineally related people from all the rest. This is done by designating as founder of a lineage some apical ancestor from whom all the unilineally related people of the segment of the larger lineage are

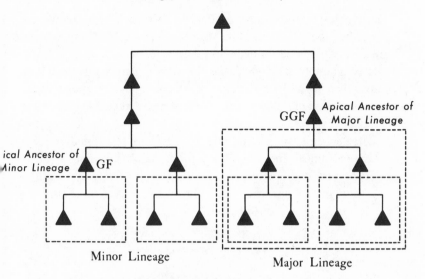

Lineage Segments

FIG. 5

said to be descended (Fig. 5). And, as the figure also shows, any person usually belongs to more than one lineage, each nested within the others, and each larger lineage designated by a different, more remote apical ancestor. The different levels of lineage correspond to different functions and/or more intense degrees of interaction. For example, a family of a group of brothers might be the lowest level (minor) lineage, whose apical ancestor is the grandfather (GF),* among whom goods are freely loaned. But the group of brothers might also be part of a larger (major) lineage composed of unilineally related men of the same village or territory, all sharing an apical ancestor beyond the GF or each group. Among the larger group there might be a moral imperative to help each other with cultivation of fields and collection of the wealth necessary for

---

*From this point on in the text, relatives will occasionally be indicated by abbreviations such as this.

marriage but with the provision that the help must be repaid within a specified time. In a real sense, segmentary lineage societies are one great lineage whose ultimate apical ancestor is the founder of the society, a remote, mythical figure. But among such people the moral imperative might be reduced to little more than a proscription against the use of lethal weapons in warfare between lineages of the society.

Later, when kinship terminology is discussed, the difference between patrilineal and matrilineal forms of organization as they relate to types of property and mobility of wealth will receive further attention, but for now the matter may be put aside.

DESCENT AND LOCATION OF RESIDENCE

It is probably true to say that the H–P complex is a form of organization that goes with patrilineality and patrilocal residence (the married couple dwelling near the residence of the husband's father) or virilocal residence (residing at the husband's place of residence, if this is not with the father). The reason is that in a sense the H–P complex *is* patrilineality in its most fundamental form. The two other forms of organization of the family which are most apparent in East Africa are matrilineal/matrilocal (the married couple residing near the home of the bride's mother) and matrilineal/avunculocal. In the former, which is very rare (it occurs, the reader will recall, among the Hadza), women stay with their brothers who are organized as a corporate group controlling land which these women work. The children born to the women through liaisons with their visiting husbands are sometimes incorporated into this group. In this arrangement, women do not hold separate lands and, in a sense, there is nothing to pass on to the children individually. In the case of matrilineal/avunculocal, this pattern is modified only in the sense that the wife goes to live with her husband at the site of his corporate matrilineage while the children return to their rightful superiors, their mother's brothers (MB), when they reach maturity. Since the husband is unable to arrange sufficient payment to her controllers, he cannot exercise ultimate control over her and certainly not over her children. He passes whatever wealth is earned by his house on to his sister's children (ZC), not to his own.

What I have been saying is not quite in agreement with Murdock's (1949, 201) claim that the rule of residence chosen or forced on a people determines the form of descent and kinship organization that they will have. It is true that there is a strong correlation between patrilineality and patrilocality, or matrilineality and avunculocality, but the form of residence, rather than determining social structure, simply reflects the structure of ownership of rights in women and their children. In this connection, Murdock has something to say that compares interestingly with the East African situation. It must be kept in mind that his generalizations about social structure were derived strictly from correlational analysis of certain social traits, such as descent and kinship, which he derives from all the people of the world. Ad-hoc explanations based on correlations are bound to be somewhat off the mark compared to those obtained through a more analytical approach where the correlations are designed to test theoretical guesses rather than pass as explanations themselves. Yet Murdock often comes close to the mark. Thus, in connection with the matter of wealth, he asserted that matrilocal residence occurs where women are the main agricultural workers (Murdock 1949, 205). The fact is that in East Africa when residence is matrilocal (the rare type of residence) this is not because women are the main agricultural workers, which they are in all African agricultural systems where the plow is not used, but because there is insufficient mobile wealth for the man to obtain the comparatively cheap (by African standards) right to take the wife to his home (and thus transform the residence pattern to avunculocal or virilocal). The most elementary right in a woman is that of exclusive sexual contact. The next is the right to take her to his home to help produce agricultural and other products. The next is the right to assert control over her children, this latter transforming the descent system to patrilineal. In this connection, two interesting conclusions reached by Murdock were that there is no evidence of a *direct* move in the opposite direction, from patrilineal to matrilineal (Murdock 1949, 193). The portrayal of descent in East Africa which I have been giving agrees with the latter point, but it provides no help in understanding the first point. Why should it be difficult to shift directly back to matrilineality if mobile wealth disappears? I do not know.

DEGREES OF RIGHTS

In anthropology the historical practice of classifying descent systems into three categories is unfortunate because it obscures more than it reveals. Despite warnings by Radcliffe-Brown (1952, 36) and others that this even misrepresents the situation, it continues to be done. We should therefore be aware when we are discussing patrilineality that we are sometimes classifying together societies in which the amount of brideprice paid is very small and almost the only right in a woman that a man can claim is to ally her children to his house, and societies at the other end of a continuum where huge amounts of cattle are transferred for rights in a woman which are so complete that the wife effectively ceases to belong to her own kinsmen and becomes a chattel of her husband. Thus, for example, Gray (1960) asserts that in Sonjo society, where, the reader will recall, only goats are raised because of Maasai theft of cattle, payments of up to 600 goats confer on the husband absolute rights in his wife.

The range of payments that occur in East African societies is shown by comparing a sample of 91 East African societies composed by myself from Murdock's (1967) *Ethnographic Atlas*. In the Atlas they are ranked according to "degree of dependence on livestock," a figure which can be correlated with the ratio of livestock to people (Schneider n.d.). This figure, in turn, correlates with the amount of bridewealth usually paid. Dependence on livestock can assume a maximum magnitude of 9. Only five matrilineal societies appear in this sample, of which three are in ranks 1 and 2 while two appear in rank 3. Some patrilineal societies also appear in these lower ranks but the interesting point is that matrilineal societies are always at the bottom. This is in line with the conclusion in the study just mentioned (Schneider n.d.) that "Matrilineality in Africa can be predicted to occur with a high degree of probability where there is no significant brideprice." A significant brideprice is ordinarily one which includes livestock (cattle, sheep, goats, camels) in any amount, although on occasion other portable valuables may also serve.

While we are on this subject, one more of Murdock's conclusions deserves attention. He concluded that matrilineality may occur at various levels of culture (Murdock 1949, 186) and is also uncorrelated with political level. In East Africa the technological and cognitive equipment of matrilineal people is identical with the patrilineal, and as far as political structure goes, the matrilineal people ordinarily have chiefs, but so do many of the patrilineal. However, we have to go south to the northern part of Zambia to find a matrilineal people, the Bemba, with a centralized kingdom. The reason for this is that matrilineality is a reflection of the rights a man possesses in a woman rather than of any stage of development. What matrilineality does correlate with, I repeat, is the nature of the goods considered to be wealth and whether they are capable of being moved (literally or in some other way) against women, something which land, for example, ordinarily is not, so that where it is the only real wealth matrilineality is common. Since states in East Africa tend to rise where there are few cattle, matrilineality and states do correlate to some extent because matrilineality itself tends to rise where there are no cattle.

THE STRUCTURE OF RELATIONS
AND RIGHTS IN WOMEN

In its most basic form, the shift from matrilineality to patrilineality is a process, the process of decreasing control by a brother over his sister as her husband asserts increasing control. This process has had a central position in analysis of social structure since Radcliffe-Brown (1924), in a classic paper on "The Mother's Brother in South Africa," made the claim that in certain patrilineal societies there is a relationship between Ego and members of the first ascending generation that can be diagrammed as in Figure 6. The pluses ($+$) in the diagram refer to a relationship between Ego and the indicated

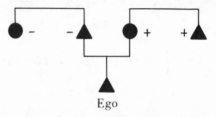

Ego

Pattern of Affection (+) and Subordination (−)
in "Mother's Brother in South Africa"

FIG. 6

person that is generally permissive, whereas the minuses (−) indicate a relationship of subordination/superordination. Radcliffe-Brown thought he had explained the peculiarly privileged way that Ego interacts with MB by asserting that this constituted an extension from mother (M) to MB of a relationship of affection, just as the authoritarian way that father's sister (FZ) acts toward Ego represents an extension from F to FZ of the F's authoritarianism. Critics of Radcliffe-Brown argued that he was attempting to explain a social phenomenon by resorting to psychology, an explanation which, in any case, would not stand up because in these unilineally organized societies MB is not necessarily literally MB but any male in MB's lineage who is of the same generation as the literal MB reckoned from the apical ancestor. How could one believe that the loving affection between mother and son could extend out laterally to a brother or mother who might happen to be her 10th cousin?

Lévi-Strauss improved on Radcliffe-Brown's formulation by widening the field of relations involved to include brother (B) and sister

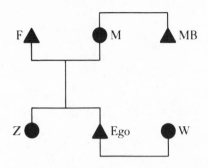

Lévi-Strauss's Basic Set of Relations
for Determining Transformations in Rights
in Affinal Relations

FIG. 7

(Z) as well as husband (H) and wife (W) as in Figure 7. The relations among these people can vary in terms of permissiveness or social distance in four permutations, which in turn may be complicated by variations in the descent principle governing the system. The types of relationships that may occur can be expressed in the following formula: "... the relation between maternal uncle (MB) and nephew (ZS) is to the relation of brother and sister as the relation between father and son is to that of husband and wife" (Lévi-Strauss 1963, 43ff). This can be diagrammed as in Figure 8. What explains this, Lévi-Strauss thinks (1963, 44), is that as a B's authority over his Z wanes, that of the husband increases. Simultaneously, the permissiveness between F and S declines as it is replaced by social distance, and the relation of ZS to MB alters in the opposite direction.

Earlier I asserted that in East Africa we should take account of changes in rights along a continuum between matrilineal and patrilineal as they vary with the size of brideprice. The probable situation that exists can be diagrammed as in Figure 9. What this suggests is that the Mat. 2 case is equivalent to Lévi-Strauss's extreme

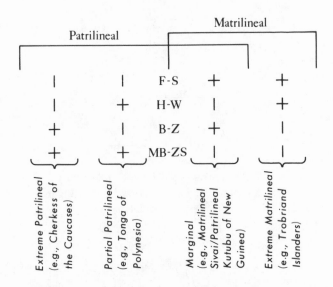

Lévi-Strauss's Transformations in Relations

FIG. 8

Mat., Mat. 1 to his marginal case, Pat. 1 also to his marginal case, and Pat. 10 to his extreme patrilineality, while his partial patrilineal falls somewhere on the low end of the Pat. scale. The one important difference between Lévi-Strauss's formulation and mine rests in the fact that mine sees the range of variation in Mat. structure as far less than the Pat. This accords with the obvious fact of variation in the range of magnitudes of brideprice, and therefore of exchanges, which is far less in the Mat. system.

All of this can be put another way. Let us assume an economy in which there is no mobile wealth so that rights in women cannot be traded. The MB has control of his Z and her children. The authoritarian attitude he displays toward them is merely the accompaniment of power and control, just as the friendly relationship he has

The East African Transformation Continuum

FIG. 9

with his wife is a counterpart to his lack of control over her. When mobile wealth does appear, he can trade off his Z while acquiring rights in his own W, transferring rights in one for rights in the other and shifting his treatment of each from the one pole to the other, the Z becoming a friend and his W a subordinate. In other words, the relationship between MB and ZS is but a reflex of MB's control of his Z and his W.

No one to my knowledge has tried to detail permissiveness and authority on a scale of degrees. Since the rights which MB gives up might be partial, one would think it worthwhile to consider the degree to which this shows up in the personal relations of MB and ZS. Some information on how a condition between + and – in the relations of MB and ZS might appear was derived from my fieldwork with the Turu, who have the following state of affairs. When a man dies, his MB, with members of his lineage (who are themselves mostly classificatory MB as reckoned in Turu terminology) come to the funeral and demand compensation from members of the deceased's lineage for the death of "our son." Although this may be said to be a patrilineal system as determined by the laws of inheritance and by various other indicators, MB acts as if he never gave up full rights in his Z and therefore in her children, and he receives some payment for any injuries that were done to "his son" during the son's lifetime. Yet Turu conform to the pattern displayed by Radcliffe-Brown and Lévi-Strauss, treating MB as a person with whom one can act permissively and particularly as one to whom one may go for help.

I suspect that there is a radical legal shift in these systems with respect to passage of property from F to S when the rights in chil-

A Turu woman and her children

dren shift from MB to F, but the "moral power" of MB, like the moral power of a wife over her property, continues over his ZS even after his legal power has passed.

To summarize, the core of unilineal descent systems is based on who controls the productive power of a woman. If it is her B the system is matrilineal; if it is her H the system is patrilineal. Matrilineality is rare because the right to exercise control over a woman can be obtained for a relatively small amount, at least insofar as it concerns rights to her sex and her children. The wonder is that it is not a universal phenomenon. The reason appears to be that mobile wealth of a type equal to the value of a woman consists in East Africa almost entirely of livestock of which even the nonpastoral people possess some. It is no accident that matrilineality is fundamentally a phenomenon of Central Africa where cattle are almost entirely excluded by tsetse fly and where other forms of valuable production are nearly limited to grain.

KINSHIP TERMINOLOGY

Turning now to kinship terminology or classification, it seems logical that systems of kinship would be tied to economies but the relationship is not always clear. I want to suggest how the connection can be made and then offer tentative explanations for the fact that East Africa is the area of Africa in which Omaha and Descriptive terminologies are statistically most prominent and why they, with Iroquois, dominate the area.

Kinship terminology has always been something of a mystery in anthropology. When Radcliffe-Brown first proposed an explanation for Omaha (1941) the novelty of his achievement was largely responsible, one would guess, for the uncritical way it was received. Not until the 1960s was his accomplishment subjected to serious second thoughts (excepting for Lévi-Strauss's previously ignored rebuttals [1969]), twenty years or more after it had been put forth. Not until alliance theory (Fox 1967) appeared in the 1960s, growing out of Lévi-Strauss's work (Needham 1962), were the tools available to make some headway at understanding terminologies in general. As Fox explained, previously marriage was treated as a "residue of lineage" since the focus was on lineage as the key to understanding African society. But kinship classification is heavily dependent on the kind of marriage system associated with it. Radcliffe-Brown's conclusion about Omaha was simply that it is a way of designating lineage membership. Alliance theory, by associating matrilateral cross cousin marriage (MCCM) with Omaha was able to claim that in fact the terminology is apt for a system which creates a circulating connubium and thereby binds a society's various lineages into a single network of linked groups.

So alliance theory must be given credit for taking kinship theory off dead center. But evidence from East Africa, as we shall see, brings into question some aspects of alliance explanations by taking them beyond a focus on marriage and relating them to exchange and economics in general, of which marriage exchanges are but a part.

As a prelude to a discussion of the economics of kinship in East Africa we should take note of a serious problem connected with attempts to study this phenomenon. Traditional functionalist methods have included the practice of treating ethnographic data statically. This disguises the fluidity that really exists, which hinges on people's calculations of costs and benefits. A single system of kinship classification, descent, and marriage rules tended to be ascribed to a group even though it now seems likely that these are not always normative but may be simply, as Leach has phrased it for Highland Sinhalese (1960), a statistical outcome of numerous independent decisions. In fact there may be important variations in any society with respect to these things, as we have already seen. In the past, aggressive application of economic analysis has been prevented by the prejudice against ascribing economic motives to Africans. But, as Rigby puts it, an economic analysis treats kinship as an expression of property relations (1969, 301), and marriage is an exchange as amenable to cost/benefit analysis as any other exchange. An economic approach asserts not that Africans are economic men but that it is worth trying to apply economic analysis to their actions to see what results can be obtained.

The path to an economic theory of kinship classification is through the exchange act of marriage. The path begins, as we have seen, with the core of the family and the question of who controls a woman, her brother or her husband. Who shall control the woman, in turn, depends on the means available for effecting the exchange. Where there are cattle or other significant forms of mobile wealth, the options open to the decision-maker tend to generate Omaha terminology in East Africa, all other things being equal (that is to say, if we hold constant for all these societies the set of technological, environmental, and cognitive conditions which characterize all the societies of this culture area), even where, as with all the northern members of the Western Lacustrine Bantu and in Busoga and Buganda, the ratio of cattle to people is less than 1:1 but still significant (Soga approximately .25:1; Nyoro .35:1; Ankole .40:1; Toro .12:1; Ganda .36:1). Where mobile wealth is lacking other means, such as exchange of women for women, must be found if possible and Iroquois terminology usually results.

Among East Africans, as was made plain in previous chapters, there is a definite predominance of types of production systems that favor Omaha. I have already discussed the problem faced by the entrepreneur who would like to attain the best organization of production and who seems to prefer to combine the production of food and children, the roles of wife and mother, in a single woman. The conditions we find in East Africa lead to three different solutions to this problem, the patrilineal solution, which seems to be the most desired, the matrilineal solution, which is the least desired, and the "Arab" solution, such as the Taita follow, in which it is possible to marry endogamously (that is, marriage to father's brother's daughter [FBD] giving patrilateral parallel cousin marriage or PPCM).

Examples of every kind of kinship terminology to be found in Africa are found in East Africa: Iroquois, Omaha, Descriptive, Hawaiian, and Crow. However, the first three predominate by far. Even though these three are most usual, we will concern ourselves somewhat with the others because of their theoretical interest.

ALLIANCE THEORY

Iroquois terminology is defined by Murdock (1959, 29), who has been mainly responsible for standardizing this subject, as a type in which cross cousins are terminologically equated and are differentiated from parallel cousins, who are equated and who may or may not be differentiated from Ego's siblings (Figure 10). Alliance theory shows this system of terminology to be apt for the practice of dual cross cousin marriage (DCCM). DCCM is a kind of "sister" or woman exchange which in its most simplified form would look like Figure 11. This model shows a society of two exogamous patrilineages whose male members exchange their sisters. The persons indicated in the model are not individuals but classes of persons such that, for example, any indicated class of males regards any female of their lineage who are of the same generation as sisters. It will be noted that in such a system the woman that any male marries is his dual cross cousin, i.e., she is simultaneously his MBD and FZD. Thus, in those cases where Iroquois terminology is used in connection with sister exchange, the two different cross cousins are in fact the same person, who are therefore appropriately called by the same term.

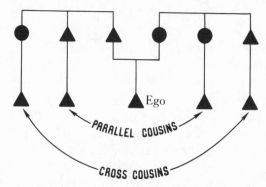

Iroquois Terminology

FIG. 10

Jack Goody, in a treatise on bridewealth and dowry in Africa and Eurasia (1973, 32) makes the statement, "cousin marriage is likely to be forbidden in Africa societies. . . ." His reason for this claim is that he finds cousin marriage to be valuable principally as a means of keeping property from dispersing widely, whereas open marriage systems do not attempt to hold a line but reach out for new marriage opportunities and thereby, through bridewealth, disperse wealth more widely.

The idea that cousin marriage may be utilized to maintain control of wealth and prevent its dispersion is useful and, as we shall see, Iroquois systems in East Africa seem to do this kind of thing. But first we must understand that the evidence clearly does not support Goody's belief that cousin marriage is rare in Africa but rather that it is common and associated with Iroquois terminology. In fact, his statement is strangely contradicted by a study of cousin terms

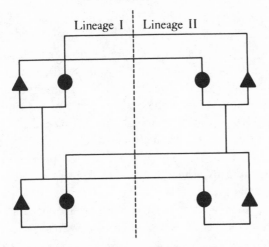

Cross-Cousin Marriage

FIG. 11

which he published in 1970 in which he said a statistical study of cousin terms showed that Iroquois terms are associated with preferred cross cousin marriage (Goody 1970, 125). This is exactly the case in East Africa where Iroquois terms are very common. (Interestingly, this study also showed a correlation of Omaha and patrilineal descent, and Crow terminology and matrilineality, while Hawaiian terms associated themselves with both matrilineal and patrilineal descent, like Iroquois. These correlations have relevance to later parts of this chapter.)

Alliance theory predicts an association of Iroquois terminology with DCCM. But it also predicts that Omaha terminology goes with MCCM, and that Crow terminology fits with PCCM (Fox 1967). This in turn fits Lévi-Strauss's theory of elementary and complex systems which asserts that marriage systems in human society have moved from the earlier elementary forms to modern complex forms through intermediate forms in a way that is appropriate to each stage of development with respect to the problem of achieving sufficient circulation of women to keep all segments of society directly or indirectly linked, a condition that has survival value. The elementary type is a sister exchange or DCCM system because the society is small and composed of two exogamous lineages whose linkage is thus assured simply by trading cousins (as many Australian aboriginal societies do). The intermediate type is one where mixing is accomplished by indirect means through marriage with MBD (producing MCCM), creating thereby a circulating flow of women (the circulating connubium spoken of earlier) as seen in Figure 12. The only way two lineages can be linked in such a system is indirectly, when lineage I gives a bride to lineage II, who gives a bride to lineage III, who are now able to return a bride to lineage I. In other words, where there is a rule of MCCM a flow of women around in a circle is created proceeding in the same direction in each generation.

The PCCM marriage system, where one is required to marry FZD, which is supposedly associated with Crow terminology, is intermediate between DCCM and MCCM because the logic of this

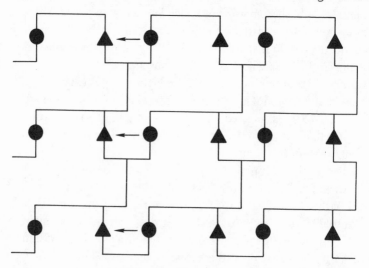

Matrilateral Marriage System

FIG. 12

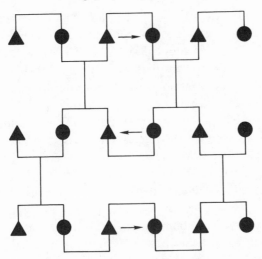

Patrilateral Marriage System

FIG. 13

arrangement leads to direct exchange between two lineages but only every other generation. That is to say, in each generation the flow is reversed (Figure 13).

In a complex system no rule of marriage is necessary because, for instance, it occurs in a large industrial society where the chances that there will be inmarriage are countered by the mobility of individuals who achieve circulation by randomly marrying along the way. Rather than an artificial, mechanical method of obtaining circulation, a "statistical" solution, as Lévi-Strauss calls it, is utilized.

All this detail about alliance theory is not irrelevant to East Africa because, for one thing, it allows me to reiterate with more emphasis that in East Africa Omaha terminology is specifically *not* associated with any kind of cousin marriage, even though there are tendencies to MCCM. Omaha, in fact, has some of the appearance of a complex system. On the other hand, three types of cousin marriage—DCCM, MCCM, PCCM—are associated with Iroquois.

What this means, I think, is that where we move alliance theory

out of a purely theoretical context to test it on the ground we discover that its conclusions depend too much on certain assumptions
about the need for mixing that are either false or unconnected directly with marriage systems. The mundane problems of production,
exchange, and optimization of wealth turn out to have more relevance and, when taken into account, show that cousin marriages of
all kinds create *intensive* marriage systems which work to maintain
closure and conserve wealth, whereas Omaha is an *extensive* or open
system where there is mobile wealth which is utilized flexibly as a
more rational and profitable way to manage affairs. This practice of
marrying strangers is referred to by Barnes (1976, 396) as "dispersed
alliance," a practice, he thinks, which means nothing in itself and
has no necessary connection to other institutions. This, we will find,
is not true in East Africa where it is not only connected to Omaha
classification but to statelessness and its corollaries.

THE IROQUOIS SYSTEM

Although Iroquois terminology can occur in a wide variety of circumstances including with matrilineal and patrilineal descent, there
is a statistically strong leaning in East Africa toward societies in
which wealth resides in people and sometimes in land rather than
being centered on livestock. This can be shown by a review of the
relationship between kinship terminology and cousin marriage in a
nonrandom sample of East African societies in Murdock's *Ethnographic Atlas* (1967, 170, 174, 182, 186). The Iroquois terminologies
are by far the most commonly associated with cousin marriage although nearly half of the cases are not (or not reported to be in the
sources Murdock consulted). For comparison, none of the Omaha
are correlated with cousin marriage. (However, 25% of Descriptive
systems allow cousin marriage, an apparent anomaly that will be
discussed in due course).

Mary Douglas's review of pawnship in Central Africa (1964)
helps illustrate the kind of circumstances within which Iroquois terminology arises. Even though she is not talking about East Africa,

her discussion is still relevant to certain southern Tanzanian people, while her view of women as wealth is entirely appropriate.

Douglas notes that over a wide part of Central Africa, including societies as distant as the Kongo around the mouth of the Congo River and the Makua in Mozambique, with Cewa, Ndembu, Lunda, Pende, and others in between, there existed before colonial authorities stamped it out a system of pawning women that was repugnant to Europeans because it seemed to them a form of slavery. In fact, the persons who were pawns were not really different from others in their society except for the fact that as pawns they could not own land. They formed lineages which were subordinate to the land owning lineages who also owned the pawns. Speaking about the Lele, whom she knows best, Douglas said that having no good land to use to attract other men to their lineage as subordinate sons-in-law, Lele men used to acquire pawned women for the purpose (just as East Africans acquire livestock). This, incidentally, fits in with a finding in my study of African brideprice (Schneider n.d.) that there is an inverse relationship between the existence of livestock in appreciable numbers and the existence of "slavery" or pawnship.

Continuing, Douglas says that this practice tends to generate a social structure composed of shallow lineages since so many are derived from pawnship, in which genealogy is unimportant due to the fact that members of the pawn lineage cannot inherit position or land. This is just the situation found by Willis among the Fipa and related societies in southern Tanzania (Willis 1966).

However, the chief point I wish to make with my example from Douglas is that in the absence of pawning the same kind of effect can be obtained by offering a wife to a promising young man who thereby becomes tied to his father-in-law as a political subordinate. A rule of cousin marriage would simply perpetuate such a state of affairs from generation to generation, although the rule need not be only one of DCCM but could include MCCM or PCCM in various circumstances. That is to say, Iroquois terminology could be appropriate to a situation where a man had the option of marrying his MBD or his FZD, depending on whether his MB or his F gave him the best deal, a condition which in fact exists in Kaguru society where men sometimes marry FZD and sometimes MBD.

Pasternak (1976, 66ff) has summarized some of the main theories for the existence of cousin marriage. All emphasize the elements of political aggrandizement coupled with low price. In other words such marriages use subordination as a component of exchange. In the case of MCCM for example, Leach feels it is valuable in loosely integrated political systems where there is status differentiation. The FL is a wife giver and in return for his SL's allegiance provides a bride. And Barth suggests that PPCM solidifies lineages as corporate groups in factional struggles, the nephew (BS) becoming a political supporter.

The Kaguru west of Morogoro in eastern Tanzania illustrate the practical implications of cousin marriage in East Africa. They have matrilineal clans (a clan is a kind of large-scale lineage) and Iroquois terminology (cross cousins are referred to as *muhisi* [Beidelman 1967, 43]). The most important part of Kaguruland is the fertile, well-watered plateau between 2,000 and 4,500 feet within which there is a great demand for land. The basic fact about Kaguru economy as it relates to kinship is that if a man desires to obtain good land he must develop good relations with the powerful men who control it: "About a quarter of Kaguru marriages are made between related kin as arranged by certain elders who thereby manage to control juniors through the form of residence these youths must thereby adopt" (Beidelman 1971, 65).

A man may marry his MBD who, in this matrilineal system, would be controlled by the BL of his MB, or by her B, or he may marry his FZD, who is controlled by his F or his B. In the first case he would then live with and be subordinate to MB and in the second to F. Beidelman then makes a significant statement (1971, 66):

In both cases, the residence pattern is of considerable disadvantage to the youth, for he is under the direct control of a kin group to whom he is in debt and to whom his wife can appeal on her own right. In the second case, he is in a particularly weak position toward his own children since the major persons with whom he must contend for his children's loyalties—the members of their lineage—reside with him, his wife, and his children. Such forms of marriage have been called "preferential" by some social anthropologists, but it should be remembered that this adjective can hardly refer to the attitude of the youth, who is generally conceded by Kaguru to have been at some disadvantage in his circumstances ever to embark upon such a union in the first place. Whatever preferences were involved refer to those of elders who gained, or at least hoped to gain, from the match.

In other words, in this Iroquois system, DCCM is not necessarily the form that characterizes marriage, but either MCCM or PCCM depending on options. As to the question of preference, Beidelman makes it crystal clear that whichever of these options a man takes up is not dependent on custom but on choice.

The Luguru, closely related to the Kaguru, are also matrilineal and use Iroquois terms. According to Young and Fosbrooke (1960), residence among them is often matrilocal with wives continuing to live with their mothers in a good percentage of cases. That is to say, in this society there is often insufficient wealth to enable a man even to remove his wife to his home. The Luguru use DCCM to preserve the unity of the land. As can be seen, this is accomplished by a man marrying the daughter of the man who is brother to his mother, thus preserving from one generation to another whatever kind of land alliance the previous generations worked out to their benefit.

The Fipa of southwest Tanzania are a double descent group among whom certain titles and duties descend patrilineally while property descends matrilineally (Willis 1966, 22). They utilize Iroquois terms (cross cousins are called *unnfyaala*) and Willis says that marriage is preferentially with FZD. The question this raises is why do the Kaguru "prefer" FZD and MBD marriage, the Luguru DCCM, and the Fipa PCCM? Willis does not say to what extent this preference is honored, but to the degree that it is, it must make special sense to those who use it. The effect of the practice is to tie two matriclans together in a reciprocal system, as previously explained (Figure 13). Whatever the answer to this question, it seems likely to reside in the fact of certain features distinctive to Fipa society when compared to our other Iroquois societies. For instance, they had a kingdom (rather than merely a collection of semi-independent or independent chiefs) and were organized into patrilineally defined village communities (despite their matrilineal inheritance of property) in which the title of subchief descended patrilineally. PCCM could, in such a circumstance, serve to keep property and titles together rather than allowing them to diverge.

The Abaha or Ha of western Tanzania, who possess a patrilineal Iroquois system, have a commoner class called Ha and an upper class called Tutsi, an arrangement common to Interlacustrine Bantu states. The Ha allow MCCM and are negative toward PCCM which, however, they do not forbid. Scherer (1965) notes that among the Ha the incidence of MCCM is in fact low compared to the Tutsi. Further, while the children of cousin marriages do not marry, their children may do so. Finally, marriages in which men raise themselves socially by taking a wife from the Tutsi class are permitted. How to explain these facts is again a problem since Scherer is not thinking of marriage as a kind of economic transaction but, to judge by his phraseology, as a kind of customary behavior. Obviously if PCCM is not highly thought of this has something to do with the fact that direct exchange of wives in alternating generations is a poor strategy. The facts that the Ha have some cattle and that in most cases these serve to effect the exchange would seem to fit with MCCM, in which indirectness of circulation of women requires payment for the bride other than by reciprocation in the next generation. And if children of an MCCM are not encouraged to marry, this seems to be related to the possibility that they do not think it wise to reinforce the link between clans effected by their parents. Finally, one suspects that if cousin marriage is more common among the aristocrats this in some way has to do with exclusiveness although one is forced to wonder whether MCCM is a better vehicle for this than PCCM.

A particularly interesting form of Iroquois system is that of the patrilineal Gogo among whom cattle ownership is high and who, as we shall see, might ordinarily be expected to have an Omaha or Descriptive system. But Gogo have special problems that generate cousin alliances, as explained by Rigby (1969, 299):

> The more general ecological conditions of periodic drought and famine ensure a residential mobility of herd-holding groups (domestic/homestead groups) and consequently the spatial dispersion and eventual atrophy of "active" agnatic [i.e., patrilineal] ties. However, such homestead groups are not economically independent, and therefore must establish ties of economic (and ritual) cooperation with other groups of the same order in the areas into which they move. This is a condition of survival and results in the importance and maintenance of affinal and cognatic ties within each, and between generations, bolstered by a highly localized marriage pattern which ensures the close residence of affines, and cognatic kin, in subsequent generations, at least until ecological or other conditions enforce a dispersal of homestead groups yet again. The cohesion of local groups is expressed in an overlapping network of kinship and affinal ties.

Conforming to this, the Gogo have no unambiguously defined exogamous groups although they do have patrilineages of a sort. Of 203 marriages which Rigby studied, 70% were between non-kin and 22% between kin while the remainder were unknown. The largest group of kin marriages were between people of the same clan, 24% between cross cousins, and 28% with the general class of affines (in-laws). Interestingly, Rigby says that MCCM is a "preferred" category but adds that although the Gogo put it this way they are simply rationalizing an accomplished fact. I think this could be rephrased to say that MCCM is strategically a very good option in the Gogo condition but not one that is always possible. Its occurrence is rationalized only in the sense that the informants try to explain that what they did was sensible.

In short, then, because of certain special problems characteristic of Gogo, including perhaps the fact that patrilineages are not able to operate as the kind of credit and help groups they are among such people as the Turu, the Gogo are forced into working out arrangements backed up by marriage with the whole group of kinsmen, both patrilineal and affinal, as opportunity warrants. Why this should be so in the Gogo case and not among other wealthy cattle people who have similar ecological problems is, however, not altogether clear. Nevertheless, the Gogo case points up the fact that the association of Iroquois with people poor in mobile wealth and Omaha with those rich in mobile wealth is not one to one.

To summarize, this limited sample of Iroquois systems suggests a number of things:

1. Iroquois terminology is not tied to either patrilineal or matrilineal descent.

2. Contrary to alliance theory, this terminology is not exclusively designed to serve DCCM but occurs in conjunction with all varieties of cousin marriage.

3. Cousin marriage is not compulsory in Iroquois systems, so that the terminology seems designed to serve conditions where this option is commonly employed.

4. Iroquois is a kind of system which facilitates alliances between families linked by marriage in three different ways:

DCCM: direct exchange of women in each generation.

PCCM: direct exchange of women in alternating generations.

MCCM: exchange of women for goods, an exchange renewed in each generation.

Most generally speaking, Iroquois facilitates the linkage of affines into more or less permanent alliances anchored in land.

THE OMAHA SYSTEM

The distinguishing feature of Omaha marriage systems is the lack of cousin marriage coupled with extensive rules, if they are rules and not merely strategies. The Nilotic Sebei of Mount Elgon in northwest Kenya illustrate. According to Goldschmidt (1967, 41–42):

A man may not marry:
1. a woman of his own clan or of a clan linked with his clan.
2. a woman of his mother's clan.

3. a woman of his mother's mother's mother's clan. (However, he may marry into the clan of his maternal grandmother. If he does so he must clip a bit off the woman's ear and throw it into a running stream to prevent a barren union.)
4. a member of the clan of any living wife, or the true sister of a deceased wife. (This is apparently no longer strictly adhered to.)
5. any woman of a clan of a prior wife's mother, or of a brother's wife's mother.
6. the daughter of any man who belongs to his age-set.

These regulations, I might add, resemble those of the Pokot, next-door neighbors, who also have Omaha terminology.

The explicitness with which Sebei and Pokot can detail their rules contrasts with the Turu. Unlike the Sebei, Turu clans and lineages are localized and corporate. But marriage is still extensive. Thus, while Turu sometimes speak of marrying MBD, which is called "bringing your mother back," this form of marriage seems to be a figment of Lévi-Strauss's statistical marriage situation in that the person is not married *because* she is MBD *but despite* the fact. If the woman suffers any difficulties in having children the closeness of the relationship (which ordinarily is not with the direct MBD) is immediately suspect and a rite of *ikiika* (cutting) is held to sever the tie so that the way for children may be opened. In this respect, the Turu are obviously similar to the Gogo who also seem not to marry MBD simply because she is MBD.

Other than this possible exception, the pattern of Turu marriage, which probably no Turu would think of as a rule, is thoroughly extensive. A man takes his first wife from whatever lineage he can (but not from his own clan) and if he then marries again he avoids that low-level lineage for another. Even among men of the same local lineage the pattern seems to be to avoid lineages with which others have connection, though this is not an absolute pattern. The reason it is not, I suspect, is that the corporacy of these lineages is tempered by the high independence of individual families. Thus, if a man should take a wife from a lineage from which a member of his village took a wife, the weak corporate links between him and his lineage mates, coupled with the weak links between families in the affinal lineage, would create no conflicting economic ties.

Fallers (1965, 103), speaking of the Interlacustrine Soga of the northeast shore of Lake Victoria, tells us that a man may not marry a woman belonging to "any one" of his parents' or grandparents' clans so that "the stable village or sub-village tends to become so intricately cross-cut by kinship ties that most of its young men must find wives from elsewhere." Obviously, Omaha-type societies, to judge from these instances and the poor correlation between Omaha terminology and cousin marriage shown in the *Ethnographic Atlas*, do not find it useful to marry cousins and do find it useful to reach out to "strangers." The question is, what is the economic justification for this, if any?

Keeping in mind my earlier suggestion that marriage rules are best treated as strategies, the basic explanation for these extensive strategies seems to lie in the area of exploitation of new options opened by the possession of significant amounts of mobile wealth. In cousin marriages, the participants seem forced into perpetual or long-term unions by the need for land consolidation or the desire for political aggrandizement. Where cattle wealth reaches a certain minimum these East African systems seem to shift to Omaha terms and extensive marriage rules. (An alternative to this is a Descriptive system, which will be discussed shortly.) The rationale is simple enough. If a man makes a marriage with another lineage or family, this involves an exchange of mobile property, ordinarily on a use basis. His affines hold his cattle while he holds their woman. A second marriage with the same group might be literally impossible without confusing the delicate balance of the first contract, not the least consideration of which would be that the groom would be putting too many of his cattle with a single management unit when he could, as in other loaning arrangements, disperse the capital more widely and thereby optimize the likelihood of the best return to himself. Thus MBD marriage seems unsuitable for Omaha systems, at least in East Africa. Cattle give their possessors a flexibility in exchange relations which intensive systems lack, and they thereby generate new, complex kinds of social patterns just as the rise of capitalism in the West generated new, extensive social structures compared to the intensive, land-oriented feudal system.

Earlier I spoke of Radcliffe-Brown's explanation for Omaha, a system appropriate to societies in which lineage is highly developed as a form of organization. Thus members of one lineage differentiate carefully their own generational differences but lump members of affinal lineages all together under a single term, the term used for MB or ZS. Besides the fact that many East African societies using Omaha place little stress on lineage as a method of grouping, Fox (1967, 250–251) points out that MB is not typically distinguished from some members of Ego's lineage. The term for MB is in fact often applied also to both sets of grandparents, paternal and materal, as in the cases of Soga and Turu. The term *kuku* in the Turu language does not mean MB but a category including MB and his lineage mates and their ascendants and descendants plus FF (father's father). By utilizing a neutral indicator, such as the letter K for this category, and neutral letters for other categories in the system, such as M for FZS and his descendants and for GS, we can diagram Turu Omaha terminology as in Figure 14. Fox thinks the people who use this system are economizing on terminology by using the term employed for paternal GF, who is a senior, to indicate members of the lineage from which mother came because they are also senior, as wife-givers. Conversely, the term for GS is used for the wife-receiving lineage into which FZ marries. However, there is another way of looking at this terminology which accords with certain economic facts and avoids having to rationalize away the equation of FF and MB. This is demonstrated in Figure 15. In preparation for explaining the diagram we must take account of the fact that the system of relations is marked by three special kinds of behavior: (1) egalitarian behavior between members of alternate generations; (2) joking between affines of the same generation; and (3) avoidance of superordinate/subordinate relations between affines of dif-

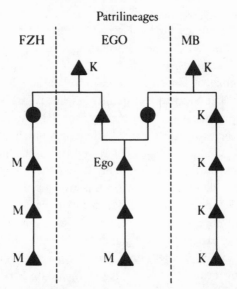

Omaha Terminology: Expanded Mode

FIG. 14

fering generations. In this figure, the concentric circles show people who are in opposition to each other with respect to property and alternate circles show people who are allied with each other against those who are in adjacent circles. Commonly, in systems like this, Ego and GF and Ego and GS call each other "brother" and treat each other as equals in other ways. Similarly, as I previously indicated, Ego has a relationship of privileged familiarity with MB. In sum, Ego has a familiar and egalitarian relationship to all the K's and, reciprocally, he has the same relationship with all the M's, to whom he is MB or GF.

On the other hand, Ego is subordinate to his F and FZ, both in adjacent circles. And he jokes with his BL's who are placed in this adjacent circle because joking (Radcliffe-Brown 1940) is a kind of negative behavior appropriate between people of the same stratum. The father and mother-in-law are also in the adjacent circle since

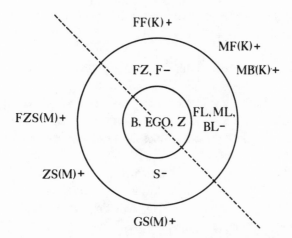

Economic Model of Omaha Terminology
FIG. 15

Ego must avoid them, which is also a kind of negative behavior appropriate to people of different strata.

This Omaha terminology reflects the following property relations which exist among kin and affines. Ego desires a share of his F's wealth in order to begin his own homestead operations but his father resists giving him any because he wishes to keep it together for his own operations. FF, who for these same reasons is in opposition to Ego's F, allies himself with GS on the principle that they should cooperate because they have a common opponent, even though, as in the case of all allies, their interests are also ultimately divergent. Simultaneously, MB, who is opposed to F in a continuous push-pull over the amount of bridewealth he should receive and the extent to which he should give up rights in his sister, allies with ZS. The diagonal line running through the set of circles may be taken to represent the division between those who are the source of wealth and those who are receivers. That is to say, although MB and ZS, or GF and GS, may pretend egalitarian status, differences are never in fact altogether abrogated. The GS may stroll into GF's house and tell his GF to leave because he wants to sleep with "my wife" (his GM), as a Turu boy may do, but he doesn't actually sleep with GM.

Two important qualifications should be added to this discussion. The first is that this model of Omaha is not to suggest that MB and FF or GS and ZS ally with each other and Ego against the adjacent circle's members. These alliances are individual. Secondly, joking and avoidance relations with affines, and egalitarian relations with MB and ZS, are not peculiar to Omaha structures. I mean to suggest here that Omaha categories seem to ally these two general forms of relations—egalitarian and hierarchical—in a special way.

Interestingly, Lounsbury (1964), debating what might be the explanation for Omaha, suggests it could be due to the laws of succession in those societies which use it. My explanation is similar except that it stresses property relations in ongoing society, not just succession. In other words, it adds a note of competition to a more static interpretation.

Another important qualification is that not all Omaha terminological systems are like that of the Turu and Soga. The Nandi, for example, equate FF and MF with each other but these are not in turn equated with MB. The meaning of this is not clear. Arguing from the Turu case, it would appear that among Nandi Ego has a different kind of relationship with the grandparents than with MB and other members of his lineage. But, on the other hand, the equation of FF and MF again argues against interpreting Omaha as simply a reflex of a segmentary lineage system suggesting thereby that it would be worthwhile to see if there are some special property implications to the Nandi system. Unfortunately, details of property relations and even of kinship classification are often not available for these societies.

The Omaha system, like the Iroquois, seems to act as an umbrella for a range of possible kinds of relations. Not all men have a MB in an actual sense because the MB relationship is normally carried out by the direct MB or his heir. Furthermore, whether MB in fact fulfiills the role depends on whether he cares to operationalize it. Presumably he will do so only when there is something to be gained by doing so. An Omaha system is one in which lineages are still important as corporate organizations but it does not require localized, highly corporate lineages. It only requires a core of mobile wealth acting as the focus of alliance and opposition.

A final point of importance is that Iroquois and Omaha terminologies do *not* correlate with nonpastoralism and pastoralism as I have defined them. The situation is more complex than that. Map XI, showing the distribution of kinship terminologies, insofar as we know them, suggests the following pattern. Among pastoral people there is a very high correlation with Omaha and Descriptive, Omaha occurring more in the south while both Omaha and Iroquois occur among the nonpastoral people, with Iroquois more common among the apparently poorer, especially as reckoned in cattle. This, in turn, corresponds with the area of most severe tsetse infestation, which is greater in the south than the north.

P. Reining (1972) has inquired into the reason why some of the Interlacustrine Bantu utilize Omaha and others Iroquois terminology (except for the Rwandese, who use Hawaiian). While she is unable to come up with a definite answer, she notes that all those with Omaha systems have extensive marriage systems combined with fertile land as important property. But, I would add, they also produce cattle, even if in ratios too low to qualify them as pastoral, and most produce bananas. In contrast, the Iroquois Interlacustrine Bantu dwell in the more fly-ridden, dry areas where they are dependent on grain crops. In short, it seems that even low levels of production of cattle can generate Omaha organization.

This attempt to explain Iroquois and Omaha systems should be seen as a preliminary step. Its main novelty, generally speaking, has been to show that Iroquois fits well with non-cattle, non-movable wealth systems that are intensive or closed, supporting marriage systems that nucleate in terms of property relations and power because this is the most rational course of action in the circumstances.

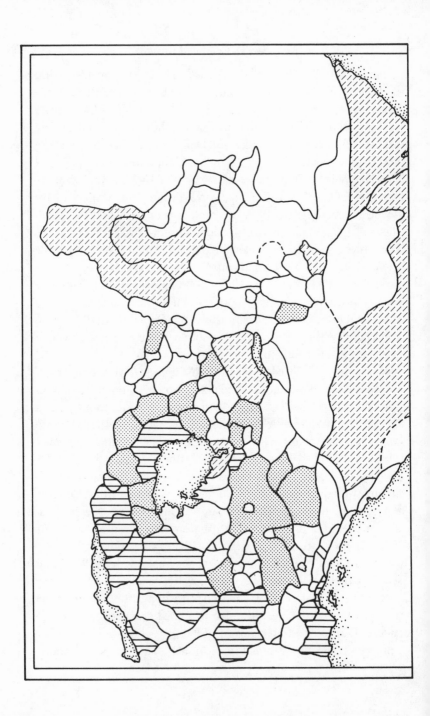

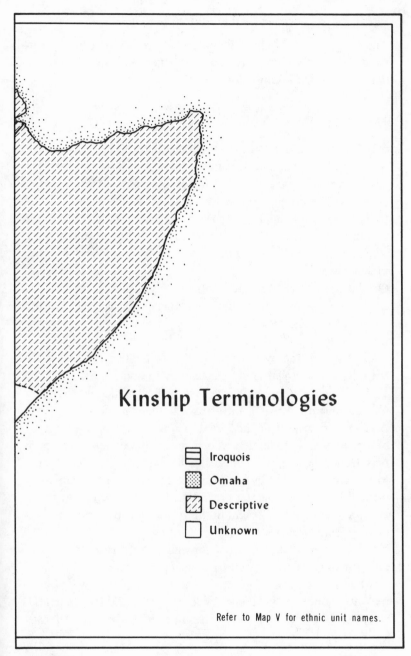

Kinship Terminologies

▤ Iroquois

▨ Omaha

▨ Descriptive

☐ Unknown

Refer to Map V for ethnic unit names.

MAP XI

And it shows a fit of Omaha with mobile wealth, non-cousin marriage and extensive property relations, which generate alliance and opposition around the wealth.

DESCRIPTIVE TERMINOLOGY

Descriptive terminology, which differentiates F, FB, MB, and all types of cousins, and which occurs among such prominent East African people as the Nuer, Turkana, and Somali, is at first a puzzle. Most of these people are wealthy pastoralists for whom Omaha terminology would appear better suited. The key to why this is not so and the reason for Descriptive terms may be found in Gulliver's comparison of the Jie and Turkana, two very closely related societies in northwest Kenya and northeast Uganda who, however, have Omaha and Descriptive systems respectively. Gulliver does not give enough information to determine whether Jie actually use Omaha terms but his description of how Jie kin relate to each other conforms to the Omaha pattern.

The most distinctive thing about the Descriptive Turkana is the friendly relations that exist between a man and his BL (Gulliver 1955), which is not usually the case in East Africa where, as in Omaha organization, hostility between these parties is the rule. Among Turkana a man and his BL act as if by virtue of exchange of a woman and cattle or camels they have become business partners. Hence the additional unusual practice of the MB contributing to the brideprice paid by his ZS, while receiving part of the brideprice of his sister's daughter's marriage. In fact, Gulliver feels that kinship is only a starting point in this relationship beyond which the joint venture of "stock associates" takes over.

Gulliver feels that this system, for which Descriptive terminology rather than Omaha is obviously more appropriate, arises out of the fact that grazing conditions in Turkanaland require a good deal of mobility by nuclear families in order to realize the large potential return on investment in herds. This, in turn, works against lineage cooperation. Interestingly, even the Nuer, the supposed paragons of segmentary lineage systems, among whom one might expect to find lineages paramount, have villages which in fact are composed of mixed people dominated by a land-owning lineage core, a state of affairs that seems to accord with their use of Descriptive terminology in that members of lineages seem in fact to be widely scattered.

In Jieland lineages can continue to operate because ecological conditions allow transhumance with regular return to a central homeland where kinship relations can be reestablished. In the case of the Jie the Omaha pattern therefore emerges with Ego treating his mother's brother as an ally against his F, a relationship he extends to MBS and the rest of MB lineage (Gulliver 1955, 209).

Descriptive terminology, then, fits an extensive economy because intensive marriage would create conflicts in the complex of relations of men relative to control of cattle and camels. But while Turkana marriage rules, which exclude marriage with members of one's own clan or of one's mother's clan, are no more extensive than Omaha, and may even be less so, the Turkana system is even more complex, in Lévi-Strauss's terms, than the Omaha because the nucleating tendencies that come with lineage localization are counteracted by the extreme mobility of nuclear families, leading to a greater probability of a "statistical" solution to the problem of seeking a mate.

While Gulliver stresses the weakness of lineages in Turkanaland and seems thereby to justify the close association of brothers-in-law, some other Descriptive societies, like the Alur, have strong lineages, suggesting that the reason for the existence of Descriptive organization is not so much the decline of lineage in the literal sense as the rise of conditions favoring cooperation rather than conflict among brothers-in-law.

Finally, there is a seemingly paradoxical association between Descriptive organization and cousin marriage. However, cousin marriage is infrequent and when it does occur tends to PPCM. Why wealthy pastoralists, such as the Bagarra or Cattle Arabs of the Sudan, who are fragmented on the compound family level by grazing demands, should resort to marriage with FBD is a puzzle which remains unsolved, even when we take into account their claim that it is a cheap way to marry.

CROW TERMINOLOGY

Crow terminology is a special problem because it is so rare. In the cases of Omaha, Iroquois, and even Descriptive, we have a fairly good selection of materials from which to derive a theory of the economics of kinship classification, even though most studies are inadequate for the job because they are short on economic information or even on the details of behavior of kin toward each other. But Crow is associated with matrilineality, which is itself relatively rare. Since most matrilineal systems in Africa are Iroquois, this leaves us with only such groups as the Iraqw, briefly described by Winter (1968), the Sukuma, insufficiently pictured by Malcolm (1953), the Luguru, partially detailed by Young and Fosbrooke (1960), and the Wambugwe, tersely portrayed by Gray (Gray MS).

Crow terminology is a kind of reverse of Omaha in the sense that the terms override generation, just as Omaha does, but it is the lineage into which FZ marries that is raised up, so to speak, and the lineage of MB that is lowered. But to conclude thereby that it is in other respects simply the reverse of Omaha would be as much a mistake as to assume that FZD marriage is but the reverse of MBD marriage (Figs. 12 and 13). FZD (PCCM) marriage, which alliance theorists associate with Crow terminology, does not merely reverse the flow of women; it creates from generation to generation a reciprocal exchange of women.

There is a tendency to see kinship terminologies moving along a continuum reflecting a move from extreme matrilineality to extreme patrilineality as follows:

$$(\text{Crow}) \rightarrow \left(\begin{array}{c} \text{Matrilineal} \\ \text{Iroquois} \end{array} \right) \rightarrow \left(\begin{array}{c} \text{Patrilineal} \\ \text{Iroquois} \end{array} \right) \rightarrow (\text{Omaha})$$

As a matter of fact, Murdock (1949, 245) finds double descent correlating with Crow, as among the Wambugwe and, perhaps, the Iraqw. That is to say, there is a correlation between Crow and mixed systems as I earlier redefined double descent. Since information on the Wambugwe is the most complete, my comments on Crow will be relative to them. The Wambugwe have some peculiar resemblances to Omaha and other extensive systems. There is no cousin marriage, and marriage rules direct totally unrelated people to marry. The Wambugwe are relatively well off with an estimated eight head of cattle per family and a brideprice running from 3 to 5 heifers which is, by my calculations (Schneider 1964) not low. And, interestingly, livestock are inherited patrilineally, as is the position of chief, although Ego also has a right to the bridewealth cattle held by his MB. However, the Wambugwe display some contrary features. For one thing they have nonlocalized matriclans whose lineages are also nonlocalized. The society is divided into chiefdoms whose heads vie for followers. If possession of cattle is unevenly distributed it could be that marriage is made for political reasons by those without cattle. However this still leaves a puzzle: why the payment of brideprice does not confer patrilineal descent in those cases where it can be paid. Unfortunately, we have no way of answering the question.

HAWAIIAN TERMINOLOGY

One last terminology, Hawaiian, is used by the Shambaa and the Rwandese (Maquet 1961, 47ff). In the statistical study of brideprice mentioned earlier (Schneider n.d.), I found Hawaiian, along with Crow, related to matrilineality even though, as Goody found (1970), it can accommodate either type of descent. In Africa, according to Murdock's nonrandom sample (1967) it also is unassociated with cousin marriage. In this terminology generation is emphasized with the generations of one's own lineage and those of affinal relatives equated. Thus F and MB are called by the same term and all cousins, cross and parallel, are equated with one's own siblings. One might expect the Shambaa to follow the path of Iroquois because they have few cattle and live in a habitat like that of the Luguru and Kaguru. The reason they embrace Hawaiian appears related to problems of land shortage which plague other eastern Tanzanian Bantu. For reasons which are not clear, the Shambaa have taken a course that leads apparently inexorably to Hawaiian, of granting rights in land to women, who may also pass them on to their sons. This practice, as earlier noted leads to a type of lineage found often in the southern Pacific and which has been labeled "ramage," but whereas in lineages (whether patrilineal of matrilineal) legal rights pass only through men, here descent may shift between men and women as the case may be. Since, so to speak, no man knows from generation to generation whether his lineage will be that of his father's people or his mother's, Hawaiian terminology allows for this by distinguishing only generations and not lineages. Interestingly, although there is a clear cognatic bias to Rwandese kinship, it is more like that of the Yoruba of West Africa, with clear patrilineal emphasis. Why Rwandese should have gone this direction is unclear, unless it has something to do with high population density. In other respects they conform to the East African pattern, their low ratio of cattle (.18:1, Maquet 1961) seeming to suggest that they would not utilize either Omaha or Descriptive terms.

CONCLUSION

This survey of family, descent, kinship, and marriage has demonstrated unequivocably a relationship between these structures of society and the economic systems with which they are associated even though the nature of the relationship is not entirely clear in the cases of the more infrequent forms.

The principle that seems to be operating is that where there is sufficient mobile wealth (ordinarily cattle or other large livestock in East Africa) descent shifts from matrilineal to patrilineal and to the house–property complex. When wealth rises to a level of a ratio of cattle to people of something like .25 to 1, Omaha kinship emerges to replace Iroquois and Descriptive arises at the highest levels of livestock wealth. Accompanying the appearance of Omaha and Descriptive, especially the former, are extensive marriage patterns of dispersed alliance.

However, when wealth is too low to achieve extensiveness, Iroquois terminologies dominate with a strong tendency to cousin marriage. All the major forms of cousin marriage are associated with Iroquois but especially dual cross cousin, patrilateral cross cousin and matrilateral cross cousin. The reason for this seems to be that in all these cases except the last a kind of exchange of women takes place, thus negating the need for an exchangeable repository of value or, perhaps, as a substitute for it. In dual cross cousin marriage a woman is in effect exchanged directly for a woman. In patrilateral cross cousin marriage women are exchanged for each other in adjacent generations. In the case of matrilateral cross cousin marriage the situation is more complicated. There is an exchange of some goods for a woman but the alliance is perpetuated from generation to generation, suggesting that the payment for the woman is insufficient to detach her more than weakly from her lineage. The wife-givers, in other words, are dominant.

Despite the special success we have had in associating Iroquois, cousin marriage, and lower levels of wealth on the one hand, and Omaha, extensive marriage, and higher levels of livestock wealth on the other, there are many facts about marriage and kinship in East Africa that are still only vaguely understood due to the poor quality of information or its rarity. Descriptive is a kind of kinship terminology that seems clearly related to higher levels of livestock wealth. But why there should also be a tendency for it to be associated with patrilateral parallel cousin marriage is not clear. Crow is a form of terminology that seems related to dual descent for reasons that are obscure.

Furthermore, the association between Iroquois and intensive social and economic operations and Omaha and extensive operation is not one to one. There are some occurrences of Omaha and Iroquois that are still inexplicable. The Iroquois Gogo are an example of a society that apparently does not fit the theory. The Gogo are wealthy cattle people whose mode of life resembles the Turkana in many ways. Why, under these circumstances, they practice cousin marriage and utilize Iroquois terminology is not clear. Similarly, the Taita, who have a high enough livestock/people ratio and Omaha terminology seem in some ways to be Iroquois. In the Taita highlands (Harris 1962) there is clearly competition for land, so much so that the Taita have resorted to the unusual practice (for Black Africa) of lineage endogamy or patrilateral parallel cousin marriage. 30% of all marriages occur within the lineage. Thus, in order to hold together valuable parcels of land, men become subordinate to fathers-in-law on a grand scale. But a non-Iroquois dimension of the system is that PPCM is not allowed within the range of second cousin, so that the closest relative a man can marry is FFBDD, a cousin marriage strategy which begins to look extensive.

All of this suggests that the real explanation for the association of kinship and economics in East Africa is some process such as the velocity of the movement of repositories of value or the rate of capital formation, a matter about which more will be said in later chapters.

CHAPTER VI

States

ORDINARILY, IN THE tradition of African anthropology, this and the next chapter would have been titled "Government," but I would like to suggest that this convention prejudices the case. The term government has gradually been expanded to cover almost any kind of overall organization to be found in indigenous Africa, whereas its original meaning was rather specific, referring to hierarchical, usually bureaucratic, organizations. In these terms many East African people had no government whatever, but they always had some kind of overall organization. So to avoid the problem of the connotations of the word government, I will talk about East African overall indigenous social organization which will include nonhierarchical systems. Thus government becomes essentially equal to a hierarchical system, which Murdock (1959, 37) and others take to define a state, i.e., a community, whether a segment of an ethnic group, a total ethnic group, or even an empire in which a political office or offices of authority exist. Thus, some of our states may consist of nothing but a few villages headed by a chief, so long as there is a chief and not merely a big man.

TYPES OF OVERALL ORGANIZATION

East Africa is known for the large degree to which government was lacking. This is not to say that states were rare but rather that nonhierarchical systems were more common than elsewhere in Africa. In addition to hierarchies, two principal types of egalitarian

153

systems existed: segmentary lineage systems and age organizations (sometimes called age grade systems). However, the three types of organization did not always exist independently. There were states based on segmentary lineage which also included age organization. And there were nonhierarchical segmentary lineage systems with age organization. Finally, some systems which were primarily age organized contained segmentary lineages. Essentially, then, classifying a society as a state depends on whether it has a hierarchical organization, whatever other organizational features it has, a definition which will be shown to be useful in our subsequent discussion of the reason for the rise of states.

TYPES OF HIERARCHY

Hierarchical systems were of two types, those based on segmentary lineage and—a residual category—those which were not. The former, of which the Alur of Uganda are an example, utilized the genealogical structure of the society to model the hierarchical structure of the bureaucratic state, the ostensible direct descendant of the founder being the chief or king and the heads of the subordinate lineages being descendants or lower-level ancestors (Fig. 16).

These states varied in the degree of centrality. Figure 17 shows how the progression manifested itself in segmentary lineage societies. At the bottom is a society like Turu, which in fact is stateless, whose organization, however, is segmentary, all the local lineages perceiving of themselves as related through common descent from the founder of the society. Kaguru represent a next level in which there is some recognized leader (*mundewa*) in the local village. This is a petty chiefdom. "The distinguishing feature of a petty chieftainship," to quote Sahlins (1968, 21) "... is its officialness." That is to say, it is an office. This is probably the most simply organized type of state. Nyamwezi had regional chiefs with numbers of villages under them but with no central organization until late in the nineteenth century and no necessary connection between the chiefs. Kimbu were like Nyamwezi but the regional chiefs were

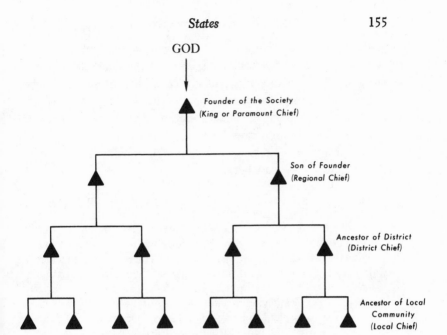

GOD

Founder of the Society
(King or Paramount Chief)

Son of Founder
(Regional Chief)

Ancestor of District
(District Chief)

Ancestor of Local
Community
(Local Chief)

Segmentary Lineage Genealogy and Model of Bureaucratic State

FIG. 16

Increasing Centrality

MAMBWE (Kingdom)

ALUR, SHAMBAA (Segmentary States or Kingdoms)

KIMBU (Linked Regional Chiefs)

NYAMWEZI (Independent Regional Chiefs)

KAGURU (Local Village Chiefs)

TURU (Stateless)

Scale of Centrality of States

FIG. 17

bound together by various kinds of connections. The Alur and Shambaa constituted what have been called by Southall "segmentary states," with a king or paramount chief but with subchiefs who competed with him for power. Finally, the Mambwe of northern Zambia, one of a group of similar societies extending into southwest Tanzania, had an autocratic king.

Shorter (1974, 42) makes an important qualifying statement about these lineage-based states:

> It must not be thought . . . that a state is segmentary only because it is composed of segmentary lineages. Segmentation is characteristic of all power competition, as M. G. Smith has pointed out, and a government takes on a segmentary form when segmentation pervades the whole administrative structure. This segmentation may or may not coincide with lineage segmentation, which need not have any political significance. In western Tanzania there exist groups of peoples having a traditional political structure of chiefdom associations, and these associations are characterized by a segmentation which is only partially identifiable with lineage segmentation. Such are the Nyamwezi, Sukuma, Kimbu, Konongo, and Galla (Tanzania), to mention but a few. Although the main impetus for the development of the associations has been the segmentation of an original chiefly lineage, a more important factor has been the challenge provided by invading alien groups. Sometimes an expanding chiefdom segmented through the peaceful or warlike assimilation of one of these groups. At other times segmentation was used by a sparsely populated chiefdom to counteract the threat of invasion, by multiplying the centres of operation in order to exploit the environment more effectively and so substantiate its claim to occupation.

In the residual class of states are, first, most of the Interlacustrine Bantu where lineage might appear as an organizing principle but where other principles are also used, sometimes to the exclusion of kinship. In these states caste, based on the myth or reality of Hima conquest (of which I spoke in an earlier chapter), places overlords above the commoners. In the second type, patron/client relations replace kinship as the basis of organization so that a subchief, rather than being a kind of relative of the king, is a client who may have no relation to him at all. It might be argued that in fact only two hierarchical principles occur, kinship and patron/client-ship, because some authors have represented the Interlacustrine Bantu states as essentially patron/client. And, ultimately, one might argue, as Shorter in effect does, that even kinship is really a façade for a patron/client system.

As to nonhierarchical systems, the Nuer of the Sudan are the prototype for so-called segmentary societies (not to be confused with segmentary states) of which the Turu are also one. They are segmented, like segmentary states, but without any chiefs. Their people think of themselves as descended from a single Creator, who produced the founding ancestor, whose sons are ancestors of the major lineage segments of the society, each of whom in turn produces sons that founded the sublineages within the major segments, and so forth. Any member of any low level village lineage can trace his relationship to any other member of the society through the common genealogy and can also determine what rights and obligations he might have toward that person. In such societies regulation of behavior is achieved by means of rules specifying rights and obligations rather than through the authority of a chief. Of course, in such societies there is a good deal less regulation than in a state, warfare between segments being a common event, and negotiations to determine indemnity resulting from violation of rules substitute for litigation. Nevertheless, because the combatants are in some sense relatives, the intensity of conflict is mitigated by constraints, such as one which limits weapons to clubs and prohibits the use of spears.

Age organization, a nonauthoritarian system, employs the concept of age to divide society into segments, even though in some cases, such as the *gada* of the Borana Galla of southern Ethiopia, age competes with other principles of organization. Unlike the segmentary societies, which make the division horizontally, so to speak, separating lineages from each other, age organization divides it vertically, creating age strata which crosscut local communities. These age strata are often corporate to one degree or another, as for example in the prohibition against members of the same stratum marrying each other's daughters, which we will remember from the Sebei.

STATES AND LANGUAGE FAMILIES

States of one size or another occur in every major language family except the Click, although some subfamilies, such as the Eastern Nilotes, have none (Map XII). The Bantu states seem more profoundly to be tied to the cult of ancestors and the principle of lineage than the others. Yet before the point is pushed too far we must note that ancestor worship in one form or another seems associated with most African societies where lineage rather than age organization is important. Nevertheless, there is a sense in which ancestor worship takes on special importance among Bantu, as can be illustrated from the Turu concept of *mukuu*. Bantu ideas about the mystical, innate power of the "eldest" are summed up in mukuu, which may stand for the eldest brother, or the oldest man or other types of senior persons who because of their position in the genealogy are thought to have special knowledge or understanding of what is right. The Turu had no chiefs, yet when the colonial government appointed chiefs these men were sometimes able to justify their positions by showing that in some sense they were mukuu.

In a classic account of the Bemba, Richards (1940, 83) summarized certain general features of Bantu political organization in Central and Southern Africa in a way that applies as well to the Bantu of East Africa who had states:

> Authority is almost invariably based on descent, whether within the family, the village, the district, or the nation, and the chief of the tribe combines executive, ritual, and judicial functions according to the pattern of leadership in each constituent kinship unit. Like the family head, he is a priest of an ancestral cult, believed in many cases to have a mystic power over the land, and he invariably claims rights over his people's labour and produce. The hier-

archy of Bantu society allows only one type of authority, one basis of power, and one set of attributes in its leaders in most of the tribes so far described.

Richards felt that this Bantu conceptual pattern is an outgrowth of the fact that states tend to form as a result of segmentation within existing clans and lineages. But I would add that it borrows heavily from the type of world view that also characterizes Bantu. After all, segmentation, as Shorter said, is normal in any state formation and does not require any specific ideology or lineage to justify it.

Western Tanzania provides us with a bridge to the interlacustrine states which, although they are Bantu, seem to borrow certain hierarchical elements from the Nilotes to whom they are, therefore, in their turn a bridge. Shorter (1973) feels that certain cultural elements in these states were borrowed from the Interlacustrine Bantu, while rejecting attempts to assert that the idea of state itself came from them. With this position I would, of course, agree, since it is my main point that a state is an exchange institution which rises where service becomes an element in exchange, a thesis that will be examined in detail later in this chapter. Shorter writes (1973, 39–40):

> Probably the best attested example of culture diffusion from the Interlacustrine region of western Tanzania is that of the Chwezi-Swezi traditions which characterize a complex of ancestral and spirit possession cults in the Interlacustrine Kingdoms, as well as in Uha, Usumbwa, Usukuma and Unyamwezi in western Tanzania. The Swezi spirit possession society of Sukuma and Unyamwezi is not, strictly speaking, a royal institution, although in recent years it has enjoyed an increasingly privileged place in the ceremonies accompanying the installation and burial of Nyamwezi chiefs.

Earlier I spoke of the presumed conquest of the Interlacustrine Bantu area and the rise of the Chwezi, Kitara, and, finally, the more recent states of Buganda, Bunyoro, and others. Mair (1962) has

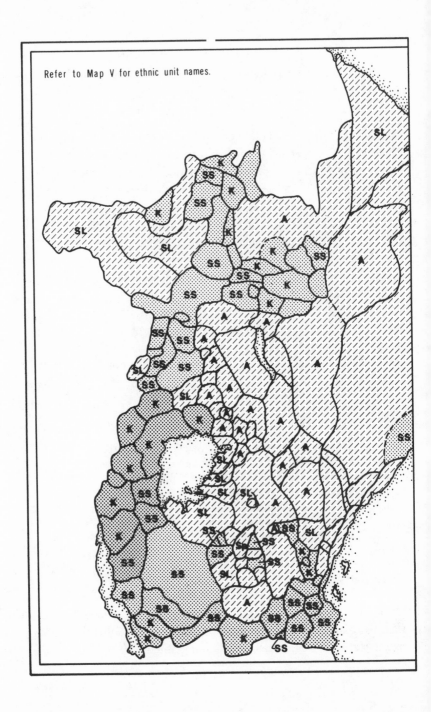

Refer to Map V for ethnic unit names.

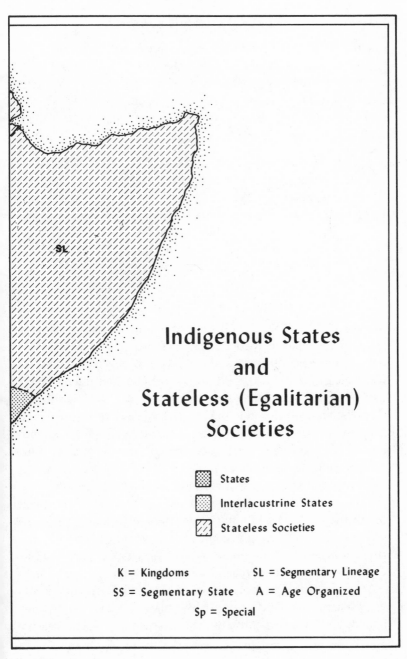

Indigenous States
and
Stateless (Egalitarian)
Societies

States
Interlacustrine States
Stateless Societies

K = Kingdoms   SL = Segmentary Lineage
SS = Segmentary State   A = Age Organized
Sp = Special

MAP XII

summarized the characteristics of the interlacustrine states. The "caste" structure, which is so unusual in East Africa, and which, according to Mair, was not even characteristic of many of these societies except in theory, is of special significance. The various western lacustrine groups were divided into castes as follows (Mair 1962, 137; Taylor 1962, 13–14):

Group	Caste
Ha	Tutsi, Ha
Haya	Huma, Iru
Nkole	Huma, Iru
Nyoro	Bito, Huma, Iru
Toro	Bito, Hima, Iru
Ruanda	Tutsi, Hutu, Twa
Rundi	Tutsi, Hima, Hutu, Twa
Zinza	Huma, Iru

Maquet (1971, 148), describing one of the more complex of these caste systems, that of Ruanda, speaks of the Tutsi as pastoralists, the Hutu as agriculturalists and the Twa as pygmylike hunters. In fact these castes are mixed with respect to production and the designations seem rather to indicate economic divisions, the Tutsi being the wealthiest and therefore the largest holders of cattle, the Hutu having few cattle and making their living mainly from the production of crops, and the Twa, a pariah group, depending on hunting but also acting as minstrels and potters.

In the simplest type system, such as that of Nkole, the Huma (or Hima) are the cattle-owning overlords (as they were in the ancient Bachwezi kingdom), claiming descent from prehistoric pastoral invaders of the land. On this simple division of Huma overlords and Iru peasants is superimposed the Bito ruling class, conquerors of the Chwezi and founders of the old kingdom of Kitara.

Much controversy surrounds attempts to explain the interlacustrine system, the complexity of the situation being further compounded by the fact that two of the interlacustrine stages, Buganda and Busoga, do not follow the caste pattern of the others. Some historians, such as Ogot (1967), feel that the present system derives from an ancient Nilotic invasion which displaced the Huma, Bach-wezi dynasty. Other scholars feel that the mythic explanation is untrue and that the system arose indigenously through certain complex processes. Mair (1962) does not agree that this is a real caste system at all. The problem is a bit like that of present-day England, where one could debate whether the royal family as it now exists derives from the Norman invasion or is, despite that, an indigenous product. After all, the queen is not queen just because of the Norman invasion. And one could also debate whether England has castes, or highly institutionalized classes, or whether the society is more complex than appears and the idea of classes is a kind of myth about the society.

My feeling is that there is certainly an historical, cultural component to these systems, equivalent to the language system in the sense that it provides the categories within which political activities are defined (much as genealogy does for the Bantu). But the system to a large extent must be explained in terms of the economics of the interlacustrine area, including the fact that although cattle are not as numerous as in the non-state areas they are in sufficient supply, particularly in the Ankole area, to provide the necessary mobile wealth to be used by ambitious people to assert power over others and defend their exercise of power in terms of what now amounts to a myth, whatever the truth of it, of Hima and Bito conquest.

Turning now to the Nilotes proper, Southall (1970, 45) notes that among the Western Nilotes (such people as Acholi, Anuak, Nuer, Dinka, and Alur) there is a universal tendency to conceive of society as divided into those who own the country and those who are settlers by sufferance. There is nothing particularly Nilotic about the idea that those who pioneered the land have perpetual right to it and continue to have mystical control over it even after they may have sold it or otherwise given it up. Such ideas are probably universal in Africa. But the Western Nilotes have elevated this idea to a principle on the order of democracy or socialism. It is manifest to one degree or another in all the Western Nilotic systems whether they are states or stateless. The most elaborate example is that of the Alur among whom five divisions are recognized: the king, the royal lineage with residual rights to succession, the more distant segments of the royal lineage whose rights to succession have lapsed, the commoners, and the serfs. Among these, the royal class is in some sense the owners of the land while the commoners are intruding settlers, and the serfs constitute an even lower status, the pawns or servile class acquired by capture or other means. In the stateless Dinka society the distinction is between the high-ranking fishing spear clans and the others.

So distinctive is this feature that it gives credence to the idea that the Interlacustrine Bantu area was conquered by Western Nilotes who brought with them this inclination to extreme social division while using it, paradoxically, to differentiate themselves from the original owners of the land. But on the other hand, perhaps possession by conquest is the highest form of ownership.

Included in the Western Nilotic groups are some states that arose in Sudan (Trigger 1969, 88). While the majority of these societies were stateless, two centers of state development were Darfur, northwest of the Nuer-Dinka complex, and at places on the Nile including, perhaps, the divine kingdom of Shilluk. Other than there, the Anuak, most of whom are in western Ethiopia, are an important inclusion.

It will be noticed that no mention has been made of the Eastern Nilotics, who with the Western form the whole Nilotic group of Nilo-Saharan speakers. The reason is simply that the Eastern Nilotic have no states. Indeed, they are a prime example of statelessness and of the use of age organization for overall organization. Treatment of this group is therefore reserved for the succeeding chapter on egalitarian systems.

Generalizing about cultural features of the Cushitic-speaking people is difficult. Besides the fact that these people are prone to nonhierarchical systems (witness the Somali and Galla), less is known about this part of East Africa, and what is known indicates that these people have been heavily influenced by the dominant Semitic-speaking Amhara society of Ethiopia (which gave rise to Coptic emperors like Haile Selassie) and the forces of various Islamic Arab groups which penetrated this part of Africa early and more strongly than elsewhere. The few states include the anomalous Galla kingdoms of Gibe in Ethiopia, such as Jimma and Limu, and a few minor systems in southwest Ethiopia, such as the Malle divine kingdom (if it is Cushitic), and the pocket of Somali chiefdoms in southern Somalia. Even among the Borana Galla hierarchy appears when the people become sedentary (P. T. W. Baxter 1975). Insofar as statehood occurred it seems to have taken on an Arab flavor, as illustrated by a quote from Lewis's account of the Horn of Africa (1955, 163):

> Mention has been made of the petty sultanates and sheikdoms which arose in the course of the Mohammedan wars of the States of Adal against Abyssinia, the largest and most influential being the Sultanate of Aussa on the Awash river in southern Danakil. Aussa represents the most extreme form of a tendency towards the formation of small centralized states as ruling islands in a sea of tribal society. The power and authority of their heads is considerable, resting as it does on the sanction of force provided by an extensive militia. Taxes are levied on produce and stock, and fines are imposed in the administration of justice. When disputes arise between surrounding tribes the Sultan of Aussa sends a deputy with his silver baton . . . to act as mediator. Arable land is worked on a feudal system for the sultan, who is empowered to grant parcels of land to chiefs and court favourites. There is thus some truth in the usual description of the Sultan of Aussa as a complete despot owning lands and people.

THE STRUCTURE OF STATES

Various attempts have been made to characterize African states, focusing on the large-scale ones, including Murdock's (1959, 37–

39), which labeled them "African despotisms" parallel in form to Wittfogel's (1957) Oriental Despotisms. According to Murdock these kings or chiefdoms had some or all of the following features:

Monarchical absolutism, in which the king or chief had absolute power (although he might not in fact be able to act arbitrarily).

Eminent domain, meaning that the king owned, in some sense, everything in the kingdom or chiefdom.

Divine kingship, the chief's power being derived from divine sources such as the Creator or the original ancestor.

Ritual isolation, such that the king did not associate freely with his subjects and might even be concealed from them.

Insignia of office, including such things as royal drums, trumpets, or shells.

Capital town, often independent of the area in which it was placed, even to the extent of being mobile.

Female cohorts, including Queen Mother or Queen Sister, who might have great power.

Territorial bureaucracy, such that the kingdom was divided into regions over which officials administered collection of taxes, maintenance of roads or levy of troops for the king.

Ministers, who were the king's instruments for running the state or conducting warfare.

Indefinite succession, such that when a king or chief died his successor was not automatically selected but might be chosen by some means involving an anarchic interregnum such as characterized some interlacustrine states where the sons of the king warred for the throne.

Mair (1962) has characterized the interlacustrine states in a way parallel to Murdock. In all of them the ruler had a palace which in the smallest states was little more than a homestead like anyone else's except that it was better built and larger because it had to accommodate numerous wives and servants. The king, to one degree or another, was treated deferentially to emphasize the difference between him and others. Hereditary officials performed certain ritual acts or maintained ritual objects of kingship, such as the umbilical cord of the *kabaka* (king) of Buganda. A "prime minister" existed in all but the little state of Zinza and the ruler chose officials to administer parts of the country. These territorial chiefs, who had no hereditary claims to their areas except in the smaller kingdoms, and who were shifted around the kingdom, organized manpower for war and public works, collected tribute, and kept the peace. In the larger states like Buganda, the prime minister was a person of great power. Finally, these officials were essentially bureaucrats, holding power by the grace of the king, whose allegiances were therefore to the office, not to kinsmen.

The Alur, who Southall says (c1953) have the most complex of the Western Nilotic states, set the chief's homestead off from others with a symbolic fence of elephant grass. Around it lived a large body of retainers including great councillors on the one side and the destitute on the other. A fire was kept burning on an open hearth during the day as the king sat in council; courtiers enforced etiquette in the chief's presence, including the removal of spears and sandals at the entrance to the palace. When traveling, which he rarely did, the king had to have his own separate ménage where he observed his special food taboos. If he had a large chiefdom, special courtiers acted as envoys semiformally accredited to different quarters of the chiefdom. But obviously, the Alur chiefdoms, despite their high devolpment, were relatively simple compared to the overwhelming majesty of the court of the king of Buganda.

If we were to continue this journey beyond the Interlacustrine Bantu and Western Nilotes to the Cushitic kingdoms and finally the Bantu kingdoms or chiefdoms proper, we could find plenty of data to give further support to Murdock's proposition that despite cultural differences in the expression of statehood, all these states had parallel structures to one degree or another. The main variation, in fact, was simply the degree to which the structure manifested itself. Some states, like Buganda, had very wealthy, very powerful kings, while tiny chiefships like those in Ukimbu had chiefs very nearly indistinguishable to the unpracticed eye from their subjects, prime ministers who were little more than housekeepers, and royal symbols, such as wooden horns, that were as humble as their possessors.

THE BASIS OF STATEHOOD

But we need not indulge this point further, turning instead to one of the most important questions about government in Africa, how to account for these parallels in the structure of states? Is the form of the state, which looks so specific, a kind of culture, invented somewhere and diffused to wherever it appears, or does it, by some process, arise wherever opportunity permits? According to Murdock (1959, 37):

> It is almost as though all of Africa south of the Sahara were permeated, as it were, by a mental blueprint of a despotic political structure, transmitted from generation to generation as a part of traditional verbal culture, and always available to be transmitted into reality whenever some individual arises with the imagination, enterprise, strength and luck to establish, with the aid of his kinsmen, an authoritarian regime over people residing beyond the limits of his local community.

I believe that the answer to this mystery is in good part simple. African kingdoms and chiefdoms (despotism is too strong a term) represent in exaggerated form the basic structure of kinship relations occurring in African societies, whether Bantu or other. Perhaps the best way to underscore this point is to describe a situation I know well, a certain Turu village. Even though Turu are nonhierarchical, the structure of relations and system of beliefs they hold is sufficient to provide the matrix for an absolute monarchy should appropriate conditions arise.

Consider first the matter of monarchical absolutism, Murdock's first trait. The Turu village is a localized lineage whose members trace relationship from an apical founding ancestor who in turn can be related to higher-level ancestors up to Munyaturu, the founder, created by God (see Fig. 16). Within the village there is one man who is acknowledged to be the main descendant from the apical ancestor (who may or may not, in turn, be the main descendant of the higher-level descendants of the founder of the society). This person, as I said earlier, is called mukuu; by virtue of his prime position, he is said to "know" what is right, and he is designated by the ancestors as the spiritual leader of the lineage segment of which he is a member. Hence, whenever councils are held he must be present. In my judgment, the mukuu of this particular village was in fact mentally incompetent. This made no difference at all. The elders would do what they decided to do whatever the mukuu's opinion. Usually, in fact, he expressed no opinion. His presence and assent were sufficient. If some man in Unyaturu were to manage to consolidate the whole society or a part of it into a state, he would without doubt first justify his position by rearranging genealogies, making himself mukuu. Furthermore, his power, like that of all African despots, would be absolute only in theory and subject to the "advice" of his councillors.

The concept of eminent domain stems from monarchical absolutism. The founding ancestor and his descendants are thought to have power over the land they settle. A man may sell or otherwise dispose of his land but the spirit of the original settler is always associated with it. Hence, when rain ceremonies are held in Unyaturu a representative of the lineage of the founder of alienated land must participate. Extending this view, Munyaturu, the creator of the Wanyaturu, "owns" all of Unyaturu while his subancestors "own" the particular segments they settled by his sufferance, so that the mukuu in a given village "owns" the whole village because he is primary representative of the subancestor who settled it. Thus, our hypothetical Turu king, having justified his position as mukuu of mukuus, "owns" all the land. But, of course, in nonhierarchical Unyaturu this ownership has no practical substance, whereas if the mukuu were able to establish his political power he could translate his ownership into a demand for tribute.

The frequency of occurrence of the position of Queen Mother no doubt relates to the fact that the typical African household is one in which a man's control of property in this world derives from his mother who created it. That kings should defer to their mothers makes them like all other African men. As to sisters, while the logic of giving sisters special status is not as clear, it probably derives from the fact that they are valuable assets, as in all African families. Where a Turu boy might depend on his sister's marriage for the wealth to help him marry or build his estate, the sister of a king does the same, if only because she can be used to accomplish a marriage of political importance.

Not all of the traits of these states are easily explained in these terms; for example, indefinite succession. The pattern of succession normally looks quite clear in the African homestead, suggesting in the case of the kingdom that if primogeniture were the rule, the king's eldest son would and often does naturally assume power. But, on the other hand, primogeniture in African families looks more clear cut than it is, the power usually passing to the eldest who has indefinite responsibility for using it to benefit his brothers as well as himself. It seems possible that when a whole state is involved, this indefiniteness could not be tolerated so that the only way to resolve it would be to allow the brothers to fight it out and to reduce the sibling group to a single member by one means or another.

Without further exploring this mode of explanation we may leave this subject, merely suggesting that in the cases of other royal traits, the similarity between the structure of states may be explained at least in part by seeing the royal institution as an expansion of social relations from the common to the royal level.

ECONOMIC BASES OF STATES

Having detailed the structure and variety of East African states, we may now turn to the fundamental question of their economic bases. As soon as the matter is raised we are confronted by the problem of traditional explanations which stress such things as conquest and royal myths. So before going on to the main subject I will say a few words to put these into perspective.

Mair (1962) is probably as responsible as anyone for establishing the point that conquest is not the only or even the most common cause of the appearance of state structure in stateless societies. Yet conquest is not unimportant. And conquest is not really noneconomic. Insofar as power brings with it tribute the subjugation of people can be a profitable business. But even when conquest has occurred, the people who are subjected, by paying tribute to their conqueror, translate the relationship from one of exploitation to citizenship or clientship, an exchange between ruler and ruled which is fundamental to all states and which can arise without conquest.

As to myth, the stress on royal myths and their function may leave the impression that a chiefdom or kingdom is secure if the myths of kingship are in good order. The myth of Mbega, founder of the Shambaai kingdom, is an example (Winans 1962, 76; Feierman 1974). In the myth the founder of the Shambaa dynasty is portrayed as having been asked to assume power.

> Whether or not it is true in an historical sense, nearly all commoners claim that their ancestors voluntarily asked for chiefs, and similarly, chiefs do not claim to rule by right of conquest but rather by invitation and right of descent.

Most western Lacustrine Bantu kingdoms utilize similar myths about the founding Bachwezi to justify present power. And we have already seen how certain cosmological notions like mukuu can be tied to positions of power. But again, mythical and philosophical sanction is insufficient to maintain power. Indeed, one may question whether these things support so much as justify power, a subtle distinction. Ultimately the state must rest on some economic base, particularly exchange relations between the powerful and the weak in which the ascription of power to the ruler is the form of payment by the ruled.

Probably the first anthropologists to entertain economic explanations of African states have been the Marxists. Maquet's attempt is well known (1923, 93). He asks why such a high proportion of

Africans living in savannah regions have experienced chiefship, and he answers:

> This pattern . . . —habitat and technique allowing production of an agricultural surplus, control of the surplus of a group by one of the members of the group, emergence and development of political power, reinforcement of the power to appropriate surplus produce —occurred thousands of times in the vast area which extends south of the equatorial belt, from the Atlantic to the Indian Ocean.

In other words (Maquet 1972, 95):

> The true wealth of a chief consisted of the number of his villages which supplied workers for his fields and young men for his army.

Carol Smith (1976) more recently has said something like this but in a way that adds precision. In her view, stratification is a defining characteristic of agrarian societies. Further:

> Agrarian societies are societies economically divided between food producers and nonfood producers in which the bulk of the population is engaged in food production. The basis for stratification . . . that which divides the elite from the peasantry . . . is without exception control over some critical resource by select members of that society. The critical resource may be a means of production, such as land, or a means of destruction, such as fire power. But it may also be a simple means of subsistence, such as salt. . . .

In Maquet's savannah of Central Africa and much of southern Tanzania, it was control of land, a scarce means of production, even large, infertile tracts, that was usually the base, although after the appearance of Arab and Swahili long-distance traders in the nineteenth century and earlier, it was often control of the supply of slaves or of ivory. In Buganda, most notably, but elsewhere too, as in Zigula and Shambaai, it was often control of fire power—guns and powder which, like the ivory and slave trade, also laid the basis for enlarging states from petty forms.

Implicit in Maquet's theory of the basis of chiefship is a theory of egalitarianism. People in "civilizations of spears" (pastoral societies) are egalitarian because they must be mobile in order to find grazing land, which makes them difficult to control. But, as we have seen, not even a majority of pastoralists are nomads so Maquet's explanation must again be modified in the direction of Smith. In East Africa (but not everywhere else in the world) domestic livestock usually cannot be monopolized by a few when the ratios are 1:1 or better, whether the pastoralists are nomadic or not. It is the "slipperiness" of pastoral wealth in contrast to land-based wealth that is the groundwork of egalitarianism, as will be shown more fully in succeeding chapters.

Mair (1962, 108), discussing the reason for the rise of interlacustrine and Nilotic chiefdoms, phrases her answer to the question of the rise of chieftainship in more specific terms than Maquet:

> The secular element in kingship is ability to attract and keep a following. Of course every leader has a following; it is tautology to say so. But what matters is the kind of following. We saw how the men who became leaders among the Luhya did so because they could count on the support in debates about village affairs of a certain number of people who were under obligations to them. This could hardly be thought of as a first step towards monarchical rule. But this first step has been taken when we find a leader who can keep permanently associated with him a body of retainers whom he can call on to enforce his wishes, and who identify themselves more closely with him than with any of the divisions of the population. This is the first essential of state power, in however rudimentary a form.

In other words (Mair 1962, 109) "people expect to get something in return for loyalty to their leader" and when the relationship becomes fixed the basis of a state is laid. This kind of exchange can occur whether people are sedentary or mobile, and it can be based on the exchange of any kind of good, grain, livestock, or whatever.

If the pattern of descent and kinship in a society is based upon the exchange relationship of marriage, the pattern of the state is built on the exchange that goes on between subordinates and super-ordinates, commoners and rulers, weak and powerful (H. Lewis 1974). This kind of exchange utilizes services, placing the supplier under obligation to his patron. While this is widely recognized by political anthropologists like Mair, she, like almost everyone else, discusses obligation in unspecific terms, making few attempts to ascertain degrees of obligation, which obviously exist. A person may be obligated to another in different amounts, and because this is possible, it is possible for a superordinate not only to obtain different amounts, depending on his resources, but for these to move in the market, the amount a person is willing to pay varying with demand for the service. A chief is an entrepreneur who is exchanging resources for obligations. As Maquet said, the wealth of a chief resides in the men he controls, their number and the degree to which he controls them.

Gamer (1976, 101) helps make the point in his discussion of patron-client relationships in developing nations:

> Many individuals who need work because the job security of their traditional village has been eroded develop complex special relationships with men who can offer them income in exchange for their services and loyalty. These men in turn develop special relationships with economic and political elites, and they form chains of individuals who exchange both economic assets and political supports. These patron-client networks have displaced clans and kingly courts as the authoritative allocators of values with a monopoly on the use of force. . . .

Gamer (1976, 105) includes a list of the types of person who may become patrons, a list which includes both traditional and modern roles: small traders, commodities middlemen, retail merchants, plantation owners, headmen and chiefs in traditional society, nobility, kings and courtiers, slave officials, military men, money-lenders, managers of estates, owners of villages, mine owners, religious leaders, bureaucrats, elected political leaders.

The nature of subservience in traditional Africa can best be brought home by citing first some gross, even trivial examples.

Stahl (1964, 129), speaking of the Chagga Chief Ndesserua, says that when he sat down he did not use a stool but rather the back of a crouching henchman. Similarly, Roscoe (1915, 9) explains that when the king of Bunyoro while on journey wished to rest, "one of his subjects immediately kneels down on one knee and offers the other as a seat for the king to sit on." Willis (1974) tells of how one of the Fipa chiefs followed the practice of blowing a whistle at night before retiring, a signal for the whole village to subside into quietness until he blew it again in the morning after which the bustle was allowed to resume. Speaking of the king of Dahomey, Burton (1893, 60) notes:

> If perspiration appears upon the royal brow it is instantly removed with the softest cloth by the gentlest hands; if the royal lips move, a plated spittoon, which, when Mr. Norris wrote, was gold, held by one of his wives is moved within convenient distance; if the King sneezes, all present touch the ground with their foreheads; if he drinks, every lip utters exclamation of blessing.

Although Dahomey is in West Africa, behavior in the court of the Buganda king was similar (Roscoe 1911, 259):

> When the king entered, everyone greeted him with the special salutation *Gusinze*, which means "May you overcome," and all bowed down their faces to the ground. No one was permitted to cough, or sneeze, or blow his nose in court; had they done so they would have been seized by guards, who stood armed with ropes, ready to bind anyone if the King gave the word.

In Busoga, like Buganda, the most prominent form of subservience was military (Fallers 1965, 137):

> This hierarchy of ruler, princes, chiefs and headmen operated as a military, judicial, and tribute-gathering organization. In case of war, each was responsible for providing for his superior a number of armed men. Each, together with his advisors, constituted a court of justice; a litigant dissatisfied with a decision could carry his appeal upward through the hierarchy to the ruler. For the support of the system, each was responsible for the collection of trib-

ute in labour, foodstuffs, beer, barkcloth and iron hoes. These were collected in the first instance by the headmen, who kept a share for themselves and passed the remainder upward through the hierarchy. At each point in the system, subordination consisted in willingness to submit to one's superior in these respects. Refusal to pay tribute, to supply military aid, or to recognize the judicial decisions of one's superior was to deny his authority and to invite reprisal. On the other hand, if such acts of independence could be carried out successfully, for example by a prince, a permanent increase in authority might be obtained.

Unfortunately, while this passage makes plain the nature of subservience, it does not show what the subordinate obtained for what he gave. The military machine that the rulers organized was used to obtain wealth from other people, and this wealth found its way to the lower classes in a fashion similar to that in Buganda, of which I will speak in a moment.

The complexity of the state and the degree of subservience demanded is related to the wealth of the state. I. M. Lewis (1976, 352) remarks:

The bigger and more specialized the apparatus of government, the greater the economic surplus needed to maintain it and hence the more extractive and intensive the economy.

But some states could not have raised the level of wealth with any amount of increased extractive pressure. Fallers recognizes this when he speaks of the economic base of the Soga state (Fallers 1965, 143):

The instability of the traditional Soga State was not entirely due to structural strains. A further factor was the simplicity of its technological and economic base. The principal weapons, the spear and shield, were simple to manufacture and easily obtainable. This meant that one man was as good as the next in battle and that a ruler could not easily monopolise the means of force in defense of his position. Neither could the ruler monopolise to any substantial degree scarce goods of other kinds. Although palace life represented a distinctly higher standard of living, it was different in kind from the life of the peasant's homestead only in its social aspects—courtly behaviour, constant entertaining, staffs of servants and the like.

Faller's point is deficient in one important respect. The economic basis of these states depended on more than the technology of warfare or even production and the level of material consumption. It depended on the production of valued goods of all kinds and the ability to exchange them, which is why the "standard of living" might be low while consumption of services was high. Buganda and Busoga were states at the height of complexity for East Africa. Compare them to the petty chiefdoms of Ukimbu and it is easy to see that the economic differences rested on the amount and kinds of goods that were produced, which could be used to obtain services. Societies like the Kimbu and Nyamwezi grew toward centralization and increased complexity principally with the appearance of a market for slaves and ivory, previously not very valuable products in East Africa.

SOME CASES

The economic structures of East African states varied considerably. Earlier, I spoke of the narrow zones of fertile, well-watered soil that form the basis of banana culture. One of the remarkable things about bananas is that they are the foundation on which one of the largest and strongest East African states was built. Bananas have also been important to the economies of other states, such as that of Shambaai. How can bananas be related to an exchange system and system of servitude on the scale of Buganda? They would seem to be unlikely trade items because they are very perishable and the supply in a country like Buganda is so great that they would seem to be too cheap to be of value. We can guess the answer from Southwold's account of Baganda society (1965, 109) where he tells us that the cost of labor inputs into banana culture is very low relative to return and that this produces a good deal of surplus labor;

this, in the old Buganda kingdom, was organized into armies which during the dry season looted their neighbors of cattle, slaves, and wives, all goods that, as we have seen, are very valuable and could certainly support the state if available in sufficient quantities. Thus there arose in Buganda the relationship of *mukama* (lord) and *muddu* (servant) or *muweereza* (emissary). Quoting Fallers (1964, 74):

> These terms, which emphasize the personal tie between the individuals concerned rather than simply differences of rank, are almost universally used today, in all phases of Ganda life. . . . A *mukopi* seeking land or a man ambitious for wealth and power "attaches himself in loyal dependence." . . . It is through such ties of a patron-client nature, Baganda believe, that a person gets ahead in the world.

Shambaai is also built on bananas but combined with maize and cassava, to name only the most important crops. As we have previously seen, the Shambaa occupy an area of fertile, productive land which is in short supply. The result is that power tends significantly to be associated with control of land. Winans (1962) explains that villages consist of dominant lineages and subordinate lineages built on matrilocal residence in which the sons of a man who has married into the village and, no doubt, subordinated himself to his father-in-law are allowed to keep the land their mother received after her marriage, although the rights they hold are subordinate to the main lineage. Subordinate lineages may, in turn, subordinate (sublet to?) other lineages. Hence, over time, the leader of the main lineage may build up a significant following:

> Such men are sometimes quite powerful if they lead large villages, and many are now recognized by the Administration [colonial administration] on the same footing as the lowest level of royal chiefs although they would have been under these lesser royal chiefs in former times (Winans 1962, 62).

I suspect that Winans is wrong and that such men in former times as well as during the colonial period would have found a way to royal status through the power they commanded. This, one would expect, is most pronounced in the chiefly lineages. Where land is scarce and labor also in short supply, and where products of sufficient value, notably maize in this case, can be secured from the land, the large land holdings of chiefs coupled with their control of labor can be seen to be the source of their power and wealth, the products of the service they exact forming the exchange commodity upon which they rely, along with land, to secure allegiance.

The use of cattle to develop relations of subordination/superordination is particularly pronounced in the western lacustrine area (D'Hertefelt 1965; Maquet 1971, 207). Maquet has attempted to generalize about this for the states of Rwanda, Bunyankole, Buha, and Burundi. In all of them there was a patron-client system which in Rwanda was called *ubuhake* (but *okutoisha* in Bunyankole and *ubugabire* in the other two states) and in which, in Rwanda, the two parties to the transaction were known as *shebuja* (patron) and *garagu* (client). The shebuja was always a Tutsi overlord and the garagu another Tutsi or a Hutu peasant. In return for cattle, which the receiver could use but which remained the property of the owner, the client was obligated, if a Tutsi, to act for the patron as a councillor, messenger, or courtier, while the Hutu performed various more menial services. This is a good example of the marketability of servitude since apparently the Tutsi client, by virtue of his superior status, could obtain cattle for a smaller price than the Hutu.

The Ankole case is especially interesting because these people apparently had a higher ratio of cattle to people than other interlacustrine groups. In this society only Hima overlords could be patrons and clients to each other. In addition Oberg (1940) says relations among the Hima seem to have been more egalitarian than in the other interlacustrine societies. Because of this I suggest that in the case of the Bunyankole we have the unique example of an egalitarian pastoral society operating as a kind of special state, the hierarchical relations existing between Hima and Hutu but the Hima being a kind of egalitarian organization.

Among the Alur we find a somewhat different situation than

with either of the foregoing two. For the most part land does not seem to have been a scarce good but, on the other hand, a greater return from the land seems to have been possible than in places like Ukimbu; the Alur chiefs also had more cattle, although not enough to support the kind of exchange structure that existed among the western Lacustrine Bantu of whom we shall speak next. The Alur chiefs utilized the labor of their subordinates to produce crops (Southall c1953, 81), to build houses and perform services, in return for which they provided cattle, wives, and other goods.

Recently Little (1978) has suggested a more comprehensive theory of the relationship between banana production and states in East Africa (particularly the interlacustrine area), which is that a large number of the societies which were heavy banana producers used that advantage, like Buganda, to organize for the purpose of raiding their neighbors. The size of each state reflected its leader's success in acquiring spoils to pay off his men. The largest (Ganda, Rwanda, Nyoro, Rundi, Toro, Ankole) were organized for offense, the petty states (Ha, Shambaai, Chagga, Haya, Zinza, Soga) for offense and defense, and the village states (Gisu, Amba, Lese, Mamvu) for defense, the latter comparative failures, at least at the time they came under European control.

In all of these state systems, then, we can see service rendered to someone who by virtue of his control of land or other goods can command this service on a continuing basis in return for dependable patronage. To say this seems trite unless it is again emphasized that exchanges do not require service as a component and the lack of this commodity in exchanges is of fundamental importance in the stateless societies.

SOME FINAL CONSIDERATIONS

Certain residual points remain to be considered before we look at egalitarian societies. One of these is the debate about the relationship between density of population and states. Stevenson (1968) has made the point that, contrary to the conclusions reached by

Fortes and Evans-Pritchard (1940), there is a connection between density of population and states. As is often the case where correlations are being debated, there is an implication of causality such that the state is thought to cause dense population or dense population the state. It seems evident to me that when we view this problem in the light of the thesis I have developed, both of these statements could be true. The state could cause increased population if economies of scale, whereby the sum total of the product from organized production groups is greater than the sum of the product of the workers producing individually, were a part of the state's production orientation. Buganda, in fact, seems to be such a case, since it is doubtful that individuals working alone could have looted neighboring societies so well as could the armies of the chiefs. But density of population could also cause the state by virtue of the fact that livestock production probably would be reduced by the competition for land from human beings, and the decrease in the ratio of livestock to people would preclude statelessness.

I have spoken frequently of fertile land as a valuable good underlying the power of petty patrons. Most land in East Africa, as we have seen, was not very valuable. How then did patrons utilize it to obtain power? Shorter, in particular, has emphasized that among people like the Kimbu, even though a particular area contained no inherently fertile land, it was still necessary for people to have land of some kind to which they could apply their labor in order to obtain a return. A chief who controlled such marginal land could therefore still utilize it as a power base, although the power he obtained from it might be relatively small proportional to the quality of the land, all other things being equal.

CHAPTER VII

Egalitarian Societies

IT IS POSSIBLE to separate states from stateless societies with considerable precision. Unfortunately, it is not so easy to determine accurately just which of the stateless societies are primarily organized in terms of segmentary lineage and which in terms of age organization (Map XII). There can be no doubt about many of them: age organization is clearly the basis of social structure in such societies as Maasai, Nandi, Pokot, Turkana, and Karamojong. Segmentary lineage indisputably dominates the framework of such societies as Luo, Taita, and Turu. But for many other societies the amount of information available, although it may be sufficient to decide whether they are states or not, is insufficient to say which kind of egalitarian society they are.

Despite this, the amount of evidence we have is enough to come to some important conclusions about these two forms of organization. The first is that statelessness is not characteristically either segmentary lineage or age-organized. It occurs in either form and sometimes in novel forms. Next, it can be shown that neither structure associates more with intense pastoralism. The following statistics, like earlier ones taken from Murdock's *Atlas* (1967), show level of dependence on livestock (as a function of the ratio of cattle, camels, and goats to people) related to type of overall egalitarian organization:

182

Segmentary Lineage		Age-Organized	
Somali	9	Maasai	9
Nuer	5	Turkana	8
Sonjo	5	Nandi	5
Vugusu	4	Pokot	5
Lugbara	4	Toposa	5
Jie	4	Kipsigis	4
Luo (Kenya)	4	Kamba	3

Obviously there is no significant correlation between type of overall organization and the ratio of livestock to people.

A closer look at the Eastern and Western Nilotes (Southall 1970) confirms this conclusion. Age organization is particularly noticeable in the Eastern group, which includes the Turkana, Dassanetch, Karamojong, Pokot, Nandi, Kipsigis, Barabaig, Maasai, Toposa, Lango, and Dorobo, while segmentary lineage predominates in the Western group, which includes the Lugbara, Nuer, Dinka, and Kenya Luo. So marked is the prevalence of age organization in the Eastern group that it might be decided that this form of organization is a cultural feature, diffused to this group from the Cushitic speakers, such as Galla, among whom age organization is often complexly developed. While certain elements of age organization do seem to be cultural in that they involve the use of concepts of cycling and other special cognitive features, age organization taken in the fullest sense is more than the special way it is conceived by those who use it. It is a principle of social organization fundamentally different from lineage in the sense that it divides generations where segmentary lineage divides lines. Not all Eastern Nilotes are age-organized, the most significant exception being the Jie who use the principle of segmentary lineage despite the fact that they are very closely related to the Turkana, who are age-organized. Further, the Kakwa, Bari, and Lotuko of the Eastern group mix the principles, as do the Arush. On the other hand, there are Bantu who have taken over age organization as a dominant feature, including the Kikuyu and Tiriki, as apparently did the Gogo in earlier days.

In fact the two principles are not exactly incompatible except in the sense that they never seem to achieve equal levels of dominance, a point which shortly will be discussed further. Lineage appears in some degree of development among most age-organized people, and lineage-organized people usually have some kind of age organization. A good illustration of this latter point can be taken from the Turu. Although they are an excellent example of segmentary lineage in a full-blown form, they have an age organization which creates a new age class each year in conjunction with circumcision rites. This might be called an absolute ranking system because each year creates a different class, whereas in the age-organized societies different years are usually aggregated into a class spanning some time, such as eight years among the Borana Galla. The Turu system's practical value is that it determines the order of seniority among men for occasions where seniority matters, as in judicial proceedings. And the system is continually reinforced in small ways, such as seating order at social events. A junior person will always give up his seat to a senior if his seat is superior.

EXAMPLES OF AGE ORGANIZATION

The most complex of the age organizations is the *gada* of the various Galla. Paradoxically, Legesse, who has written the most comprehensive account of the gada, which he observed among the Borana Galla of southern Ethiopia, says that it is not really an age organization at all, at least not in the usual sense of a society divided into horizontal categories which separate men (and sometimes women) at various levels of age. His point is that the meaning of the system is to distribute privileges equitably across generational lines through separation of father and son whatever their absolute ages, rather than simply separating older and younger generations (Legesse 1973, 113). In the gada this is undoubtedly the case but in the other, simpler, East African systems, the separation of father and son is ordinarily coincident with separation of older and younger generations.

Gada is far too complicated to describe in a short space. For that we will look more completely at one of the simpler East African systems, contenting ourselves with a hint at the nature of gada. The system is so multifarious that Legesse has written a whole volume, 340 pages, on nothing but how the Borana Galla version works, including a section on a computer simulation of it which supports, he thinks, his claim that the automatic operation of the system has a built-in positive feedback element inexorably leading to a decline in the number of legitimate children (men in some grades are not allowed to marry and have legitimate children) with the threat of demise of the whole society due to declining legitimate population.

Gada is a crosscutting system of peer groups in which an individual belongs to one peer group calculated in *chronological age* and another in *generational age* (i.e., a man is equal to his FBS although that man might be much older or younger than Ego, depending on such things as when he was born and the relative ages of F and FB). Both of these systems form their peer groups every eight years. A young man enters the age grade (chronological) at a specific age but the generational group exactly 40 years behind his father so that F and S are always five generational grades apart (5 x 8 = 40). Consequently, all genealogical grades contain members of widely varying ages, while the age grades contain members of approximately the same age.

As Legesse indicates (1973, 114), various rights and duties, including authority to govern, are assigned to various gada groups but

The essential fact about this design of the life cycle is that the individual has the full support of his age mates as he confronts each critical transition in his social development. The words of Philip Gulliver—in his discussion of the role of age differentiation in human society—adequately describe the spirit of peer group structures in Borana (Gulliver 1968). "Wherever a man goes in the course of his nomadic pastoral movement or in traveling, he finds men who are his age-mates, comrades, and supporters. He finds also his seniors and juniors to whom he can fairly easily adjust his attitudes and behavior. He can never become socially isolated."

But we should also note that, according to Legesse, Borana children are not obsequious toward grownups, adolescents speak up in the most serious adult conferences and are listened to, and children take part in sacred rituals side by side with men of great age. Whatever organizational benefits age organization confers on society, it also provides a means for maintaining order by some method other than the subservience of some people to others. The Borana Galla thus show in this trait, which has been remarked repeatedly when discussing societies with age organization, and which is implicit in the meaning of the term "pastoral democracy" applied by I. M. Lewis to the lineage-organized Somali (I. M. Lewis 1961) or "Gada Republic" applied to the Galla by Murdock (1959), that individualism, even arrogance, marks the behavior of many livestock husbandmen.

The age organization of the Eastern Nilotes is simpler than that of the Galla. Among the former, the most complex systems are those of the Nandi and Maasai. The Nandi system (Huntingford 1953a), which is similar to that of most Eastern Nilotes (Sutton 1973), consists of seven age sets with fixed names that continually cycle through time: Kipkoimet, Kaplelach, Kimnyike, Nyongi, Maina, Juma, and Sawe. Each set recruits new members through circumcision rites over a 15-year period after which it is closed and a new set begins recruiting within one of the revived cycled categories (Fig. 18). Ordinarily a son occupies the second set below his father so that as in the case of the gada the system has generational as well as chronological dimensions, but unlike the gada there is a much closer correlation of the two so that the senior set at any time will be filled with elderly men only. Nandi age sets were given a military dimension, described earlier, and generally speaking the age set systems have been interpreted as military by Europeans. But, as Legesse and Gulliver both say, this is an incorrect interpretation. The age set

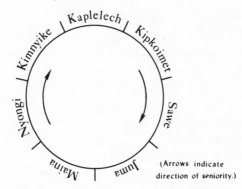

Nandi Cyclical Age Set System

FIG. 18

system ascribed rights and duties. In places where warfare was important these included military activities but where it was not important the age sets were more pacific if no less significant.

By the way these age organizations are usually described, the impression is given that the recruitment and assignment of duties as well as the gradual movement of the age sets through time was automatic. But in fact the division of society in terms of generation seems, like Omaha terminology, to reflect a degree of antagonism between generations, what Spencer in detailing this for the Samburu (1965, 44ff) calls "ambivalence."

It seems clear that age organization was not used mindlessly but in situations where it made sense. The sense of it was to provide some method for sharing responsibility among individualistic, antiauthoritarian people and between antagonistic generations, as a substitute for a hierarchical system in which power was a property of certain people who obtained it through the social marketplace. But age organization was also used as an alternative to segmentary lineage organization, which was also an alternative to hierarchically derived authority. Why one form should have been selected over another is an important question. As Gulliver implies, the need for

individual mobility within the ethnic area was an important consideration. Sedentary pastoral people seem to have less need or desire for it although, paradoxically, they do seem to need unilineal
descent.

But some wealthy pastoral people, like Kipsigis, did not have to
resort to transhumance to support their cattle. And some mobile
people, like the Somalis, continued to depend to an important degree on segmentary lineage. Thus nomadism is not the complete
explanation for age organization.

The possible answer to the puzzle is competition for land. It is
not necessarily only fertile land that is competed for. Semidesert
land may be in great demand if there is pressure for grazing, as
among Somalis, and where there is no other poor agricultural land
it may be highly desired, as among the Kimbu. Lineage segments,
whose members need to cooperate in order to hold and exploit land,
may have more importance than among people like Turkana who
for one reason or another can move freely about the society's general territory. But even allowing for this, there is still a question
about such people as the Kipsigis, age-organized but also heavily involved in both agriculture and pastoralism.

AUTHORITY

The negative attitude toward authority displayed by people in
East African stateless societies helps characterize them relative to
people in states. I have already recorded Legesse's comment that
Borana children are independent. He further remarks (1973, 112):

> What little restraining authority is exercised over the behavior of
> youths is not assumed by the father. It is mainly the gada peer
> group and the age-sets that regulate the behavior of their individual
> members.

Since gada groups contain members with widely varying ages, Legesse is really saying that authority is exercised over men of all ages
by the members of their peer groups. And since authority is checked

as well as bestowed by the system, gada can be understood as a method not only of assigning authority but also of severely circumscribing its use. The democratic, antiauthoritarian character of all Galla, except those of the Galla Gibe states, is demonstrated by H. Lewis in his account of their history (1965, 28).

Just as there has been a tendency among ethnographers to think of people with age organizations as having the most cattle, there has been a tendency to think of individualism and warlike propensities as characterizing the wealthy and as being tied to age organizations, particularly those of the Eastern Nilotics and Cushites. The Maasai, most specifically, have this reputation. Huntingford (1960, 55) has called these pastoral people the most warlike in East Africa. Speaking of the Nandi and other pastoral people, Huntingford calls them "conservative" (1950, 83), a term which seems generally to occur to people writing about East Africans of this type, who treat it as synonymous with individualistic, taken to mean unsubservient. The Maasai have repeatedly been described as "aristocratic" and "free" (Huxley 1949, 89).

But truculence, combativeness, and other manifestations of independence are not confined to age-organized societies. Evans-Pritchard described the Nuer as living in a state of "ordered anarchy" (1940, 6). Butt, speaking of the Nilotes as a whole, says (1952, 41):

All who have come into contact with the Nilotes have remarked on the proud, individualistic and truculent behaviour which they display towards each other and particularly toward foreigners. They consider their country the best in the world and everyone inferior to themselves. For this reason they despise clothing, scorn European and Arab cultures, and are contemptuous and reserved with foreigners, so that it is difficult to get to know them. Their attitude towards any authority that would coerce them is one of touchiness, pride, and reckless disobedience. Each determines to go his own way as much as possible, has a hatred of submission, and is ready to defend himself and his property from the inroads of others. They are thus self-reliant, brave fighters, turbulent and aggressive, and are extremely conservative in their aversion from innovation and interference.

That this independence is not directed simply toward outsiders is well illustrated in Gulliver's account of judicial processes among the agricultural Maasai or Arush of Mount Meru (1963, 299):

> The solution of a dispute between Arush does not come from authoritative decision, but through agreement resulting from discussion and negotiation between the parties which are in conflict.

Despite being a nonhierarchical system in which there is no designated authority, there is still law, and disputants recognize right and wrong. But men who are equal negotiate rather than submit.

I. M. Lewis' account of the Somalis tells much the same story (1961, 228):

> Where . . . parties of different dia-paying groups have recourse to a panel of arbitrators the court has no direct sanctions with which it can enforce its rulings. This will become clear from the description of *guddi* procedure which follows. Indeed whether or not litigants or rival dia-paying groups accept the decision of the arbitrators whom they summon to judge between them, depends very much on the structural context. If their kinsmen wish to reach a peaceful settlement, either through fear of war or pressure from the Administration [colonial], and if they consider that the judges' decision is a reasonable one, they will see that it is executed.

My experience with two nonhierarchical societies, the Pokot with a Nandilike age organization, and the Turu with a segmentary lineage system, supports these authors' claims about how order is maintained in a nonhierarchical system. Among the Pokot, a complainant could cause a court to convene and summon defendants and witnesses to listen to his charge. But the parties might or might not appear at the appointed time. And the decisions of the court were carried out only by marshalling public opinion while the defendant, if he lost, might simply move away, leaving all his troubles behind.

In the case of the Turu, a *mwandu* or court could be convened and render a decision. The loser might refuse to honor the court's

Pokot council

decision and sometimes, if the stakes were high enough, the settlement might be accomplished by force of arms. Certainly no Pokot
or Turu would ever accept without question the assertion by another
that he was guilty of anything and should pay. Backing up the system of law were notions about right and wrong enforced by super-
natural powers, in the case of the Pokot the idea that a person who
had violated the law had thrown out of balance the cosmic gyro-
scope, making himself unclean and automatically causing a punishment to feed back on the miscreant resulting in suffering or death.
Upon his deathbed a man with a guilty conscience is very much
aware of the misdeeds for which he never received formal retribu-
tion but for which, he speculates, he is being punished.

One feature of the age-organized societies that implies the existence of authority is what Huntingford (1953b, 15) calls "chief ritual
experts" or "chief diviners" who have also been described as war
chiefs. These personages, known as *laibon* to Maasai and Kipsigis,

orkoiyot to Nandi, and *werkoiyon* to Pokot are, however, not authorities. They have great influence because of their messianic power to foresee the future and decide the propitious times for cattle raids, rain making, and circumcision. But they cannot order people to do anything.

EGALITARIANISM AND EXCHANGE

How does the presence of large domestic animals in significant numbers cause this egalitarian, nonsubservient, nonhierarchical state of affairs? The answer to the question rests ultimately on a correct grasp of the nature and quality of exchange relations in society. Both hierarchical and egalitarian systems are fundamentally exchange systems. That is to say, any society is an exchange system (if we do not define exchange as narrowly as Boulding [1973] for whom the term refers only to material or "economic" exchanges). As we saw in the last chapter on hierarchical systems, people exchange women, land, food, and other valued goods including, most significantly, service or obligations which represent conforming to the will of others in some degree. In most of these societies there are also small and large livestock, but in the nature of things, the amount of value that can be stored in a goat or sheep is so small, along with the limited size of goat and sheep populations in most nonpastoral systems, that these animals cannot carry the weight of an exchange system that will produce nonhierarchical forms. (The Sonjo and perhaps the Kikuyu, who concentrate on goat production, are exceptions.) And the proportion of large livestock to people is insufficient to create a flow of livestock exchanges of sufficient magnitude to overcome the need to exchange obligations.

In the egalitarian systems all things are exchanged that are transferred in the hierarchical except that cattle or camels are added in larger amounts and service, at least among men, subtracted. Service can appear in these societies but it is so muted and tenuous that it never reaches institutionalized form. Even slavery seems to be absent, as I have said, because the effect of egalitarian exchange conditions and attitudes leads to a decline in the importance of labor. In most of these systems, as we saw earlier, the opportunity costs associated with maintaining agricultural output as herds increase seem too great so that emphasis on agriculture declines.

The substitution of cattle for service is explicit in many of these societies. When a Turu man contracts for marriage, one element of the contract is a period of brideservice extending over a year during which time the groom is supposed to visit his father-in-law's house to help in various tasks contributing to the wealth of the house of his wife's mother, tasks such as harvesting bulrush millet. If he wishes to avoid this (and all men do if they can), and if he can afford it, he substitutes for this service an additional brideprice cow. Through Central and East Africa the amount of brideservice in marriage seems to vary with the amount of livestock paid, from extremes such as among the cattleless Yao and Cewa, where the husband is perpetually engaged in some form of brideservice, through situations like that of the Bemba of Zambia where five years of service must be paid before the husband can take his bride to live at his home, to conditions like that of the Turu, and to the other extreme in the richer pastoral societies where no service whatever is rendered.

The important economic fact about the societies in which brideservice is lacking is that because of the large quantities of mobile, reproducing wealth equality is accomplished by setting up wide-ranging, crosscutting, balancing bonds between people which keep anyone from obtaining a monopoly of wealth which can be turned to creating hierarchy.

This "balancing" or counterchecking of debt is achieved through what Gulliver (1955, 196) calls "stock association" of which the stock loaning practices I spoke of earlier in this book are illustrations. As was pointed out there, the economic and political meaning of these transfers, of which marriages are a part, seems always to be underestimated by students of East African pastoral people.

Gulliver's extensive examination of *ngitungakan* ("my people," or stock associates) among the Turkana is an exception (1955, 198):

In both Jie and Turkana societies each man is the centre of a field of direct, formalized, interpersonal relations some of which are established by birth—cognatic relations, some by conscious acts of marriage—affinal relations, and some by deliberate pledge—relations between bond-friends. Whilst the emotional and practical content and the moral values inherent in these types of relations differ considerably in some respects, yet they exhibit two vital factors in common which give them essential similarity and mark them off from the fortuitous relations with acquaintances and casual companions, and from those social relations sustained by compulsory ritual co-operation.

These two vital factors are (1) that people related by kinship and bond-friendship are a man's particular friends, the circle in which he finds affection, sympathy, assistance, and confidence; and (2) with each of these people a man maintains well-recognized, reciprocal rights to claim gifts of domestic animals in certain precise circumstances.

Earlier I spoke of the fact that Turkana kinship is unusual because of the strong ties which develop between affines. This, Gulliver explains, is due to the importance of the stock associate system, which overrides kinship. (This system also characterizes the neighboring Dassanetch—Almagor 1978, 9). The strong relations between affines should therefore not be viewed as a peculiar type of kinship but as a bond friendship which converts a marriage relationship into a kind of business partnership. In Turkana society, kinship is just a starting point in the development of stock association. In the end every man develops a unique complex of such relations, one of which is illustrated in Figure 19. Another way of putting Gulliver's point, which brings home soundly my point about the special extensive nature of such economies, is that if Turkana had no cattle they could not have extensive bonds of this sort and might be forced into intensive kinship relations whether they liked it or not.

The Somali system of *heer*, or what I. M. Lewis calls contract (1968, 161), is somewhat different from that of the Turkana in the sense that these contractual relations are much more closely tied to the segmentary lineage structure. As we have already seen

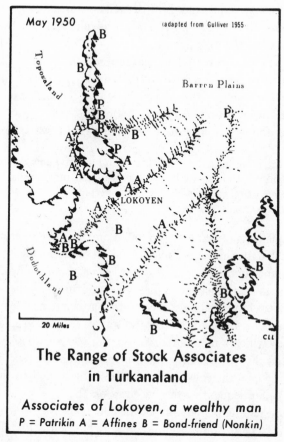

The Range of Stock Associates in Turkanaland

Associates of Lokoyen, a wealthy man
P = Patrikin A = Affines B = Bond-friend (Nonkin)

FIG. 19

this is partly explained by the competition for water and grazing, which gives lineages an importance lacking among Turkana. Lewis (1968, 168) stresses that these lineages and clans are held together by contracts (heer), agreements running from generation to generation, which provide a temporal and special counterpart to kinship obligations. The basic Somali lineage is a *dia*-paying (bloodwealth paying) group, whose members give each other support for collecting and dispersing dia as a result of homicides related to struggles for water and land. But heer relationships may go beyond the lineage and therefore involve the individual in a network of associates wider than his lineage.

The difference between Turkana and Somali is not as great as might seem because in both cases the authors are saying that the contractual relations between men, based on livestock exchanges, dominate kinship to one degree or another.

Gulliver found a similar situation among the Arush (1963, 79):

> When the father dies the bonds [between brothers] now disappear as compulsory factors but they are transmuted into mutually advantageous, cooperative relations. They become relations between autonomous equals. . . .

The equalizing of status is also found among the Pokot where it is manifested in the term *apoi* applied by all adult men to each other. After a youth passes through the *sapana* ceremony which elevates him to adulthood he applies the term to his father, as his father does to him. Pokot also have a stock association system called *tilia* (Schneider 1953, 264ff). On the surface it looks like a simple method by which a man obtains a steer for some purpose, such as a sacrificial rite, from another man by giving him a cow. The two then jointly own the cow (because it is worth more than the ox it replaced). Subsequently, the receiver of the cow is obligated throughout its life to give some of the cow's offspring to its former owner. In fact the ramifications of this exchange are, like those of the Turkana and Somali, far more significant than this. Tilia may be instituted for the purpose of cementing a relationship with another man who is trusted as a competent manager, who thereby becomes a kind of partner in economic affairs, one on whom the bestower can depend for help with substance, advice, and loans. The exchange is formalized with gifts, and gift giving between the partners continues throughout the relationship. Technically it is terminated with the death of the cow, but if the relationship has been good for both parties it may be reconstituted and may even be carried on by their sons. The value of the relationship to the parties can be estimated by the fact that it is created only with people who are not already clansmen or best friends (just as marriage is only contracted with strangers). Its effect is to construct a network of credit relations transcending kinship and extending out spatially to remote areas. But the extent to which tilia can be instituted depends on the amount of wealth a man controls. It favors the rich and, consonant with that, it is highly utilitarian despite the fact that it is clothed in professions of friendship. While parties to tilia have legal, moral, and personal claims on each other, the institution is easily perverted, most commonly by the cow holder claiming the animal has died while fraudulently presenting a substitute hide to prove it, thus ending the relationship. Pokot legal proceedings concern themselves extensively with disputes between tilia partners. But it can be strained, if not perverted, in a more subtle way, as Haaland (1977) found among the Toposa, a people living north of the Jie in the Sudan who are members of the Eastern Nilotic group. He concluded that the system of "delayed cattle exchanges," as he calls the stock associate system, benefits most the individual who delays as long as he can paying his debts and cashes in other peoples' debts to him as soon as possible (1977, 183). If, as Haaland remarks, following Barth (1973), pastoralists differ fundamentally from agriculturalists in having at all times to be engaged in management because the herds are always growing and declining so that decisions must constantly be made about saving and investment, to such managerial preoccupations must be added continual decision-making about the payment and collection of debts.

Pokot consider marriage to be a kind of tilia and express this by reference to the bride as a heifer, who therefore is being exchanged for the brideprice cattle. And after marriage is established, the affines are expected to exchange gifts with their sons-in-law, giving up some of the calves born to the brideprice cows. The analogy with tilia is not exact, of course, since, in effect, cows are being exchanged for cows. But this simply proves that tilia is more than just a trade of a cow for an ox.

Moving more than 400 miles south, all the way down East Africa to the Turu, we find a stock association system called uriha, also described in certain respects in the chapter on production. It is remarkably like that of the Pokot although it has certain differences special to the Turu situation. The similarity, no doubt, is due to the fact that throughout East Africa, whenever people get sufficient large livestock, it seems always to occur to them that a good stratagem is to create networks transcending kinship by means of the creation of stock association.

On the surface, uriha looks somewhat different from tilia. The exchange is often described as one in which a man who has too many cattle gives some to another man to hold for him, the receiver's compensation being the milk and manure he gets from the animals. In fact it is a stock association instituted at the suggestion of either the giver or receiver with the expectation of a long relationship, one which may even pass from generation to generation. Legally speaking, the giver of the cattle retains absolute right to their disposal and can charge a holder who uses any without permission. But in fact the holder, if he and the giver are on good terms, may do almost anything he pleases with the animals, although he must compensate for them in some way if he disposes of them.

In the previous discussion of uriha I described some of the reasons for the uriha partners to enter into the pact. Essentially these come down to the desire to establish wide-ranging ties of mutual help with people other than those with whom one already has them. Apparently in the Pokot case one has them by birth with patrilineal relatives and so these are excluded. Among the Turkana the same may be true. But, interestingly, the Turu are more like the Somalis in that they vitalize lineage membership through uriha, just as they use it to cement ties with affines. Figure 20 shows the extent of intravillage and intralineage association in one Turu village along with the lines of association to outside areas. These outside ties, like those of the Turkana and Gogo, are frequently with affines, which is consistent with their view of marriage as a kind of uriha, an interesting parallel with the Pokot and probably a widespread phenomenon among pastoral people, to judge by the extensiveness of

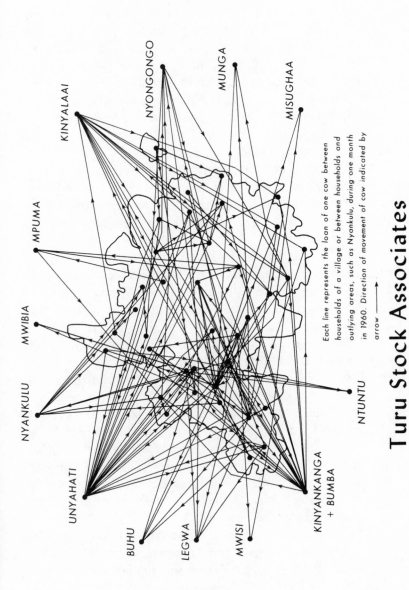

Each line represents the loan of one cow between households of a village or between households and outlying areas, such as Nyankulu, during one month in 1960. Direction of movement of cow indicated by arrow →

Turu Stock Associates

KINYALAAI

NYONGONGO

MUNGA

MISUGHAA

MPUMA

MWIBIA

NYANKULU

UNYAHATI

BUHU

LEGWA

MWISI

KINYANKANGA + BUMBA

NTUNTU

FIG. 20

marriage ties as described in the last chapter. As in uriha proper, marriage is a loan, but in this case a mutual loan, of productive property in which the owner of the woman receives bridewealth to use, not to own, his profit being the same as that obtained by the holder of the uriha cattle, while the holder of the woman receives her productive labor. There are differences, the most important being that marriage is a reciprocal loan. Also, in uriha proper, if the cow being held by a receiver dies the relationship terminates unless the parties wish to revive it with another cow. In marriage, if the bridewealth cows die they must be replaced or the marriage is ended. And when the bride dies the bond is ended and brideprice cows must be returned but minus the number necessary to compensate for depreciation of the dead wife's capacities during the term of her marriage.

Among Turu stock association is a prime means of extending ties of association into areas other than those provided by the basic lineage structure of society. In different cases this means creating ties with strangers, affines, and even with distant members of one's own lineage.

The Gogo also have a stock association system called *kukuza* which resembles that of the Turu in many ways. I mention it only to call attention to an important point about it which Rigby (1969, 50) makes. He says he prefers to call the institution "trusteeship" because it implies no social or political inequality between the partners. In order to establish firmly my point about the lack of exchange of service in pastoral societies it is essential to recognize that the balance of agreements between stock associates is not one in which subservience is an ingredient. But, more importantly, it is not part of the contract precisely because in the nature of the exchange subservience ordinarily cannot be instituted.

While extensive descriptions of the operation of stock association are rare, it seems a good guess that the patterns detected in Turkana, Jie, Somali, Pokot, Gogo, and Turu societies are not peculiar to them. No doubt the Nandi *kaptich*, Kipsigis *kimanagen*, or Nuer *math* operate in similar ways and no doubt such systems exist widely even where they have not been reported.

KINSHIP AND STOCK ASSOCIATION

In the accounts of stock association the matter of the relation between kinship ties and stock association has appeared several times. Gulliver informed us that kinship is only a starting point for association, being replaced in time by stock association. I. M. Lewis tells us that Somali heer contracts vitalize kinship relations. Arush were seen to abandon kinship as a basis for association after the death of the father, and Turu reinforce relations with members of the local lineage through stock association. Traditionally relations among unilineal kin have been presented as ones that have rights and obligations inherent in them to which stock association would be redundant. Obviously, then, the fact of widespread stock association in such groups raises questions about the adequacy of the traditional views of kinship. The resolution of these questions is a task for the future. But I would like to suggest how this may be done.

Our examination of stock association makes it plain that people who have large livestock to manipulate can do things about the way they relate to other people which people without livestock cannot do. Most specifically they can create mutually advantageous relationships in which these animals play a focal role, a role which importantly cancels the growth of hierarchy even in kinship relations. In other words, it is possible that in hierarchical, nonpastoral systems kinship contains an element of subservience that gives it a special character lacking in pastoral kinship. The introduction of livestock makes possible a nearly complete deemphasis on kinship in some cases, and a reformulation of kinship into a more contractual relationship in others. To add another point, perhaps Iroquois systems are essentially hierarchical systems whereas Omaha and Descriptive are essentially egalitarian.

This raises the question, of course, of why lineage and kinship do not disappear altogether where livestock allow a man to create his own personal network of relations. There are only suggestions of an answer to this in the works we have examined. The idea that land is a factor has been considered by many and is surely an element. If pastoral people continue to exploit the land horticulturally they are faced with certain production problems tied to labor-intensive operations which make lineages useful as devices for short term, intensive mobilization of labor. But the mobile, noncultivating Somali suggest to us that land is not the only consideration. It is true that Somali lineages seem to persist because of the need for cooperation in protecting grazing rights and wells, but this is land use in a different form, suggesting that the question of the persistence of lineages ought to be framed in more general terms. Wherever joint action within some territory by groups of people has value this will promote lineage, whether this joint action is for production of crops, protection of grazing land, or, as in Australia, hunting and gathering. Where capital-intensive operations predominate, stock association based on individual production units may be allowed to manifest itself at the expense of lineages if necessary, and leads to the creation of alternative forms of organization, such as those based on age, whose functions are essentially different from lineages.

An interesting aspect of this businesslike association is the apparent low level of witchcraft accusations among East African pastoralists (P. T. W. Baxter 1972). Actually this claim should probably be qualified to apply to "East African pastoralists who are detached from important kinship ties," the nonlineage-oriented. Witchcraft accusations, in other words, seem to coincide with relations of intense kinship. Thus even where such relations exist, charges of witchcraft remain in the local kin group and do not intrude into stock association.

To these considerations I would add one more suggested by Horowitz (1975, 394). There is an interesting tendency in Africa for the various ethnic groups to coincide with ecological niches; Turkana live in the arid zone west of Lake Turkana and differ from Jie, to whom they are extremely closely related, who inhabit a different zone. The Wahi Turu dwell in the inland drainage marshes of southern Singida, the Chagga in the fertile banana belt on Kilimanjaro, and the Kikuyu in the Aberdere forests. Horowitz feels that this is best explained as a kind of economic specialization coinciding with intense exchanges among the specialists. Thus, systems of stock association in East Africa are largely ethnically oriented and tied to opportunity costs, there being a lower cost for establishing ties with persons whose production problems are similar to one's own. A Turkana can bargain more easily with another Turkana because each can adjust his calculations more precisely in terms of costs and benefits than he could with one whose production problems he does not understand.

KAMBUYA'S CATTLE

In my discussions of pastoral cattle manipulations the one thing lacking up to this point is some idea of the magnitude involved in the production and exchange of the animals. Such information is very rare because East Africans do not keep records and are usually rather secretive about it. The one major exception is a study of Kambuya's cattle published by Goldschmidt (1969). Kambuya was a wealthy Sebei (a people living on Mount Elgon in west central Kenya) who died leaving a herd of about two hundred head of cattle. Goldschmidt was able, through extensive conversations with the deceased's eldest son, to obtain some idea of the extent of his cattle manipulations throughout his life. He was unable to obtain complete information, unfortunately, but the results he did obtain are revealing.

The cattle over which Kambuya exercised control during his lifetime, insofar as Goldschmidt was able to determine, totaled 704 head. These were animals obtained through birth (72.9%), brideprice (3.9%), gifts, largely from his father (1%), purchase (3.4%), outright exchange (8.7%), *namanya* exchange or stock association (8.3%) and miscellaneous other sources (1.5%). As indicated, the largest source of animals for Kambuya was calving from his heifers. The second, if we aggregate brideprice, stock association, and "outright exchange," is exchanges with other people, which total 20.9%. Obviously, exchanges are of very great importance in the composition of herds if Kambuya's history is any indication.

BIG MEN AND CHIEFS

Egalitarianism does not mean that there are no differences in wealth in stateless societies. Huge variations in the number of cattle or camels owned by different men may exist. In the subtribe of Wahi in Unyaturu the range seems to have extended from 0 to 1,500. The ranges are even more extreme in some of the richer societies.

And egalitarianism does not mean that there is no respect for rich men. They are listened to, given special treatment and attention, and are the subject of great interest to other members of society. But as in America, any attempt by the rich to translate wealth into power is resisted. One of the best descriptions of big men, in Gusiiland on the east short of Lake Victoria, is LeVine's (1962, 523–524):

The social status of a homestead head and his influence in community affairs were largely dependent on his wealth. A rich man (*omanda*) was respected and listened to, while a poor man (*omoraka*) was despised, at least covertly, and ignored. This pattern of invidious distinction is most explicit in Gusii terminology used for referring to these categories of men. The word *omonguru*, literally "man of power" and used in Gusii versions of the Bible to mean "the Lord," is invariably defined by informants as a big polygynist with many wives and cattle. For monogamists there are several terms of abuse. One of these is *omworo*, "weak man." Another is *nyakekemo*, "one basket," referring to the fact that he has only one wife to prepare a basket of food to offer visitors when they come. Every wife prepared a basket of dry porridge for the main meal, so that a polygynous homestead would have abundant food for guests, while the monogamist shared his single basket with them. A rich

Turu big man

man would also slaughter a bull to feed visitors from far away, while the average person would slaughter a goat or sheep—and a poor man, merely a chicken. These differences in capacity to entertain guests were among the most important economic differences within a community, for the lavish hospitality of the wealthy polygynist attracted many guests, particularly lineage elders (*abagaaka begesaku*) who would congregate at his homestead to eat and adjudicate disputes. The wealthy host often dominated such judicial proceedings and people would bring their cases to him because of his dominant position. Thus was wealth translated into power in the local community. The rich man exercised power in other ways as well. The leader of the young men in a cattle-village was often a son of the richest homestead head represented in the cattle-village, since his cattle formed the largest part of the joint herd. A wealthy elder with many sons was often feared and respected because of the retaliatory power of his sons as a military force. There are indications that the wealthy used their power to dominate and exploit others in a local area. This is expressed in the Gusii proverbs: "The property of the poor man is used by the rich man"; and, "The property of the *omworo* is grabbed by the *omonguru*." Furthermore, there was rivalry between wealthy homesteads in a given area ("Rich men fear each other") resulting in the emigration of one or more of them, leaving one homestead head in undisputed dominance over the area. In the large tribe of Getutu, which alone among Gusii tribes developed a hereditary chieftainship, the military–judicial power of the chief was solidly rooted in great wealth. Bogonko, most famous of the chiefs, who lived in the 19th century, is said to have had fourteen wives and many sons. A song still sung boasts of Bogonko's herds of cattle so great that many men were needed to herd them without losing any. His descendants claim that Bogonko would slaughter four bulls just to feed his sons to make them strong in warfare. The association of wealth, as indicated by polygyny and cattle, with political power was a pronounced characteristic of the traditional Gusii social system.

Traditional Unyaturu seems to have been like Gusiiland in this respect. Big men were called *axai*, strong men, who used their wealth to develop followings which transcended lineages and who tried to establish hegemonies. But as in Gusiiland most seemed to have failed.

I. M. Lewis echoes this theme for the Somali (1961, 197):

> Despite the fundamentally egalitarian character of Somali society, there are often considerable variations in wealth, as much in the interior in stock-wealth as in riches acquired through successful trade in towns. Somali are well aware of the power which wealth brings, and at the same time, of the responsibilities which it entails in the support of poorer kinsmen. A rich elder does not lack a friendly hearing for his opinion from his less well-off kinsmen, and can usually rely on their support for his views in lineage affairs.

Everywhere among stateless people, it seems some word exists for the big, important man. Among the Bari he is literally a "big man" (*ngutu dumu*) as he is also in Arush society (*ilkituak*). Nuer call him *gat twot*, "bull of the camp." Otherwise there is a local term for a big man which is ordinarily bestowed on one with wealth: *rwot* in Lango and *ruoth* among Kenya Luo. The Nandi call him *poiyot ap kokwet*, the leading spokesman in the kokwet councils. And among certain of the Nilotic people, such as Lugbara or Lokuya, his position was associated with rain making, although the Lugbara differentiated the rain makers (*opi-ezo*) from wealthy men (*'ba rukuza*).

   I. M. Lewis, reflecting on man as a political animal, has reached many conclusions parallel to mine in addition to which he has stated what amounts to a theory of big men which I will attempt to summarize here (1976). Rather than being a stage in the evolution of government, the state, or rather the monarchy, is but a point on one end of a spectrum whose other end is stateless societies containing only big men. Most states are internally torn by pressures which on the one hand push them toward greater centralization while on the other hand they are pulled toward decentralization by segments of the state which seek autonomy from the center. Power is a relationship of domination and the powerful seek always to dominate further while the dominated seek to get out from under domination (I. M. Lewis 1976, 284, 314). Tribute, he goes on, "is a symbolic statement in tangible terms of loyalty and submission" (1976, 220). The exchanges between the wealthy and their followers are such that for some gifts the rich man receives submission and tribute whereas in other instances he receives little more than support. The latter are big men, the former chiefs and kings.

CONTRADICTIONS

   To avoid appearing to be too pat in my theory of egalitarianism I want to end this chapter by referring to some important contradictory cases. The Sonjo are one. Gray argues a thesis that despite the fact that the Sonjo have a complex irrigation system they did not develop a state (Gray 1963) as they should have if Wittfogel's

(1957) theory of irrigation as the foundation of the state is true. Yet when one examines wealth and position in Sonjo society it seems to contain some of the elements of statehood in a very rudimentary form. The *wenamiji* are an oligarchy controlling rights to irrigation. This is unusual in the sense that rather than a chief appearing as a consequence of land control, a group of men emerge. There are wealthy men, *wakiama*, whose superior position is based on goats which they exchange for irrigation rights. But they can get such control only by paying tribute to the wenamiji. Of course if the Sonjo are then in fact an elementary form of state, the fact that they have no cattle, but only goats—albeit in large numbers, would accord with my thesis, at least as it applies to state formation. But there are still problems with respect to their marriage system, which seems fully extensive.

On the other hand, the Kikuyu pose an opposite problem. They were clearly a stateless society organized in terms of age. But there is no sure indication that they had many cattle, although they appear to have owned plenty of goats. A possible solution to the Kikuyu enigma lies in a better understanding of their relationship with the Maasai. There are increasing signs (Muriuki 1974, 83ff) that Maasai and Kikuyu societies were heavily intertwined (for example, President Kenyatta's mother was Maasai) and it would not be surprising if that connection had as an element large Kikuyu livestock holdings in trust with Maasai.

Among other contradictions that need to be resolved are the fact that the Luguru, agricultural matrilineal people in eastern Tanzania, who "should" have had chiefs, apparently did not. However, it would be surprising if the thesis I have developed in this book held true without exception. We could expect that shifts in important parameters that determine the structures of most East African societies would lead to variations in control of resources so that, as among the southern Bantu, states might appear with high ratios of cattle to people, and in some cattleless areas egalitarianism, as among the Tiv of Nigeria, would appear based on some kind of capital other than livestock.

SUMMARY

In this chapter I have detailed the high correlation between egalitarianism and ownership of high ratios of cattle. People in stateless societies in East Africa display a characteristic independence and negative feeling for institutionalized authority. This disdain can be traced to the fact that cattle are a form of wealth which by their nature provide great opportunity to crosscut hierarchical tendencies and for the rich to fall and the poor to rise. Hence hierarchical relations, which depend on the extraction of service, symbolized by tribute, cannot arise.

More generally, summarizing the thesis of the book so far, in preparation for further examination in the next chapter of the economic theory of egalitarianism and the question of the causes of states and egalitarianism, two major forms of overall social organization have been identified in East Africa. I have termed one of these hierarchical or state (following Murdock), and the other egalitarian or stateless. The East African hierarchical systems are marked by the presence of differential status caused by the exchange of submission, obeisance, or tribute in one amount or another for gifts or payoffs from patrons. In such societies there are chiefs, persons whose role is distinguished by the fact that they receive submission and whose position is demarcated by myths, legends, and symbols of authority such as drums. That is to say, their higher position is institutionalized, an office rather than merely a rank. The degree of power (i.e., ability to command) that chiefs hold is widely variable from a low point of minimal control over a minimal number of people (a petty, local chief), to a high point, that of a king or emperor, whose control over other people extends to his ability to take their lives in some cases, and who may rule over very large numbers of people. All these persons, from petty chief to emperor, have in common the fact of authority, a value lacking to anyone in the stateless society except in a vestigial form and except in the relations of men to women and children.

While these hierarchical systems may be built on segmentary

lineage structures, in which the ascribed positions of authority are defined in terms of proximity to important ancestors, they need not be; the fundamental element of hierarchical formation is the exchange of goods for some degree of submission, which may occur between non-kin as well as kin.

The economics of these hierarchical systems may be described as intensive because exchanges tend to be within established circles, between people whose relationship tends to endure from generation to generation, as in marriage where cousins are joined (and thereby generate Iroquois terminological systems for classifying kin). Just as the debt to the king is cemented by subservience, which is a relationship that extends through time, marriage exchanges have an element of subordination to the kinsmen of the bride and debts continue from generation to generation thereby concretizing status differentiation.

The nonhierarchical or egalitarian systems, it must be emphasized, leveled only men. As in the hierarchical, women occupied permanently inferior positions in most cases. These egalitarian systems may be negatively characterized in terms of the lack of submission as an exchange item, and positively as having multiple opportunities for acquiring new wealth so that men of substance, big men as opposed to chiefs, were seldom able to translate wealth into power since those whom they sought to dominate had resources, derived from multiple opportunities and wide-ranging systems of stock association credit in an atmosphere of rapid capital formation, which allowed them to escape submission. It seems to be a workable rule that in both types of societies men sought to dominate others, egalitarianism being not just an ideology but a reflex of economic opportunity. All men seek to rule, but if they cannot rule they prefer to be equal. Those who have wealth are unable to institutionalize it and legitimize their attempts to control others, any attempts to do so resulting in scornful and sometimes violent reaction by others against whom the wealthy are unable to retaliate sufficiently to establish authority.

Egalitarianism may occur either in segmentary lineage systems or in age-organized systems (as well as some less common systems), the former seemingly dependent on the degree to which land continues as an important production asset while the latter is dependent on the degree to which livestock production is dominant and possible without close control of land. In both cases, however, the ideology of the structure, whether lineage or age, provides a framework within which duties necessary for the protection of social order may be ascribed without assigning power to anyone. Another way of putting this is to say that they provide for rules, norms, law, and adjudication, but not for power to enforce these rules, enforcement tending to be diffusely sanctioned, expressed as an exchange process rather than as punishment. The criminal is fined, not constrained or killed.

The economics of egalitarian systems is based on the production of large livestock, mostly cattle but sometimes camels, where the ratio of cattle to people is one cow or more to a person. This reflects the fact that egalitarianism is not merely the product of cattle raising but the volume of production as expressed in the ratio. The marriage and kinship systems mirror this, marriages in the most developed egalitarian systems being extensive, moving out of the local circle to new, noncousin relations, while the system of classification of kin becomes Omaha or Descriptive, reflecting in the first case the conflict between categories of people over control of wealth and in the latter the demise of kinship as a framework for the control of wealth as economic individualism and entrepreneurship assert themselves in extreme form. These are wheeling and dealing systems, composed of "the thickest-skinned capitalists on earth, people who regularly risk their lives in speculation" (I. M. Lewis 1975), spreading out both in terms of social relationships and in space as their members range about, sometimes becoming literally nomadic but otherwise simply peripatetic between sedentary homesteads and villages.

CHAPTER VIII

The Causes of Egalitarianism

IN THE COURSE of describing the two types of socioeconomic systems which exist in aboriginal East Africa I have had some things to say about the causes of egalitarianism. This chapter considers this question more closely while exploring the opinions of others who have also had something to say on the question.

The title of this chapter may seem rather unusual. While concern with the question of egalitarianism and hierarchy is pervasive in the social sciences, it is usually phrased in terms of the reason for the rise of states. Until very recently egalitarian systems have been considered to be somewhat primitive, an early, inferior condition of human development, as in Trigger's view of the rise of states and "civilization" in the Sudan (1968, 88ff). But more and more theorists are reexamining this assumption and are coming, like I. M. Lewis, to feel that egalitarian social organization is a legitimate alternative to the hierarchical.

STATES AND SURPLUS

Probably the most widely held view among anthropologists today concerning the rise of states, a view which has been with us for a long time—since V. G. Childe at least—is that they are built on surplus production. The classic view of the Neolithic held that in the pre-Neolithic stage, allowing for some possible exceptions such as the upper Paleolithic Magdalenian people, man lived close to starvation. Society lacked differentiation, except for sex roles, because all members of society were nearly continuously engaged in food production, allowing no time or food surplus to support craft and political specialization. With the invention of agriculture and the domestication of animals, surpluses became possible. These could be used to build two new social roles: producers of other goods— pots, tools, minerals, clothing—and bureaucratic personnel, who could coordinate large social entities. Both had positive benefits for people.

Probably the most profound modification of this point of view has been launched in recent times by Sahlins, particularly through his concept of the Domestic Mode of Production. This theory, based importantly on Richard Lee's study of the !Kung San (Bushmen), claims that during the undifferentiated "tribal" state of society domestic production units are independent of each other to an important extent, highly productive, and production decisions are ruled by Chayanov's Law, which predicts that the level of production is determined by the number of mouths there are to feed. Production per worker increases with the birth of children, who must be fed but who do not produce, and declines as they become producers. Sahlins feels that chiefdoms are tribes in their most "developed" form while states, which he thinks of as more elaborate than chiefdoms, have even more complex and productive systems, because through coercion and other devices these authorities coax out of the domestic units "surplus" production that they would not otherwise bother to produce, which is used to maintain and expand the hierarchy. Sahlins' position is strangely ambivalent toward the chiefdom, in a Marxist way. While accusing chiefs of exploitation he also seems to feel that they are necessary for progress because they push the domestic units off dead center and begin the positive process of building wealth, which culminates in more democratic forms of social organization that could not otherwise evolve.

Adams (1975) takes a similar position, best illustrated by the following quotation (1976, 700–701):

. . . I explicitly do regard religion to be an important predecessor to the appearance of chiefdoms; and chiefdoms I see to be the first major centralization above the family centralization that has been achieved by man as a primate. . . . The appearance of centralized chiefdoms required a basic centralization of power that was, on the technology available at the time, dependent on the higher allocation of power. . . . However, the reason that I regard this as being important is that it was the only way that *seemed to be available* to concentrate *allocated* power, that power granted by one individual to another in the absence of physical threat.

In other words, if I may interpret Adams, technological advancement or improvement in the means of production is a good thing; in order to obtain it chieftainship was necessary; therefore centralized, hierarchical systems are superior to egalitarian ones. In the course of constructing this syllogism Adams seems to have bypassed egalitarian organizations and, perhaps inadvertently, relegated their modes of production and capital-intensive exchange operations to the scrap heap.

Recently Jonathan Friedman (1975), reconsidering Leach's writings on the Kachin of highland Burma, where Leach found within the same ethnic group both egalitarian (*gumlao*) and hierarchical (*gumsa*) structures, has come up with a rather complex explanation that parallels the ideas of Sahlins and Adams in certain ways, in which the egalitarian again is seen as a rather inferior system. Friedman is concerned specifically with the question of why the egalitarian (E) and hierarchical (H) structures oscillate, beginning as E and growing into more and more elaborate H systems until they reach a point where they collapse back into E. To simplify Friedman's argument, he sees chiefdomship arising out of exploitation of the swidden possibilities of the land through the application of as much labor as possible, producing a surplus which its holder turns into power over others by giving feasts and otherwise obligating people. In the process, he incurs debts which he can pay only by increasing production and further exploiting others. This spiraling of production and debt finally leads to a point where the chief is overextended and cannot pay his debts, leading to the demise of the chieftainship. An incidental effect of this oscillation is that in the drive to continually increase production of food the ecological system is irreversibly damaged to a small extent each time the cycle recurs, but as the oscillation goes on generation after generation a new ecological zone—grassland—is created, which in turn affects the political outcome of the struggle for hierarchy leading to long-lasting states but then, also epicyclically, to nearly permanent degraded egalitarian, headhunting societies. Thus in Friedman's view E systems among the Kachin are crashed hierarchies and they are also systems of low production, ultimately benighted.

Finally, in a classic study of egalitarian and hierarchical systems in Oceania, Sahlins (1962) presents the egalitarian systems of Melanesia, in contrast to the chiefdomships of Polynesia, as "underdeveloped," too bankrupt to grow, and their people as self-interested and cunning, seekers, predominantly, of personal power.

The idea that states are built on surplus is one that seems to appeal to Marxists in general, no doubt because it takes off on Marx's idea that inherent in the capitalist system is a structure of exploitation in which capitalist managers in effect force workers to labor because the workers own no means of production and must work to live while at the same time the managers do not pay them the full return of their labor but only enough to reproduce themselves, the surplus over that (the profit) being extorted for the benefit of the capitalists. But such pure Marxist notions, when applied to social conditions like those described by Sahlins, Adams, and Friedman, run into some serious problems. Besides the problem with the notion of surplus itself, which economists question because it in effect argues that the cost of capital, land, and management is zero and therefore does not have to be paid for, at least one Marxist (O'Laughlin 1975) has pointed out that such ideas are not applicable to tribal people because the workers do own their means of production. And Sahlins' belief that domestic units in tribal societies are producing only to feed themselves and that their operations are not subject to economic analysis, which assumes that producers are trying to maximize utility, is increasingly under attack (e.g.,

Massing 1977). In other words, there is evidence, some of it in this book's earlier chapters, that people in an E condition may be engaged in maximizing activities even though they are producing only for home consumption. Cancian (1976), in a recent review of theories of social stratification in anthropology and sociology, has asserted persuasively that the idea that "the greater the surplus, the greater the stratification" has little support.

EGALITARIANISM AND MODERN SOCIETY

There have been a number of theorists in the history of social science who have considered an alternative view to that of the Marxists and an increasing number of modern scholars who have moved steadily in that direction, seeing the egalitarian condition not as primitive but as a legitimate alternative to the states. A notable recent example, for instance, is Clastres (1977, 20) who has written an impassioned defense of the Indian societies of America:

> ... most Indian societies of America are distinguished by their sense of democracy and taste for equality. The first explorers of Brazil and the ethnographers who came after often emphasized the fact that the most notable characteristic of the Indian chief consists of his almost complete lack of authority. . . .

An early theorist who concerned himself with this question was Sir Henry Maine. In practical fact he should be classed with the evolutionists I just discussed because of his theory that society has evolved from an inferior to a superior state. But Maine, contrary to these, saw the path of evolution as proceeding not from E to H but the reverse. In the archiac society man's position is fixed by rights and duties much as is true in the H systems, but as evolution progresses relations between people become more flexible and contract emerges as the basis for interaction. If we set aside Maine's evolutionism, we can see that his status and contract categories are equivalent to H and E in important ways, and he may be credited with having uniquely ascertained that there are two basically different types of social systems, one in which position is relatively fixed and the other in which social mobility is more possible.

I. M. Lewis, whose views of East African pastoralism parallel mine in many ways, would reject Maine (Lewis 1976) on the grounds that, among other things, Maine did not see that the rise of modern, supposedly contractual, society has been accompanied by increasing centralization and more and more law, both conditions which are contrary to E organization. But Lewis does this only to underscore his claim that in egalitarian systems like that of his Somalis, settlement of disputes is pronouncedly in terms of reparation and restitution, not in terms of abstract notions of law and authoritarian decisions. Thus, while Maine perceived the difference between E and H structures, he mistakenly, or so Lewis thinks, saw Victorian England as E.

But Lewis's conclusion is not without challenge, notably in the recent work of Dumont on egalitarian and hierarchical systems. In *From Mandeville to Marx*, which he thinks of as a treatise on *Homo aequalis*, balancing his earlier work *Homo hierarchicus*, Dumont asserts the thesis that the rise of the "ideology" of classical and neo-classical economic theory has occurred in conjunction with the rise of capitalism, the two together representing the emergence of what he terms equalitarian individualism out of holistic, hierarchical feudal society. As Dumont sees it, precapitalist society was economically a system dependent on land and rent for the production of wealth. This immobile, characteristically scarce, good laid the basis for feudal hierarchicalism in which nature was seen as the creator of wealth, not man; land was the chief property, not labor; morality was stressed over individual self-interest; subordination to lordly authority was inevitable; and the state triumphed over "society." Thus, as in Sahlins' scheme, the state is opposed to man but unlike Sahlins, Dumont represents the equalitarian state as superior.

What Dumont perceives in western history as different socio-economic—ideological systems can easily be transported to East Africa, as the perceptive reader has no doubt already concluded. It is precisely the control of land that in most cases transforms the East African society into a chiefdom, although other kinds of property also became important in kingdoms, and it is the emergence of cattle as a volatile, mobile resource that generates the rise of individualism and of antiauthoritarian ideologies. But it will also be apparent to the reader that schemes like Maine's as well as those of a host of Western economic and social historians (Polanyi, Riesman, Eisenstadt, Toinnes, Mauss, and Weber), which see E or contractual social structure as emergent in history, seem to have missed the possibility—apparent in Clastres' defense of American Indians, demonstrated in the societies of western Melanesia, and clear cut in East Africa—that E is not necessarily an emergent quality of society but an alternative to H.

THE ECONOMIC BASIS
OF EGALITARIANISM

The economic basis of egalitarianism, and of hierarchy, is gradually becoming clear. Dumont's treatment of the subject speaks to this point with his association of H with immobile land as a means of production and mobile capital with E. Various students of pastoral societies, who increasingly tend to refer to them as capitalist (I. M. Lewis, P. Spencer, Goldschmidt 1972), whatever the degree of their sophistication in economics, have sensed certain basic economic elements peculiar to pastoral societies. Gray (1963, 153), speaking of power and wealth in the Sonjo villages, remarks that political power is derived predominantly from control of the irrigation system, which is susceptible to monopolistic control in a way that goat ownership is not. I. M. Lewis (1976) stresses the idea that fundamental to statehood, compared to the stateless egalitarian people, is exploitation of people, by which he means that the chief is able to extract greatly unequal amounts of goods from his subjects by virtue of his position. This, he seems to feel, is the central fact about the relationship, even though the subjects and their chief or king, as well as the anthropologists who study them for the most part, justify the state as a necessary institution for the well-being of society. As Lewis notes, the professed arduousness of the king's role as benefactor of the people, as the king sees it, looks more like exploitation when seen by the person at the bottom.

These views of Gray and Lewis are echoed in a more sophisticated form in Carol Smith's theory of the spatial distribution of elites (1976). To Smith, stratification is a defining condition of all agrarian societies, and the basis of stratification is control of some critical resource, usually land, but also such things as firepower or even salt. That is to say, "imbalanced" exchange is characteristic of such societies and the imbalance, she argues, can derive not only from control of the means of production but also from control of the exchange of goods, as in markets, leading to stratification. Smith's is a theory of hierarchy but a theory of egalitarianism is implicit in it. Where no one can obtain control of critical resources, such as land, firepower, salt, or the means of exchange, no basis for authority exists. In pastoral societies such as those in East Africa and many in other parts of the world, under certain circumstances, cattle generate this condition through their inherent reproducibility and mobility, making them difficult to control both because they can easily be moved around and because they continually change in numbers.

Kenneth Boulding, whose fertile mind always produces insights into anything he choose to focus on, has examined the problem we are discussing in his theory of the "economy of love and fear" (1973), a theory of "grants economics." To Boulding, grants are offers of "economic" goods to others for which there is no return. But he recognizes that there is in fact a return of "noneconomic" goods, which confer prestige on the giver and generate hierarchy. Compounding his theory is allowance for the fact that grants may be given in return for security or release from fear. According to his way of thinking, in fact, the core of Marxist philosophy has to do with the immorality of grants made by workers to capitalists in the form of surpluses of production for which they are not paid.

In Boulding's scheme (1973, 28–29), "exchange" refers to the reciprocal transfer of economic goods and exchange is therefore the opposite of a grant. Grants create community where exchanges do not and, he feels, this is the reason why capitalistic society is weak since its dependence on exchange rather than grants leads to a lack of community, components of which are loyalty, devotion, and affection.

At the heart of Boulding's concern is a question central to Marxist thought, the morality of the worker/capitalist relationship. He feels that exploitation exists only if the worker feels exploited and the real question, in cases where workers do not feel exploited, is whether it is private property or central planning which will be most productive. At this point in Boulding's analysis I perceive a certain failure. In the first place, there seems little question that in at least some instances of capitalism, the worker is in effect a client or subordinate by virtue of the fact that the capitalist owns the means of production and the worker than has no alternative but to work for him. It is under such conditions, one might speculate, that the worker might perceive himself as being exploited. But if the worker had real alternative options, such as becoming a capitalist himself, such feelings would not occur to him. In the former case the worker is equivalent to an East African client tribesman, in the latter to a pastoralist. But, we should also note, the locked-in worker would not necessarily feel exploited, any more than the East African client, although he would certainly be ready at any time to leave his subordinate position and eschew any ideology that supported his subservience if he could. Thus, what makes "social payment" inferior to material payment, as in the case of the pastoralist, is that social payment *must* contain a claim on behavior over time (service) whereas the material payment *can* be totally nonsocial and so give the payor freedom.

Thus, the question of exploitation turns out to be quite complex. If we are to accept the Marxist view that all clients are by definition exploited whether they think so or not we would have to believe that egalitarianism is the road that all men should and can follow. But, as we can see, egalitarianism is not a path which one may choose if it suits him, but one which occurs when the objective economic conditions make it possible. The most ironical thing of all is that Marxist programs for achieving the state of nonexploitation seem always to be framed in terms of increasing the power of the state, not reducing it.

AN ECONOMIC THEORY
OF PASTORALISM

The confusion in the debate over capitalism results, I think, from the unquestioned association of capitalism with the exploitation of labor. A better definition, which fits the East African facts, allowing for the special case of exploitation of women, is one that defines capitalism as a mode of production in which it is capital, not land or labor, that is central to the production of wealth, whose manipulation brings the best return, the application to which of labor might be irrelevant.

In East Africa the beginning of a theory of pastoral capitalism is now apparent. I alluded above to Barth's idea (1973, 12) that pastoralists (not just East African pastoralists) necessarily must be involved in investment decisions:

> ... I am working on the hypothesis that the pastoral regime of production has essential properties which contrast with the other productive regimes of a region, and which in various modulations determine the form and relations of nomads, dependent on this regime for their maintenance, to the other populations of the region.

In pastoral societies, he goes on, the nature of pastoral capital opens up options for management decisions that are lacking in agricultural regimes. Most notable of these options are that saving and investment are *necessary* (his italics) under all circumstances. Further, such investment is possible without benefit of economic institutions since a main product of herds is offspring. In the agricultural regime land is essentially imperishable and cannot be consumed by the management unit, so saving and investment are not inherently essential, and land cannot be increased except through its crops, which in turn cannot be produced without economic institutions to effect its conversion into crops:

> The consequences of these basic differences in productive regime are striking, particularly with respect to the growth potential of the units of enterprise that engage in them. Expansion of the enterprise must depend on increased investment in one or several production factors (including technical innovation). Enterprise in the pastoral sector is always faced with the possibility of rapid growth (or decline) regardless of what the public economic institutions and facilities may be, because part of its product comes automatically in the form of capital gains, which only an active management decision to slaughter will remove from reinvestment. Enterprise in the agricultural sector, on the other hand, has no such ready way of growth; unless special institutional public facilities for conversion exist, it will stagnate from lack of investment opportunities.

Särbo (1977) claims that the pull of pastoralism for Sudanese Shukriya in the eastern Sudan is its potential for economic growth, which is nonexistent in purely agricultural operations. Haaland (1977) goes further to claim that the low rate of consumption of cattle and low marketing rate are due to the degree to which they are tied up in credit relations. He thinks that it is a basic strategy for pastoralists to delay paying debts as long as possible and to try to collect debts as soon as possible. This constitutes a basically financial view of livestock management.

Pushing to another level of sophistication, Bates and Lee (1977) have pointed to the obvious but often overlooked and profoundly important fact that in situations where livestock are acceptable as currency in exchange for food with those who specialize in food production, the degree to which pastoralists will "specialize" in herd production is dependent not only on local environmental conditions but also on *the rate at which the exchange can be made*. Otherwise put, the number of animals (and, I might say, the structure of the herd) needed to support a pastoral family varies with the rate of conversion of pastoral products to food obtained from others (as well as the rate of return for other values, such as wives, which these authors do not discuss).

Unfortunately, all these positions are deficient in some respect in terms of economic theory. Take Bates and Lee, for example. Their profound economic insight that the structure and management of a herd will depend in part on ratios of conversion (prices) for agricultural products is juxtaposed against an assumption that the management of herds is otherwise purely for subsistence, not realizing that even among pastoralists as a group, the fact that animals have purchasing power with agriculturalists will produce a climate of valuation of livestock that will lead inevitably to their partial departure (and sometimes full departure) from subsistence use to financial use and capitalistic manipulations. It would be a foolish pastoralist who would continue to manage his herd to produce food at a high cost when he could buy all the food he wanted with his livestock managed as currency and thereby, in effect, obtain his food at a lower cost.

It is possible to bring to bear on pastoral operations even more sophisticated and systematic economic analysis. (Such analysis, I am convinced, could now be done at a level far beyond my competence.) A beginning could be made with Einzig's (1966) theory of money, a sort of summary of views current at the time he wrote. Einzig has no doubt that African cattle are money and the third part of his revised edition of *Primitive Money*, on monetary theory, makes clear that this has important implications for both economy and society. Communities may differ at the polar extremes with respect to the kinds of money they have. On the one hand are communities in which the currency is so weak that it cannot act as a store of value. And it is the form of a commodity the demand for which as a commodity is so great that it limits the supply of money causing economic stagnation (or stability, if one prefers to look at it that way, as a chief might) because the demand for the currency outdistances the supply. Furthermore, the supply is being replenished too slowly to repair the deflation, with the result that credit is hard to come by and, ultimately, hierarchicalization of the community results as those who are without means to create wealth are dependent on those who have it, whose power is derived from past savings or past accumulations of wealth. As a matter of fact (although Einzig does not seem to see this), in such a situation it is in the interest of patrons to advocate "monetary policies" which help continue the shortage of money, thereby supporting the basis for their power. Einzig thinks that all "primitive monetary policy" is ordinarily deflationary, a view with which I tend to concur if it is applied principally to agrarian production systems.

But in economics in which livestock act as currency, the situation is about the reverse of the one just described. In the first place, livestock, particularly large ones, are a strong, hard currency (for whatever reason; the value of a currency, as Einzig asserts, has no necessary relationship to its intrinsic or commodity value) and can act at the same time as a medium of exchange, store of value, unit of account or standard of value, and standard of deferred payment, and they are highly liquid, all characteristics which need not coincide. For example, something which acts as a medium of exchange may have little use as a store of value because its value changes rapidly (like the present U.S. dollar?). In order for these features to coincide, Einzig argues, there must be a high degree of confidence in the currency.

When a commodity (in this case a food source) takes on monetary functions, the two functions have consequences for each other. In the first place, the values of the two functions are not necessarily correlated. If the commodity function is predominant this leads, as I said, to deflation of the currency taken as a financial item. But, on the other hand, if the currency function dominates, Gresham's Law comes into play, the poorer milkers and meat producers moving in the financial market while the good are withdrawn or simply not produced. The goal is then to turn out the largest number of animals possible at the lowest cost. When livestock become currency of this type, pressure on grazing land is inevitable (as Spencer [1974] has seen) since, compared to long-term ecological considerations, livestock finance is short term in its view. This is where Meyn (1970)

Penned cattle

goes wrong in concluding that poor range management indexes poor management of livestock as "bank accounts."

Another consequence is that as the supply of the commodity currency increases, with accompanying inflation and therefore rise in prices of the commodities against which it moves, the commodity aspect becomes more attractive and so absorbs the increase, thus stabilizing the currency function and tending to keep the currency in short enough supply to act as a hard currency.

Livestock as currency have an especially important feature, their reproducibility at very low cost. All currencies tend to deflate because the volume in circulation steadily declines and must be replenished. With nonself-reproducing currencies this may be costly, requiring application of labor to the production process (as in cloth money making) or to land (as in crop currencies), both instances in which a patron may control the means of reproduction and thus maintain a deflationary posture. But livestock reproduce naturally and at a high rate (although, Dahl and Hjort say, not as fast as some people think, their simulations showing a doubling of fertile cows in a herd in 9½ years. This creates an inflationary condition which is augmented by the fact that since they are a hard currency, whose exchange value is tied to storage of value, they can be used as the basis for long-term credit and so further augment the supply of money (defined as purchasing power). They therefore provide the basis for widespread opportunity to obtain wealth because the supply is high relative to demand. To which we may add that since they are mobile they are difficult to control, not just because of the volume but because they can be easily moved around. Hence livestock provide, through their inflationary character, the condition for economic growth and also the condition for political decentralization.

When a good is valued sufficiently to take on monetary characteristics, no matter what the reason for this valuation, managers of that wealth will conduct management strategies differently than if it were merely a commodity, if the return from managing it as a financial asset is greater than managing it for other, subsistence, reasons. In the case of cattle, the production of milk and of stores of value seems to coincide because both emphasize keeping a large proportion of the herd in females. But the two aims may have different management consequences. As Dahl and Hjort have shown, milk in indigenous East African economies has poor storage capabilities and so poor marketability. In any case, the milk is supposed to be produced to feed the family and so must be produced essentially as a subsistence operation. The manager in a situation where herd size correlates with level of milk production, as it would in East Africa, to judge from Dahl and Hjort, would seek to optimize his operations at the point of maximum product, the largest amount of milk that could be produced regardless of cost (unless the costs exceeded the value to be obtained). The manager would be willing to assume the high costs that accompany achieving maximum product because, as we have seen, it is nearly impossible to produce sufficient milk to feed a reference family in the circumstances in which East Africans must operate.

However, the manager who is producing cattle as stores of value would seek the economic optimum, where the greatest separation between cost and numbers of cattle would be achieved. Where cattle are stores of value and liquid, such a management strategy would bring clear and recognizable profit for the producer, who would know that any degree of increased spread between cost and herd output would be a benefit to him. Put another way, if East African herd managers are indeed managing cattle for financial return rather than maximum milk production, they are not producing as much milk as they could if they were willing to incur added costs.

CAPITALISM AND FREEDOM
IN THE WEST

A surprising result of this view of pastoral capitalism is that it seems to fit with what Milton Friedman (1962) has been saying about capitalism and freedom for some time. However, Friedman the mathematical economist must be separated from Friedman the spokesman for equality. Although he might think his theory of equality, or freedom as he calls it, is embedded in his rational model of the market, the two are separable, since a somewhat intuitive case can be made for the model of a free society based on the idea of resisting closure, a model which is not totally isomorphic with his rational model of the market system. Friedman has stated his position as follows in *Capitalism and Freedom* (1962, 9):

> The kind of economic organization that provides economic freedom directly, namely, competitive capitalism, also promotes political freedom because it separates economic power from political power and in this way enables the one to offset the other.

Or (1962, 15):

> Political freedom means the absence of coercion of a man by his fellow men. The fundamental threat to freedom is power to coerce, be it in the hands of a monarch, a dictator, an oligarchy or a momentary majority. The preservation of freedom requires the elimination of such concentration of power to the fullest possible extent

and the dispersal and distribution of whatever power cannot be eliminated—a system of checks and balances. By removing the organization of economic activity from the control of political authority, the market eliminates this source of coercive power. It enables economic strength to be a check to political power rather than a reinforcement.

It is not too much to suggest, then, that the conditions for the rise of hierarchy are not just East African. Friedman suggests that they are the same conditions framing what we think of as a capitalist or market system (1962, 171–172):

> A major problem in interpreting evidence on the distribution of income is the need to distinguish two basically different kinds of inequality; temporary, short-run differences in income, and differences in long-run income status. Consider two societies that have the same distribution of annual income. In one there is great mobility and change so that the position of particular families in the income hierarchy varies widely from year to year. In the other, there is a great rigidity so that each family stays in the same position year after year. Clearly, in any meaningful sense, the second would be the more unequal society. The one kind of inequality is a sign of dynamic change, social mobility, equality of opportunity; the other, of a status society. The confusion of these two kinds of inequality is particularly important, precisely because competitive free-enterprise capitalism tends to substitute the one for the other. Noncapitalist societies tend to have wider inequality than capitalist, even measured by annual income; in addition, inequality in them tends to be permanent, whereas capitalism undermines status and introduces social mobility.

If we allow for the fact that Friedman seems to feel that whether one type of system or the other is to be is merely a matter of political choice, he could be talking about hierarchical versus egalitarian societies in East Africa.

Controversial as Friedman's theories have become in recent years, especially the notion that unfettered capitalism will lead to freedom, these statements of his put alongside those of others to whom I have referred in this chapter (Dumont, Boulding, Maine) and alongside the data from East Africa do not appear radical at all. The most he can be accused of, if that, is that people have the power to choose whether they will organize society in terms of exchange (capitalism) or hierarchy. While it may be possible to some degree to control the conditions under which the economy of freedom may arise—in fact it surely is possible—this control is at the least not complete and at best problematical. As just noted, to no small degree the present high egalitarianism of Western countries and Japan rests in good part on the wide availability of cheap energy, a condition which may not continue indefinitely. By the same token, as we shall see in the next chapter, present conditions in East Africa which are raising the cost of producing cattle are promoting the rise of hierarchy.

SUMMARY

In sum, then, it should be clear that egalitarianism, wherever it exists on this planet, whether in modern capitalist systems or in the New Guinea highlands or East Africa, rests upon an economic base which is such that by its nature (and sometimes perhaps by legal arrangement) it cannot be monopolized. But in addition, and probably not accidentally, the content of this economy is wealth which is volatile, mobile, and not easy to bring under containment by a few. It is difficult, says Goody (1969), to centralize cows. This wealth, furthermore, is probably capital rather than land or labor and so Boulding, Dumont, and Friedman are probably right in associating capitalism in the larger sense with freedom and equality as defined here.

The one large issue posed by the juxtaposition of pastoral capitalism and industrial capitalism that remains unresolved by this discussion, to which I. M. Lewis seems to be alluding, and which is probably inherent in the Marxist debate over exploitation, is the fact that the clear emergence of egalitarianism in industrial societies is mixed with hierarchy, proliferation of laws, and inequality in ways not found in the less complex pastoral societies. What this suggests is that a theory of industrial capitalism as it relates to equality and hierarchy is more complex than a theory of pastoral capitalism, and remains to be written.

Through this discussion of the issues of egalitarianism and hierarchy it seems plain that except perhaps for the Marxist evolutionists, equality and freedom are states to be admired. Modern development philosophy, turned off by the results of development strategies of the 1960s, which tended to increase gross national product but also status differentiation, seems to say this when it specifies that development must not only increase product but the breadth of distribution of product, thereby promoting equality. Yet there are few people in the world for whom national builders and developmentalists seem to have much less sympathy than these pastoralists who, in a kind of pristine condition, have achieved the freedom and equality so many others search for. John Omer-Cooper puts the point more strongly, suggesting that historians—as well as anthropologists and other scholars—are also at fault in this matter (1972, 302):

> It is worth remembering that our current preoccupation with scale is relatively recent. In earlier times, historians tended to take other values, such as the development of democratic institutions, or the quality of artistic, cultural and intellectual life, as their yardstick for assessing the historical significance of a particular past society or epoch. . . . In African history, similarly, may it not be true that the less complexly structured and smaller-scale societies made possible the development of certain social values and a quality of life which were not attained to the same extent in the larger kingdoms and empires which tend to engage our attention?

CHAPTER IX

An Epilogue on Development

THE SOCIETIES and ways of behaving described in this book for the most part no longer exist. However, the degree of change has varied since the early part of the nineteenth century and most particularly since the onset of colonial rule after 1885. The hierarchical societies were affected first, by virtue of the monopoly of power by the colonial powers, although the kinship, ideological, and production systems were less affected. The more nomadic pastoral societies were least touched right up to modern times, some still continuing relatively untouched to the moment. Of the pastoral societies the more settled bore the brunt of contact, competing with settlers for prime agricultural land, but even they, due no doubt to the fact that they had no chiefs in the first place, were not as directly and overtly upended because the colonial powers did not know how to take hold of them the way they could the chiefdoms, whose leaders were apparent and could thus be controlled. Today the impact on their production systems is more and more severe as pressures by national governments increase in favor of agriculture over pastoralism.

In a book designed, as this one is, to explore the economic basis of social organization, it is of theoretical interest to examine the effect on social organization of these colonial and postcolonial intrusions. But it is also of humane interest since people's lives are being heavily affected. How have East African societies fared as a result of modern developments?

231

THE ARAB IMPACT AND
EAST AFRICAN STATES

Although historical evidence to show it is usually lacking, it is safe to predict that East African societies have never been static or unaffected for long by events, both internal and external, which caused major disruptions in established order. We saw early in the book how the introduction of bananas must have caused radical centralization among interlacustrine societies, like Buganda, and had important implications for the people on whom these banana military powers were thereby able to make war. The Hima invasion of East Africa was unsettling, to say the least, for the indigenous Bantu inhabitants and fed back on the Hima themselves because altered agricultural practices apparently led to tsetse infestation and the decline of herds. The great rinderpest epidemic of the late nineteenth century was devastating to social systems as well as to herds of cattle, if the thesis of this book is correct.

The value of reviewing the impact of the Arabs is therefore not that this was the beginning in East Africa of important intrusive forces but that there is enough historical evidence to measure with greater accuracy the way African societies, with their intensive agricultural and extensive pastoral structures, responded to it. The Arab intrusion occurred on such a broad front that it constitutes a kind of historical laboratory within which we can infer some social laws by comparing reactions of different peoples. The Arab penetration was certainly the most intensive occurrence of long distance trade in East African history up to that time. I. M. Lewis (1955) speaks of the fact that coastal Arabs and Persians have been trading with Somalis since the tenth century, exporting slaves, ivory, skins, hides, gums, ghee, ostrich feathers, myrrh, and frankincense in return for such goods as cotton cloth, metal wire, beads, guns, powder, and percussion caps. This coastal trade was carried on from many enclaves in Somalia and further south. But it was not until the nineteenth century, because of the rise in world demand for ivory and slaves, that Swahili (Arabized Coastal Bantu) and Arab excursions into the interior began in earnest.

By the time Germany and Britain took over East Africa during the last quarter of the last century, especially after the Berlin Conference of 1885, which divided East Africa among them, the Arabs had very extensive networks of trade going inland from southern Tanzania, central and northern Tanzania, and southern Kenya and Somalia, stretching as far as the lower Congo, western Tanzania, and western Uganda. The earliest, begun before 1837, started at Kilwa on the coast, crossed southern Tanzania to Lake Nyasa (Lake Malawi now) and Fipa and went on into Zambia and Zaire. The Fipa, according to Willis (1974), were already growing cotton and weaving cloth when Livingstone reached them after the middle of the century and although we do not know for certain that Arabs and Swahili were responsible for this, culture theory (see Chapter III) would suggest this to be the case since weaving was not indigenous to Africa and occurred otherwise before modern times only in West Africa where it was probably a Mediterranean introduction. The main trade route changed after 1837, going from Bagamoyo, opposite Zanzibar, the trade capital, through the *nyika* or "bush" to Ugogo and on to Tabora, a center of ivory trade, from whence it continued to the coast of Lake Tanganyika at Ujiji, another trade center, where Stanley met Livingstone. A later development was a route northwest from Tabora to the old kingdom of Karagwe in northwest Tanzania after which it bifurcated, one branch continuing to Bunyoro and Acholi in western Uganda (where it met an Arab route coming down from Khartoum in the Sudan), and the other to Buganda, the two major trade centers of precolonial times.

A route from the northern Tanzania coast at Tanga (the "nyika" behind Tanga gave Tanganyika its name before being changed to Tanzania to include Zanzibar) inland past Shambaai to Mount Kilimanjaro and Mount Meru to Burgenej on Lake Victoria (Beachy 1967). But this was never as important as the more southerly routes, partly, no doubt, because the area beyond the coastal hinterland was dominated by pastoral people with whom, for reasons I shall discuss shortly, trade was restricted.

The volume of this trade naturally varied with time, apparently growing steadily until stopped by the colonial takeover. Feierman reports (1974) that after 1820 the demand for slaves and ivory rose rapidly and by 1870–80 was the main basis of chiefly power in Shambaai. Beidelman (1971, 11) estimates that shortly before colonization 100,000 persons in caravans passed annually through Kaguruland. Abraham (1967), discussing the trade in Unyamwezi, notes that in 1891 one caravan on its way to the coast had 600 elephant tusks, 2,000 head of cattle and 2,000 small stock which it had obtained in exchange for cotton cloth, metal wire, beads, guns, powder, and percussion caps. And Beachey (1967) says that by 1885 it was not unusual to have 2,000 porters in a single caravan.

Our interest in this trade, however, is not so much with its particulars but the general impact. The first thing to notice is that the trade was mostly with and through state areas, the major exception being Ugogo, apparently because Gogo territory could not be avoided in getting to the lucrative areas beyond, mainly Unyamwezi but also the eastern Congo, if the shortest route from Zanzibar was to be taken. It is possible to argue that egalitarian areas, because they had fewer people, were less interesting to people whose main demand was for slaves and ivory, the volume of which would probably be proportional to the number of people producing them. But I suspect the reason is more profound than this. It lies in the types of exchanges that were possible. The goods which Arabs had to offer were in demand by all Africans. As we saw in Chapter IV, beads, cloth, and guns, to name only three items, qualified as money and the pastoral people desired them as much as the state people. But these pastoralists, ironically, despite their wealth, had difficulty coming up with the goods with which to pay. In the first place, the egalitarian nature of these societies meant that there were fewer people who could qualify as slaves, and because of the importance of herding as a specialization perhaps they had little skill in ivory hunting. The

Kamba appear to have been an exception. Thus, it seems that the pastoral people were not favored by trade and trade routes because they could not supply the goods the Arabs demanded in quantities sufficient to overcome the attraction of the state societies where hierarchical social structure and more experience in hunting, including hunting in groups, provided the basis for a good supply of ivory and slaves. The best thing the pastoralists had to offer was livestock, for which there was probably a limited demand among Arabs since they did not regard them as repositories of value able to compete with ivory and slaves. And, in any case, the pastoralists probably would have regarded the trading off of large numbers of livestock as irrational.

In addition, the pastoral people seem to have been more hostile and less willing to trade peaceably. Muriuki (1974, 138) recounts how the Kikuyu got their aggressive reputation by attacking traders in their area. Both the Gogo and Maasai had the same reputation although the Gogo profited by assessing duties against caravans through their territory.

The successful Arab penetration was based on three techniques. The first was to establish armed, fortified trading posts in principal areas such as the Shambaai foothills and Tabora in Unyamwezi. These posts were built only after the trade became very profitable. Before that local people controlled it, as did the Nyamwezi until the Arabs took over. The second technique was to use mercenary bands or armies to back up local strong men or chiefs who then repaid the traders with slaves and other booty. Such operations were intended to be self-supporting, the booty paying for the hired army. The third method was simply to buy off the local strong person or persons. In the case of the Gogo this was done in order to secure safe passage. In the state areas the payments to the chiefs made it possible for them to secure their positions and thus serve themselves and the traders simultaneously.

This latter method points up the impact of this trade on internal affairs in these states where it often led to important structural changes, usually in the direction of greater centralization, based on the ability of strong men and chiefs to obtain greater followings through ability to pay increased patronage. Shorter (1973) has analyzed this process most completely as it manifested itself among the Kimbu, who were on a main segment of the southern trade route. Up to the time of the beginning of the trade, the Kimbu were matrilineal with a level and type of production which could support only petty chiefs. The land was poor and the people had continually to shift to virgin territory to institute a new slash and burn cycle. Chiefs' powers were based on the ability to scout out new territory and hold it for their people. With the rise of the Arab trade these chiefs asserted their ownership of the land and its products in order to gain a virtual monopoly on the disposal of ivory, whose profits they shared with the hunters who killed the elephants. Chiefs and their sons organized long distance caravans to the coast during the eighteenth century to trade the ivory for cloth, beads, copper wire, guns, and gunpowder. This led to the growth of an enriched patrilineal hierarchical system in which only nobles could wear colored cloth and beads, and only free women could wear copper. The guns were used to conquer neighbors thereby enabling successful chiefs to extend further their control over ivory by taking rights to it from the chiefs they conquered. Ultimately, around 1884, the increased movement toward centralization based on returns from the trade and expanded gift giving led to a centralized kingdom for a short time before German rule under Nyungu-ya-Mawe.

In Unyamwezi a similar process of centralization seems to have taken place with the added element (Oliver and Atmore 1967) that a subsidiary demand for slaves grew up within the society itself in order to maintain agricultural output while the free men were off hunting ivory and slaves for the Arabs and themselves. Along similar lines, Beidelman (1971) tells us that Sultan Mamboy of Kaguru, whom the Arabs installed in 1870 as their man, supported his power with patronage of cloth and beads in exchange for which the Arabs secured his support and labor, building materials, and food for their station.

In Buganda, guns again had an effect by giving the king greater power than in the past, when he had to depend on the patronage system to keep chiefs in line. He monopolized the small number of guns (Wrigley 1964) and with them displaced these chiefs whose positions were then given to pages of his court, who owed more to him because they did not have chiefly rights to fall back on. Unfortunately for him, however, these pages eventually organized a military coup which in 1888, just before the British took over, grabbed possession of the country, much as did Idi Amin Dada in more recent times.

Feierman (1974) has detailed how the trade led in the case of the Shambaa kingdom to its breakdown. The kingdom was based on an indigenous system of production and goods which was sufficient to create a centralized state. The king, having no desire for Arab goods to secure what he already had, was less sensitive to the advantages of guns than were his neighbors, such as the Zigula to the south. But when the Zigula got guns for ivory and slaves they were in a position to threaten the nearby chiefdoms of Shambaai. This created a demand among the outlying Shambaai chiefs for guns which, when they got them, were used to assert their independence from their king.

In summary, Arab penetration of East Africa seems to have been selective, aimed at the state systems where supplies of ivory and slaves unmatched by stateless societies were available which, in any case, did not sufficiently desire Arab products to be willing to deplete their herds to obtain them, even if the Arabs would have wanted them. The chiefs in the states used the goods and guns that they obtained to alter the balance of power, conquering other chiefdoms where they could, breaking away from sovereigns where they were subordinate to them, or, as in the case of Buganda, further subordinating chiefs who were already somewhat subordinate. Arab influence cannot be said to have created states, but rather to have changed their structures in various ways and to have had a general tendency to increase the size of states and perhaps their despotic quality as a function of an increased base of wealth and greater monopoly of valued goods.

COLONIAL AND NATIONAL PERIODS

During the colonial period, extending from about 1885 to about 1961 (during which the British were the dominant force, especially after 1918, when German Tanganyika was mandated to Britain by the League of Nations, while German Ruanda and Urundi were given to Belgium), both states and stateless societies were affected. In the case of states, the principal effect was the virtual abolition of patronage as a basis for statehood since it was considered by colonial authorities to be corruption. Buganda is again an instructive example. According to Wrigley (1964), after British power was established in Uganda the wealth which the Kabaka used to reward his clients was cut off by the abolition of warfare, but the state hierarchy became, in effect, agents of the British Crown, collecting taxes. The British conceived of the policy of indirect rule as one in which an indigenous state bureaucracy was to be maintained under the control of the British government. However, by abolishing the traditional economic structure of the state, the indigenous state became, in effect, a façade acting as a colonial bureaucracy which the British would have had to create if it had not already been present. The old system did not fade immediately and for a long time the role of chief was confused by the fact that chiefs tried to continue in the previous manner while still adhering to the demands of the role assigned them by the colonial government, a tricky and contradictory task.

In the stateless societies, chiefships were created to accomplish administrative tasks. The Pokot tribal area, for example, was divided into "locations," each with a chief who reported to the District Commissioner. And in egalitarian Unyaturu large clans were assigned chiefs. During the 1940s and 1950s one of these chiefs actually rose to the position of Paramount Chief, partly on his own initiative. The role assigned to chiefs in the indigenous states at least bore some resemblance to its old form and such chiefs were usually able to act with some authority. In the stateless societies they were often ludicrous, seen by the colonial authorities as executives and by their own people as, at best, messengers. They certainly

did not ordinarily attempt to assert authority, for which they had
no economic or ideological base, except insofar as the fact that they
were backed by the British gave them some new basis for action.

Both kinds of societies again underwent changes in the nationalist period from about 1961 to the present. The colonial period had
been characterized by a certain uniformity, since almost all of East
Africa—including the Sudan and much of Somalia—was under British control. But when the new independent governments appeared,
they all took differing tacks and followed varying policies due to the
fact that they were individually searching for the right direction to
suit each one's special circumstances. For example, Tanzania abolished chiefs and tried to institute a kind of egalitarianism based on
the establishment of villages and local corporate enterprises (*ujamaa*). In Kenya chiefs were retained but their roles were revised in
accordance with the policies of the central administration to bring
them closer to the local level in order to encourage plans for development. Chiefs continued also in Uganda but along the lines they
assumed under colonial rule. The most significant thing that happened all over East Africa was implementation of various programs
at various levels to create new wealth by altering traditional production, in the hope of establishing the new nations as viable entities in
the international scene. These efforts may be characterized in very
general terms as state socialism based on "villagization" and ujamaa
in Tanzania, capitalism in Kenya, and military dictatorship in
Uganda. The Sudan today also employs military control, as does
Ethiopia since the fall of the Emperor Haile Selassie in 1974, while
Somalia has taken an even different course, one which is interestingly like the old stateless system, according to I. M. Lewis (1973,
352).

During the periods of colonial and nationalist rule, the people of
the former state and egalitarian societies have responded differently
when development opportunities presented themselves. The people
of states may be dealt with most briefly because they reacted in ways
that may generally be considered predictable. In many cases these
people, after the disappearance of the market for ivory and abolition

of the slave trade, had little to build on. The most successful new opportunities, besides the rare positions in government, and other positions dependent on advanced European education, were agricultural. Many people entered the labor market (some were forced to do so in Kenya through passbook laws). A few were able to acquire new crops and make money from these; two such examples are the Baganda and Wachagga, both of whom profited greatly from coffee production. The Chagga have been the most successful agricultural innovators in Tanzania in the past, although in recent years the Sukuma have successfully taken to cotton production, and successful cash cropping appears in other places as well.

Among the former stateless, pastoral people, a remarkable pattern emerged. Although they had a form of wealth which might have seemed to give them an advantage because development of an international and national market for beef was an obvious possibility, their cattle were considered to be too poor for world markets and they were reluctant in any case to sell them in sufficient numbers. There thus grew up a legend of pastoral conservatism which had a large element of truth in it. Reluctant to sell their cows and thereby acquire the cash to "develop," they also were loath to enter the labor market or turn their energies to cash cropping because, as we have seen, these activities are considered to be less than optimizing in terms of indigenous calculations as well as demeaning when pursued without cattle. In short, these pastoral people shrugged off the colonial system, which many former state people were exploiting, and seemed to try to perpetuate the indigenous, egalitarian systems based on cattle and camels.

However, this was not always the case. In some instances former stateless people were shoved into new agricultural enterprises whether they liked it or not although many, if not most, were saved by the fact that the marginal habitats which served their animal husbandry so well were poor for agriculture. It is instructive to see how some of these pastoralists responded to the new pressures.

Probably the most famous case is that of the Teso, living in east central Uganda, north of Busoga, who have been affected so long by the results of pressures on them to produce cotton with ox plows that we no longer know for sure what their social system was previously like. Indications are that they were a stateless, Eastern Nilotic, cattle and finger millet raising group similar to other agricultural Eastern Nilotics of the Karamojong cluster. Their rangeland is well watered, with an average of 40 to 50 inches per annum from north to south, so they were able to live in settled villages around which they grazed cattle and raised their crops. Their overall social structure was based on age, which supported individual mobility that produced villages of mixed clans.

About 1910 the colonial government forced the growing of cotton upon them in order to provide them with income with which to pay head and poll taxes and to serve rising markets for cotton in Britain and India. The chiefs (originally a product of conquest of the area between 1895 and 1900 by the kingdom of Buganda, who were continued by the colonial government) were the first target, required to attend training sessions on the use of ox plows and cotton growing. The innovation was successful and by 1925 there were 1,154 plows, by 1934 11,615, and by 1946 25,200, a linear increase over twenty years of over 21 times. Today 90% of all Teso farmers in Uganda own plows. Since all grow cotton, this means that about 10% have to hire plows and oxen, although considerably more who have plows must still contract for at least some of the oxen needed for a team.

Why did these pastoral Teso take with such alacrity and so well to what would on the surface seem to be for them an unsuitable activity? The answer is not completely clear because, although there have been at least two extensive studies of this phenomenon (Uchendu and Anthony 1975), which included economists in their complements, focus has been exclusively on production possibilities in line with the common developmentalist idea that there is something unquestionably proper about encouraging people to increase production no matter what its meaning to them. It appears that what happened is this. There was, first of all, a good market for cotton so that those who grew it could sell it for enough to make it worth their while. Its appeal was strengthened by the fact that the cost to the producer was relatively low (i.e., low opportunity costs) because (1) they already had access to cattle which could be trained relatively easily to pull the plow leaving only the plow to be bought; (2) they could use the cotton fields as seed beds for finger millet in the second year of rotation and could thus increase production of finger millet both because the area for planting was enlarged without extra cost and because the plowed seed beds made for better crops (there was always a good demand for finger millet); (3) the labor for plowing was available since that is men's work and men were not deeply involved in the production of millet, which is women's work; and (4) it did not interefere with cattle production because the fields did not have to be fenced. So cotton could be grown at low cost without interfering with the indigenous production system which, indeed, it enhanced.

But why did they wish to obtain the new income? In part the answer is that they needed the cash to pay taxes and so avoid depleting their herds some of which, otherwise, they would have had to sell; in part it is that they desired some of the new goods being imported into the area by Indians and other traders; and in part it is because they desired to use it to increase cattle holdings. The Teso qualify as pastoral people. In 1963 they possessed over 578,000 head of cattle. If we add to this their sheep and goats on a liberal estimated ratio of 10 to 1 cow, we get another 17,000 head, making nearly 600,000. With a population of about 403,000 (Uchendu and Anthony 1975), this makes a ratio of cattle to people of 1.4:1. This ratio may have been increasing over the years if the inflation of brideprice that has been occurring is a measure (from five head in 1938 to 16 in 1975). But it is possible that this increase in brideprice is simply a reflection of the inflation of cattle values or a change in the value of women.

Besides continued focus on cattle, other aspects of the Teso system show that this is still an indigenously oriented economy, not merely a facet of a national, Western-oriented, system. Finger millet is still the main food crop. Women still produce it with old methods. Brideprice is still paid to obtain female labor for this kind of production. And farmers have not tried to develop cotton growing beyond the point where costs of its production would upset the indigenous system. They will not use profits from cattle sales or from cotton sales to purchase machines for weeding, a bottleneck to production, and confine themselves to weeding by hand. They will not purchase fertilizers. They will not fence fields, which would interfere with cattle raising. They will not use tractors for plowing. In short, it appears that the Teso have used cotton as a means of maintaining and even increasing an indigenous economic system based on cattle as repositories of value and the source of at least intra-Teso political freedom.

The Kipsigis, one of the Nandi-speaking group, have also been changing for a long time. Manners (1962), who has detailed this, leaves the impression that Kipsigis are radically detached from their former stateless system. These people live in southwest Kenya in an area of good agricultural land and high rainfall, whose appeal was so great that when British colonists appeared in Kenya they moved into the adjacent lands on the north and northeast and even intruded themselves into what became designated as the Kipsigis reserve. In accordance with their usual policy, the colonial government imposed various taxes on the people which had the effect of forcing them to sell cattle. They were also required to give 70 days' labor a year to settlers in order to be allowed to remain on their land, and they used the income from this to pay taxes and thus reduce the number of cattle they had to sell.

At the same time a large demand for maize was created in the Kipsigis areas by the fact that the government had to feed its administrative, military, and police personnel who were being used to subdue the pastoral Nandi, and for whom the settlers were not growing enough since they had become specialized in tea production. In 1907 the District Commissioner urged the Kipsigis to grow maize and took direct action to remove their war leaders (laibons) because they counseled resistance.

The Kipsigis did take to maize production, a task which was entirely in the hands of men. On the one hand, they gradually increased the production of maize, later adding tea, to the point where the scarcity of land caused the appearance of individual tenure, while on the other hand they displayed a noticeable lack of zeal about hiring themselves out as laborers on neighboring plantations. In addition to cash cropping they began to sell cattle, which became their second largest money earner. But it is noteworthy that cattle sales were carried on in such a way that by 1966–67 (Daniels 1975) they still had about 300,000 head to 175,000 people, a ratio of 1.7:1 which, as we have seen, places them well within the pastoral category.

In sum, even though the Kipsigis, by Manner's account, made radical changes in their production methods, they have continued to hold large numbers of cattle and have apparently used the production of maize as a means of avoidance of plantation labor and of maintaining their large herds.

Further, Daniels shows that in other respects the Kipsigis, like the Teso, have clung to a way of life which relates to the indigenous economy. They still practice polygyny, pay brideprice, initiate males into age sets, and are opposed to institutionalized authority. The spur to their engaging in these cash activities seems to have been the low opportunity costs in both the material and the social realms. In the material they had cattle which could be employed for plowing and they had surplus male labor, the two main considerations. And they were able to do these things without becoming any more subservient to anyone than they already were as colonially dominated people.

Gulliver's account of Arush (1969b), like many other such accounts of pastoral people, seems to explain their negative attitude toward change as being due to a preoccupation with tradition. For this reason he is slow to tell us about Arush cattle holdings. We therefore form the impression that these agricultural Maasai living on Mount Meru devoted themselves exclusively to the cultivation of bananas and, more recently, of coffee. But the 1948 Blue Book of Tanganyika (whose figures admittedly are not entirely reliable) show the Arush as having 75,000 head of cattle, with enough goats and sheep to make about 10,000 more units, to a human population in 1957 of 63,000. If we allow for the possibility that the Arush also have Maasai cousins herding cattle for them in the plains, the number might be even greater.

Like the Kipsigis, the Arush from the beginning of the colonial period were unwilling to offer themselves for employment in the building of the town of Arusha or at the plantations which grew up in that area. They were also negative toward Christianity and schooling, another common characteristic of stateless people. The Arush originally went up into the mountains in the last century to escape Maasai internecine wars. They appear at that time to have been cattle owners who aimed at the exploitation of the grazing, but they early set out to trade goods produced on the mountains for livestock with the Maasai down below. There followed a process of gradual filling up of the mountain agricultural zone while at the same time grazing land was acquired on the plains.

In the end the Arush system seems to have been composed of a mountain agricultural zone and a plains grazing zone and, like the Kipsigis and Teso, they took to cash cropping of coffee because the opportunity costs were low: coffee does well in banana plantations and can be introduced without interfering with banana production (Ruthenberg 1968, 217). The money they obtained paid taxes and allowed them to avoid selling off cattle. The reluctance of Arush to have much to do with missions, schools, or plantation labor is an expression of their livestock wealth and continued commitment to a nonsubservient existence.

There are other examples which parallel these three cases. Hammersley (1969, 192) tells us that while the Sukuma have taken to cotton growing on a large scale, the proceeds of the crop are put into indigenous cattle production. The Gusii (LeVine 1962) now grow coffee but continue cattle raising and their reluctance to engage in plantation labor is comparable to that of the other pastoralists. The Turkana who are now engaged in fishing as a cash crop also turn the proceeds back into livestock. Finally, although the Maasai have not become cash farmers, Gulliver (1969b, 240) feels they are willing to accept innovations that are of direct utility to cattle keeping and would even plant if the opportunity costs were low enough. To summarize, this survey of some stateless societies shows that they all seem to have been able to maintain egalitarian systems by exploiting nonsubservient forms of production which fed into the modern sector and gave them wealth with which to resist it. Egalitarian peoples in other areas have not found this necessary because they were not pressured to the same extent. The Turkana and Pokot, for instance, live in remote areas whose value to the modern sector is not apparent and where attempts at development have therefore been rather sporadic and listless.

The governments of East Africa have had great difficulty dealing with these pastoralists, partly because they have not understood the economics of pastoralism and partly because even if they do understand they do not know how to effect changes in these economies that will bring them in line with national development. On the whole, government and developmentalist attitudes toward pastoralists have been hostile. Pastoralism has been characterized as "primitive," an inferior way of life, and proposals for its continuation are made in a form which will limit its use of the habitat (e.g., cutting down on overgrazing) and increase its contribution to national development. Probably the most extreme example of negativism toward pastoralism is that of the Karamojong (Baker 1977) where, as a result of the failure of various development schemes to which the Karamojong would not respond, the government has thrown up its hands, so to speak, and has started to work around them, moving agriculturalists into their western rainy-season grazing area and thereby severely undermining their ability to maintain the pastoral system. In other places manipulation of pastoralists for national purposes is more the rule, as in Tanzania where Rigby (1975) sees the government's villagization of Gogo as an attempt to obtain political control over them (at the expense of pastoralism), or in Kenya where ranching and agricultural schemes continue to be fostered, especially in the prime agricultural areas.

Probably the most frequently utilized method of coping with pastoralists is through ranching schemes, which are pervasive in East Africa. The need for "better" range management, which is at the heart of ranching, is well stated by E. E. Russell, formerly Director of the East African Agriculture and Forestry Organization (Pratt and Gwynne 1977). He claims that the pastoral people make little contribution to the national economies by their livestock operations and some are a real threat because as numbers of livestock have risen at abnormal rates severe overgrazing is threatening actual damage to the land. But he also recognizes a paradox: the returns to be expected from ranching schemes, which will control land use and prevent damage while increasing the productivity of animals, are so low that they won't justify the costs of the schemes. Then Russell makes a point which is macabre in its implications: that the tsetse fly-infested areas, which wild game can inhabit although domestic livestock cannot, produce more revenue as tourist attractions than the pastoral areas! Should the pastoral areas then be allowed to be taken over by fly?

Elaborating on Russell's theme, which was the foreword to their book on rangeland management and ecology in East Africa, Pratt and Gwynne (1977) assert:

> In most cases . . . the people [pastoralists] are tied to a way of life that limits their own development and that leads to overstocking of the land. Without incentives for social and technical advance, further mismanagement and deterioration is inevitable, producing malcontent and suffering among the people, [and] irreparable damage to the range resources.

Such views are to be expected from Europeans who never showed any sympathy for pastoralism as a mode of production (although pastoralists had a romantic fascination for them), but one wonders whether present African leaders who may have an acquaintance with the truth of pastoralism as an economic system agree that pastoralists are "without incentive." Nevertheless, they seem as ready as Europeans to propose rangeland management if only because of the incompatibility of the pastoral economy with national development.

Very recent information on ranching schemes is not readily available but indications in the available literature are that the general situation described by Meyn in 1970 holds. The 1969 Kenya Development Plan proposed a comprehensive program of range development aimed at converting pastoralists to commercial livestock production by subjecting 2.2 million hectares to intensive operations and 11.4 million hectares to extensive production operations. The intent of the scheme was to increase the average annual takeoff of cattle from 12 to 14% by 1975. The plan envisaged the fostering of communal cooperative ranching operations whose *raison d'être* was to be able to secure official rights to land where there were none, this despite the fact that the planners recognized that experience with communal ranches showed that they tended to make great progress in the first two years after which they deteriorated due to "lack of discipline" among the members, a statement I translate to mean that the members ultimately refused to limit the number of livestock on the range to the level determined by the ecologists and agricultural economists, a sure indication that the people were still thinking of livestock as stores of value and not as beef.

Parenthetically, one ecologist (Talbot 1972), insisting that proper range development requires that "ecological principles" be taken into account, excuses Maasai overuse of the land on the grounds that they were in balance with nature before development caused them to get out of balance, and, like Russell, above, seems to advocate turning Maasailand into a zoo because wild animals would be less degrading!

In Tanzania the 1964 Range Development and Management Act was first applied in Maasailand and then extended to Sukumaland in 1967-68. Its purpose was to convert pastoralists to a "cash economy" and bring capital and management to the underpopulated range, thereby shifting pastoralism into "full production." The Act proposed model ranches based on government capitalization of water, ranges, etc., in short a variety of ujamaa applied to ranching.

And in Uganda large scale ranching efforts began as early as 1947 with clearing of tsetse-infested bushes and in particular with the Ankole ranching scheme.

It will be useful to have a closer look at attempts to implement ranching in these various areas, beginning with Kenya. Kenya's plans seem to have been focused primarily on the Maasai (Davis 1971), who are the major cattle holders and hold some of the best agricultural land. While the plan envisaged over five million hectares—only 10% of the total rangeland of Kenya—to be allocated to a form of private ownership by 1974, all of Narok and Kajiado divisions of Maasailand, southwest and south of Nairobi, were targets. Narok, in fact, has been eyed for agricultural programs too, specifically wheat growing, and within Kajiado plans were developed for fourteen group ranches in the Kaputiei section. The rationale of the scheme was the idea that traditionally Maasai did not engage in better range management practices because communal ownership did not allow for long-range investment plans. Interestingly, there seemed little consciousness in these plans of the possibility that shifting to beef production would be a radical, perhaps impossible, change for Maasai. Beef production seems to have been viewed as merely an extension of indigenous practices, whose messiness would be made orderly by proper ranching. Probably because of this, in 1976 Hjort could report that there had been little success with the livestock development project and that what new cash was being obtained through it was being used by Maasai to increase the number of cattle they had in terms of management strategies relevant to the indigenous economy.

Nevertheless, there was one significant deviation from this pattern of intransigence. In 1971 Hedlund delivered a report on activities in the Kaputiei area in connection with the implementation of the ranching system. In 1960–61, as mentioned above, a major drought had struck in East Africa, killing 65% of the total herd of 300,000 animals in the Kajiado District. As a result, the Kaputiei Development Committee was formed, apparently consisting of local Maasai big men, who split up 56,000 acres into 28 individual ranches. The "owners" of these new ranches, the big men and their families, had what they thought was clear title to the land, granted by the Kajiado Council (who in fact had no legal authority to grant title to land), and they withdrew from traditional stock associate memberships, closed their ranches to grazing by other Maasai, and would not lend money or cattle to Maasai who were not of the group. Most importantly, they started to sell more cattle than others and opened bank accounts. The significance of this development in Kaputiei, as I see it, is this. After the famine caused by the 1960–61 drought, and the huge loss of wealth they must have suffered, these Maasai big men, who must have had some acquaintance with the way banks operate, decided that the potential for speedy recovery of wealth through beef ranching was greater than through the traditional methods, which means that they saw the opportunity cost of shifting to beef production as low, at least for people who still had some means. This shift, of course, was incompatible with communal ownership of land, stock association, and other forms of cooperation with indigenous Maasai. In other words, having decided to go for the European economic order, a whole range of changes in their mode of operation was perceived by them as necessary. The apparent result of the banding together of the big men to help each other accomplish this change was probably to institute an incipient hierarchical system since land, by being shifted from open range to closed range, becomes, like agricultural land, a potentially scarce commodity that lends itself to exclusive control, ensuring that in the end some Maasai will be without land and be forced into relations of clientship with rich Maasai patrons. In short, the seeds of polarization of wealth were laid, a seemingly common outcome of development schemes all over the world.

The present situation in Tanzania with respect to range development is unknown, but there is no reason to believe that there is any more sympathy for indigenous pastoralism or any more success in challenging it, except that the current powerful move to villagization would seem inevitably to threaten traditional pastoral economic modes, if only because of the limitations on mobility that urbanization imposes.

The story of the Ankole ranching scheme, which seems to have been the major attempt in this direction in Uganda, where agriculture is more generally the focus of production activities, brings out again, like the events among the Kaputiei, the social implications of ranch development. The Ankole are the major livestock-raising people in the Interlacustrine Bantu group. The evidence is that they are more tractable than pastoralists in the northeast section of the country—the Dodoth, Jie, Karamojong, Uganda Teso, and such. Begun in the 1940s, when the British controlled the area, the scheme continued to develop after independence, at which time United States AID money became involved. In this later development more than a hundred ranches were to be set up for beef production (Doornhas and Lofchie 1971). AID was concerned that the allocation of the necessary land be accomplished on an egalitarian basis, a concern they urged on the Uganda government. But they were unable to make this specification stick, with the result that the overrepresentation of Huma aristocrats (only 5% of the population) in Uganda's national politics, compared to the Bairu peasants, led to Huma control of most of the ranches.

According to Rapp (1976), the Sudanese government seems also to be inclined to promote ranching but is less dogmatic about it than, for example, Kenya. And whether Ethiopia has any policy at the present time is not known, although in the past she seems always to have had only marginal control over the pastoralists residing in her peripheral areas including the now well-known Ogaden Somalis.

In Somalia, range enclosure is something that seems to have begun spontaneously in the north, based on laws established during the British colonial period which allowed laying claim to private title. This process, according to Box (1971), which allows 20 hectares to be set off per individual, has now proceeded so far that it is irreversible. The land is used by nomads as an agricultural backup but, since they bring a portion of their herds with them while utilizing the land, the concentration of livestock is causing damage to the range itself. Other than this, past attempts at range management, according to Box, have all failed.

To summarize, attempts at range management, involving most importantly limitations on the number of animals that can be held, and an orientation to the production of beef, have consistently run into problems. The only seeming successes are the Ankole scheme and the individual Kaputiei Maasai ranches, although the present comparatively high beef sales in traditional pastoral places like Embu and Kamba suggest that over a long period the Europeanization of areas of Kenya close to the developed centers has had its effect on the indigenous pastoral economy. Otherwise, the political polarization in Ankole, paralleling the polarization of wealth that is inevitable in ranching, and that also seems implicit in the Kaputiei development, is something that must be recognized as part of the whole future pastoral development process.

In Somalia the government seems inevitably to be headed toward a confrontation with pastoral nomads. Somalia may be thought of as being divided into two parts: the north, with 600,000 people, of which 85% are pastoral nomads; and the south, with 1.6 million, of which 70% are nomads; or an aggregate of 73% nomads for 2.2 million people. The south is where most agriculture and cattle raising is to be found. It seems to have been government policy for some time to settle at least some nomads on the unused arable lands in the south (7 out of 8 million hectares). In this attempt they have no doubt been encouraged by people like Konczacki (1967), who believes that they keep overlarge herds only from a "precautionary motive" and can be induced to become agriculturalists when they are shown that it provides a more reliable food supply. (I suspect, however, that a problem with this position is that since almost everyone in Somalia is a nomad or has nomadic connections, Konczacki's argument, and those like it, would be seen by Somalis to be based on fallacious notions about the causes of nomadism.) Buxton (1977) tells us that the Marxist government of Somalia considers the nomads to be its most intractable problem. While they earn more than half of its foreign exchange from the products of camels and cattle (mainly camels), there is no real future in expanding the production of camels. Yet it is clear that the nomads are not eager to farm. After the drought of the early 1970s, 268,000 nomads were left destitute. Of these 120,000, "without much coercion," chose to take up fishing and farming. Up to the time of Buxton's report in 1977, about 10% of these had drifted away but the remainder were living on foreign foods while their farming and fishing operations were still nonself-supporting.

A great irony in the Somali story is that, according to Buxton, the government feels that an ideology of scientific socialism is more suitable for Somalia than capitalism because it is a poor country. Which raises the perennial question, when discussing pastoral economies, of what is a proper definition of poverty.

So, as we have seen, the future for pastoralism in East Africa is not bright, although to a certain extent it can be claimed that after more than fifteen years of independence the confrontation between pastoralists and national governments is a standoff.

The pastoral problem, as I see it, may be summarized as follows. On the one side we have a pastoral mode of production and social structure based on the fact that livestock, notably cattle and camels, act as currency and stores of value whose high liquidity in all sorts of transactions makes them amenable to financial uses, resulting in growth economies based on inflation derived from the natural propensity of herds to increase. Furthermore, this inflationary process has political consequences because when combined with easy accessibility to the means of production, principally as a result of the need to disperse herds, it leads to egalitarianism, just the kind of social relational system advocated by development planners. In contrast, the deflationary process that marked nonpastoral East African economies was the basis for traditional states. While the present growth of cash cropping in these societies has resulted in a move toward egalitarianism in some cases, the broad trend all over East Africa (outside of Somalia and a few other places) is not egalitarian.

And if current development plans like the resettlement scheme for nomads in Somalia, or the World Bank-supported rush to increase agricultural production in Kenya, are carried through, we may expect further drastic reductions in pastoralism, economically and politically.

On the other hand, pastoralism is viewed by governments and planners as essentially irrelevant to development and as often damaging to the habitat. It is popular to advocate various ranching schemes as a means of reshaping the pastoral way of life to conform with national development plans. Such schemes have in fact rarely been successful, since ranching is really a form of agriculture and as such a radical shift from pastoralism.

The colonial and nationalist periods, then, have been ones in which the former state and stateless societies have responded differently to the opportunities provided by these new developments. At the risk of overgeneralizing it may be said that state people have been prone to abandon the old structures for opportunities that provided new freedom and a reduction of subservience to others, through wage labor on plantations, production of cash crops, or education, while the former powerful chiefs have been neutralized by being incorporated into the bureaucracy or abolished. On the other hand, the former stateless people have either resisted and ignored these new opportunities, which they saw as a threat to their freedom, or have exploited them in order to extend their freedom even further, ordinarily by maintaining their cattle holdings or building them up. However, developments in Maasailand and elsewhere suggest that sooner or later the egalitarian pastoral systems will break down.

REVITALIZATION

So far I have had little to say about revitalization processes (of which revolution is a subtype) except a passing reference to the fact that Turner (1969) has taught us that much ritual is in form mini-revitalization. It is time here to rectify this omission because of the importance of the revitalization process in social reform. Revitalization, which is often thought of as unusual, as a deviant kind of behavior based on a breakdown of normal social order, is so common in human society that an adequate theory of society, we now realize, would include revitalization as a normal component of any social system over time.

Revitalization is a group process in which a class of people, perceiving themselves as thwarted in pursuit of some just goal, begin to act en masse, throwing off individuality and melding into a kind of superperson, verbally or physically attacking other people who are viewed as the source (rightly or wrongly) of their frustration. These revitalized persons (members of evangelical religious sects or radical and extreme conservative political movements spring to mind as cases in point), acting ordinarily under the leadership of a prophet or messiah, espouse extreme altruism and externalize their frustrations in symbols which often employ reversals of normal values. For example, among the Meru of Mount Kenya, a kind of shaman or prophet called the Mugwe (Needham 1960) treats his left hand as sacred. As will be remembered from Chapter III, in East Africa world views based on binary classification make the right hand superior or less tension-producing. Thus, the sacred left hand symbolizes the reversal of normal order in the revitalization process of which the Mugwe is a part, the way ragged clothes and long, unkempt hair symbolized the revitalized person during the counterculture movement of the late 1960s in America.

Revitalization shows up most frequently in East Africa in male initiation rites, no doubt because of the friction between older and younger generations. But it can also appear at other points of friction and frustration, as in the relations of women with men. (I have not chosen to deal in detail with the subordinate role of women in East Africa but have taken it as a given because it is a topic that deserves more attention than I can give it in this book. But it is clear from my discussion of these societies that women are extremely servile to men in most cases, even in the egalitarian societies, and this sometimes expresses itself in special rites such as the cycle of Turu women's secret society, which is essentially anti-male.)

Male initiation rites represent, in a sense, controlled revitalization, coping with frictions and frustrations inherent in the relations of generations. Certain revitalization symbols commonly occur in them, such as refraining from washing or "washing" with dirt during the months of the ceremony, hunting for unusual animals, using peculiar weapons, and living in communes. But revitalization can break out anywhere. There certainly must have been times in the prehistoric period when frustrations led to unique mobilizations of classes of persons acting in a revitalized fashion. The revolts in Rwanda and Burundi by peasants in recent years during the shift to nationalism may only be examples of common events in the prehistories of East African societies. Revitalization has been a regular feature of the impact of the colonial and national periods, one that is often not recognized for its frequency. I shall not here try to make an exhaustive list of these movements but will say enough about them to suggest how general they have been.

One of the most famous is the Hehe (a state people of southern Tanzania) rebellion, called *maji maji* (literally "water water") after the fact that the Hehe, typical of the way revitalized people think, felt they had nothing to fear from German guns since their faith would turn the bullets to water. Similarly, Willis (1974) reports a Fipa revitalization movement headed by Kajwa in reaction to the German occupation in 1898. Davidson (1969, 200ff) mentions a revolt by Swahili on the Tanzania coast that was led by Abushiri bin Salim of Pangani against the Germans. And he also tells of an impassioned statement made by one Masemba, apparent leader of a resistance group, put in writing to the Germans and translated from Swahili as follows:

> I have listened to your words, but I can find no reason why I should obey you. I would rather die.... I look for some reason why I should obey you and I find not the smallest. If it should be friendship that you want, then I am ready for it, today and always. But I will not be your subject.... If it should be war that you desire, then I am also ready.... I do not fall at your feet, for you are God's

creature just as I am. . . . I am sultan in my land. You are sultan
there in yours. But listen to me: I do not say that you should obey
me, for I know that you are a free man. . . . As for me, I will not
come to you, and if you are strong enough for it, then come and
fetch me. . . .

Masemba's statement is instructive. There is a temptation to glorify
rebelliousness and revitalized persons, especially in the colonial
situation. But one would be hard put to do so in the case of Masemba who, Davidson says, was a "notorious slave trader" as well
as a chief. Obviously Masemba objected to the fact that the Germans desired to make him subservient to them and insisted that he
would not give up his just position of dominance over others in his
own society! However, we should also be aware that hierarchical
structures were accepted, working systems, which even the subservient clients within them must have resisted giving up to be replaced by an unknown or, what is worse, by even greater or less
institutionalized subservience. Not all rebellions are revitalization
movements, and it is possible that Masemba was a representative of
the more mundane type. But the way he phrases his resistance ("I
do not fall at your feet, for you are God's creature just as I am")
suggests that he is.

Dini ya Msambwa is one of the lesser known revitalization movements which occurred in Kenya and Uganda in the late 1940s and
the early 1950s, especially notable for the fact that it took hold
among some egalitarian people. Begun in the Abaluyia area, it
spread to areas like West Pokot where, in 1950, it led to an attack
by spear-wielding Pokot on Kenya police that had been sent out to
observe one of their meetings, some of whom were killed. Like
many of these movements, this one was "nativistic," which is to say
it had as a central tenet, a return to precolonial ways, symbolized by
a refusal to use European utensils. Another minor movement, led
by a woman (in this case symbolizing elimination of discrimination
and fostering of equality) occurred in Unyaturu about 1903 (Jellicoe 1969, 4) and led to the establishment of a permanent police
post in the area by the Germans.

In 1962, the Bakonjo of Uganda revolted in an attempt to detach themselves from rule by the Toro Kingdom, under which they had suffered since indirect rule was instituted in the area in 1900 (Alnaes 1969). Feierman (1974, 162) tells of the Bondei revolt from the rule of the Shambaa, which can be seen to be, like the Bakonjo revolt, an indirect result of the historical contact period. Whereas the revitalization processes were set in motion among Bakonjo by the implementation of indirect rule, this revolt between two indigenous societies was stimulated indirectly by Arab trade for slaves, which upset the local balance of relations. People's rage against injustice is specific to their socioeconomic circumstances. Just as Masemba cried out against the injustice of not being able further to lord it over others, the Bondei cried out against the following injustices, so specific to indigenous African lives (Feierman 1974, 163):

> The capture of our children and their being given in marriage by force without our receiving dues or cattle.

> Their slaves and guards robbing people whom they meet in the road.

> If a man is accused of witchcraft no evidence is called but he is killed and his children are taken and sold.

> If they want food they send men into our towns to take goats and chickens and if the owner says a word he is beaten.

> If one of their wives has parents they do not allow her to visit her father or mother.

The best-known revolts and revitalization movements, of course, are those which occurred at the national levels. Included among these are the Mau Mau Rebellion led by Kenyatta, which was instrumental in establishing Kikuyu dominance of Kenya, the Hutu-Tutsi conflicts in Rwanda and Burundi, as well as the other various national movements such as TANU in Tanzania. Those which occurred in Rwanda and Burundi are interesting for the fact that although they were national, they were also ethnic, because these two states have moved from ethnic to national status without significant violation of indigenous ethnic boundaries. However, in both cases the removal of colonial authority, in this case Belgian, created the condition (opportunity to take power) for revolt (and also, incidentally, raised questions about traditional analysis of these societies which tended to portray the subservient peoples as content with their lot). In Burundi the Tutsi ruled from the time of independence in 1962, surviving a Hutu revolt in 1972 after which President Micombero, a Tutsi, is said to have instituted a counter-revolution (or counterrevitalization) movement in which more than 100,000 Hutu were killed. In Rwanda, just the opposite occurred; the Hutu revolt succeeded and the Tutsi were demoted and slaughtered.

Revitalization is so common because relations between people are never without friction and because systems viewed as just, even if unequal, often degenerate into contradiction and injustice. If we were to explore all the societies of East Africa at any stage in history, we would find revitalization occurring at one magnitude or another in all times and places. The wonder is that people are able to work out relations in such a way that revitalization is not the dominant process but rather the seemingly aberrant one.

DEVELOPMENT AND SOCIAL INTERACTION

The desire to achieve something called development in East Africa is up against a problem inherent in the concept of ethnocentrism. The term development seems usually to mean increase in output of goods (sometimes also increase in general consumption of goods as opposed to a condition in which a few get most of the rewards) of kinds that are valued by those instigating development, the Western and industrial nations. And the term is up against a second problem, the tendency to see development only in material terms. Furthermore, as I shall try to show, these two problems are interrelated.

At the beginning of this book I talked about the difference between culture and society, emphasizing that culture is knowledge which, by its nature, is randomly created. It is a product of accident. That men now have domestic animals or, more specifically, domesticated cattle, is an accident rather than an inevitability of history. Society, on the other hand, is situationally determined, a system of interrelations among people. Hence, societies of similar types (Iroquois terminology, cousin marriage, segmented lineage structure) may appear independently (East African and northeastern United States). The kinds of goods a people produce are determined by the laws of cultural innovation. But the amount of goods produced, the way the goods are exchanged, or the type of status system that exists is a social/economic phenomenon dependent on social processes.

Development properly refers to social processes, although it is commonly confused with culture. That is to say, whether a people produce a certain kind of good in a certain quantity depends on the value of doing so in their relations with each other, Marx's relations of production. Development does not mean rediscovering the wheel. That is change or innovation. The basic technology which a people need to become industrialized must be imported from those who have it (because innovation of important ideas is in fact rare and difficult although refinement of known technological principles may occur locally). But whether it is then used or not depends on the value of doing so relative to the way people relate to each other.

It is plain that planners (European and African) interested in development are not interested in just any kind of development, but only in the kind that serves the values of the industrial nations. There is little interest in whether pastoral people increase the per-capita output of their skinny cows. There is much interest in changing their herding practices to produce different kinds of cattle, bred and raised for high beef and milk output. Thus, development requires not just that people increase output but that they shift their social, technical, and ideological orientation to Western industrial patterns.

While the implications of development are therefore social and economic in this sense, they are importantly so in another sense. At the heart of development programs in an ethic about egalitarianism versus hierarchy which parallels that which we found in the indigenous East African societies themselves. When developmentalists increasingly call for programs that introduce new production methods, attack indigenous social systems to replace them with Western styles (democratic, socialistic, or whatever), and urge that consumption per capita must increase along with output, they are, I believe, asserting that these new social systems must be egalitarian, nonhierarchical, and extensive. They are asserting that increased consumption per capita is essential because it is necessary to counter hierarchical tendencies. They are against concentrations of new wealth which will generate hierarchy.

If we look at how development programs have proceeded in the various East African countries, we can see that advocacy of egalitarian developmentalism is most overt in Tanzania (van Hekken and van Velzen 1972, 11):

> With the Arusha Declaration Tanzania has irrevocably committed itself to socialism. The country's firm resolve to create an egalitarian society has found expression in numerous party resolutions and this has decisively moulded government planning.

As Blue and Weaver's (1977) recent assessment of the Tanzanian model of development stresses, the aim is to achieve both growth and equity simultaneously for rural as well as urban people by refusing to subsidize the urban sector through cheap agricultural prices. There is to be collective leadership in government, industrial management, and agriculture (which would mean collective management in ranching, no doubt, where ranches are established) and a move to expand political consciousness toward freedom, independence, and responsibility. In short, equality is to be achieved by law, not by process, by structure rather than dynamics. But as Blue and Weaver point out, the economy has not grown since 1967–68 and 60% of the government's budget comes from foreign aid. So much money is spent on service rather than capitalizing production that it has become a kind of welfare economy. And the consequence of all this, of course, is that in order to pursue these goals the government must inevitably reduce, perhaps destroy, the freedom and equality of the pastoralists whom, at one point several years ago, they even tried to force to wear pants. Rigby's (1975) poignant account of the villagization of the Gogo is the most revealing yet of the impact of Tanzania's development policy on pastoralists. The method by which equality was to be achieved is the now famous plan of ujamaa villages whose basic principle (Shorter 1974, 131) is that villagers operate a block farm in which work and profits are pooled. In theory, at least, the farm is voluntarily formed around some production scheme capitalized by the government while a committee supervises the work and the sharing and spending of profits.

It is no secret that ujamaa has had some problems, as is illustrated by Shorter's mention of the development of the Matwiga tobacco scheme in Ukimbu during the 1960s. Those who took part, he says, did so in expectation of obtaining high individual incomes (Shorter 1974, 131) and at the first hint of the introduction of the ujamaa concept they began to flee.

There is some irony in all of this. Tanzania is unlike some of the other East African countries in having been born on a wave of revitalistic idealism. By contrast, although Kenya was boosted toward independence by Mau Mau, the actual accomplishment of nationhood and its subsequent mode of operation have been far less idealistic. A feature of revitalistic thinking, as I have remarked, is egalitarianism, the lowering of the high and the raising of the low. In this sense, then, the ideals of revitalization are in apparent accord with the normal ideals of people. Those of former stateless systems in East Africa valued equality and freedom and those who were part of states desired to obtain it. Yet in the pursuit of this goal the Tanzanian government may be employing a method which works against it since Tanzanians do not see cooperative organizations as free. In fact Tanzania has promoted the notion, through the concept of ujamaa, that group actions based on merging of individuals into large corporate entities like lineages are natural to indigenous Africa. Our examination of East African societies would lead us to question this. More recently, due to the failure of ujamaa as a voluntary method, the government has taken to villagization (Rigby 1977), attempting to force the issue.

If I am correct in my analysis, egalitarianism of the nonrevitalization kind, which recognizes individual equality rather than mass equality, can be achieved only with a requisite economic base, a certain kind of production and exchange that provides widespread opportunity for individuals to get ahead. As Feldman (1969, 110) remarks in his *Economics of Ideology*, "The ethical values of a country's leaders are insufficient to ensure a particular form of social organization." It may even be that since Tanzania places its hopes for the future on agriculture, raising the specter of land shortage, it is creating conditions like those in parts of hierarchical indigenous East Africa that will ensure a nonegalitarian society. Van Hekken and van Velzen (1972, 30), in a study of land scarcity in Rungwe District of southern Tanzania, have charged just that. Rural inequality and the rise of patron/client relationships are its product. It might therefore be well if the administration and popular opinion were not so prejudiced toward pastoralism (as Rigby has charged [1970]), and instead treated it as a legitimate sociological phenomenon with which it is necessary to come to terms.

But it is easier to identify problems like this than to come up with solutions. Obtaining the means for promoting egalitarianism is harder to do than to wish for. If Marxists have had a tendency to promote industrialism as the wave of the future they may have done so because industrialization has tended to have the desired egalitarian effect in the United States and Europe (not to mention Japan), contrary to Marxists' claims. But, on the other hand, it has also generated massive environmental problems.

When we look at East Africa as a whole, we can see a strange isomorphism (probably accidental) between modern national governments and the general social conditions that characterized these areas in the past. Tanzania, in general, was a country of petty states and there seems to be a tendency now for this country, whose resources are still poor, to create a petty bureaucratic system (Rigby 1977) of patrons and clients. Burundi, on the other hand, along with Rwanda and Uganda, had the most highly centralized despotic systems in the recent past and today they still tend to be ruled by despots on the order of Idi Amin Dada. Kenya was the most stateless of these areas, along with Somalia, and today Kenya is the most capitalistic, free swinging of the states. As for Somalia, Lewis (1973, 352) makes a case for believing that its statehood is a façade behind which a traditional Somali stateless system operates. The southern Sudan was also an area rich in egalitarian societies whose friction with the northern dominant rulers may stem from that fact. And in Ethiopia we have seen in recent years a highly despotic indigenous kingdom replaced by a highly despotic military system.

CONCLUSION

The lesson for development in all of this seems clear. In the first place, promoting nonrevitalistic egalitarianism must be seen as only one of two possible directions that can be taken by East African nations seeking to gain a foothold in the world system. Insofar as it is obtainable, it is probably a goal desired by everybody. But it is not inevitably obtainable, in which case there must be recognition of the fact that hierarchy, based on patronage, is not altogether evil; it may in fact be unavoidable (Gamer 1976).

A second lesson is that, whichever type of system evolves from the economic facts of life, attempts to control and manage the system must draw upon the lessons we have learned from the study of revitalization processes. We must be aware that to some extent the kinds of relations which people develop—egalitarian or hierarchical—must be generated out of freedom to act, to exchange and make commitments. Insofar as these people see the possibility of making such arrangements and regard the ability to do so as their right, interference with them will generate the very kind of frustration required to launch revitalization phenomena, with all the irrationality and turmoil which characterize them.

Bibliography

The following bibliography contains all the sources cited in the text. In addition, for those who would like to explore more deeply aspects of East African societies that are not covered in the book, I have included a selection of other important books and articles. Where applicable, when the society or societies to which the piece refers is not obvious from the title, this information is placed in brackets.

Abrahams, R. G.
  1967 The Peoples of Greater Unyamwezi, Tanzania [Nyamwezi, Sukuma, Kimbu, Konongo]. International African Institute, London.
  1967 The Political Organization of Unyamwezi. Cambridge Univ. Press.
Adams, R. N.
  1975 Energy and Structure. Univ. of Texas Press, Austin.
  1976 Commentary, Reviews in Anthropology, 3, 700–701.
Aldington, T. J. and F. A. Wilson
  1968 The Marketing of Beef in Kenya. Institute of Development Studies, Univ. College of Nairobi, Occasional Papers No. 3, Sept.
Allan, W.
  1965 The African Husbandmen. Barnes and Noble, New York.
Almagor, U.
  1978 Pastoral Partners: Affinity and Bond Partnership among Dassanetch of South-West Ethiopia.
Alnaes, K.
  1969 Songs of the Rwenzururu Rebellion [Toro]. In Gulliver 1969a.
Alpers, E.
  1973 Rethinking African Economic History. Ufahamu, 3, 97–130.
Arens, W.
  1975 The Waswahili: The Social History of an Ethnic Group. Africa, 45, 426–437.

266 Bibliography

Assad, T.
  1966 The Kababish Arabs; Power, Authority and Control in a Nomadic Tribe. Hurst, London.
Baker, R.
  1977 Polarisation: Stages in the Environmental Impact of Alien
Ideas on a Semi-Pastoral Society [Karamojong]. In P. O'Keefe
and B. Wisner, Land Use and Development. International
African Institute, London.
Barnes, R. H.
  1976 Dispersed Alliance and the Prohibition of Marriage: Reconsideration of McKinley's Explanation of Crow–Omaha Terminologies. Man, II (n.s.), 384–399.
Barth, F.
  1967 On the Study of Social Change. American Anthropologist 69,
661–669.
  1973 A General Perspective on Nomad–Sedentary Relations in the
Middle East. In C. Nelson (ed.), The Desert and the Sown.
Univ. of California Press, Berkeley.
Bates, D. G. and S. H. Lee
  1977 The Role of Exchange in Production Specialization. American Anthropologist, 79, 824–841.
Baxter, P. T. W.
  1972 Absence Makes the Heart Grow Fonder. In M. Gluckman,
Allocation of Responsibility. Manchester Univ. Press.
  1975 Some Consequences of Sedentarization for Social Relationships [Borana Galla]. In T. Monod (ed.), Pastoralism in
Tropical Africa. Oxford Univ. Press.
Baxter, P. T. W. and U. Almagor (eds.)
  1978 Age Generation and Time: Some features of East African
Age Organizations. Hurst, London.
Beachey, R. W.
  1967 The East African Ivory Trade in the Nineteenth Century. J.
of African History, VIII, No. 3.
Beattie, J.
  1960 Bunyoro, An African Kingdom. Holt, Rinehart, New York.
  1971 The Nyoro State. Oxford Univ. Press.
Beidelman, T. O.
  1961 Right and Left Hand Among the Kaguru: A Note on Symbolic Classification. Africa, Vol. XXXI, 250–257.
  1967 The Matrilineal Peoples of Eastern Tanzania. International
African Institute, London.

1971   The Kaguru, A Matrilineal People of East Africa. Holt, Rinehart & Winston, New York.

Bernardi, B.
1959   The Mugwe, A Failing Prophet [Meru]. Oxford Univ. Press.

Blue, R. N. and J. H. Weaver
1977   A Critical Assessment of the Tanzanian Model of Development. Agricultural Development Council, New York, No. 30, July.

Boserup, E.
1965   The Conditions of Agricultural Growth. Aldine, Chicago.

Boulding, K.
1973   The Economy of Love and Fear. Wadsworth, Belmont, Calif.

Box, T. W.
1971   Nomadism and Land Use in Somalia. Economic Development and Culture Change, 19, 222–228.

Burton, R.
1893   A Mission to Gelele, King of Dahomey. Vol. I. Tyson and Edwards, London.

Butt, A.
1952   The Nilotes of the Anglo-Egyptian Sudan and Uganda [Nuer, Dinka, Acholi, Luo of Kenya, Shilluk, Lango, Burun, Alur]. International African Institute, London.

Buxton, J.
1963   Chiefs and Strangers; A Study of Political Institutions among the Mandari. Clarendon Press, Oxford.
1973   Religion and Healing in Mandari. Clarendon Press, Oxford.
1977   Greener Pastures for Nomads [Somali]. Financial Times, April 19, 12.

Cancian, F.
1976   Social Stratification. Annual Review of Anthropology, 5, 227–248.

Caplan, A. P.
1975   Choice and Constraint in a Swahili Community. Oxford Univ. Press.

Carsten, M.
1974   Change and Development in East African Cattle Husbandry. Akademisk Forlag, Copenhagen.

Cerrulli, E.
1956   Peoples of South-West Ethiopia and its Borderland [Ingassana-Mao, Suri-Surma-Mekan, Burji-Konso, Didinga-Longarim-Murle, Gimira-Maji, Ometo, Sidamo-Darasa-Kambatta].

International African Institute, London.

Champion, A. M.
1967 The Agiryama of Kenya. Occasional Paper No. 25, Royal Anthropological Institute, London.

Clark, J. D.
1970 The Prehistory of East Africa. Praeger, New York.

Clarke, P. H. C.
1960 A Short History of Tanganyika. Longmans, Nairobi.

Clastres, H.
1977 Society Against the State. Urizen Books, New York.

Codere, H.
1973 The Biography of an African Society, Rwanda, 1900–1960. Musée Royale de l'Afrique Centrale, Tervuren.

Cohen, D. W.
1972 The Historical Tradition of Busoga, Mukama and Kintu. Clarendon Press, Oxford.
c1972 Wumunafu's Bunafu: A Study of Authority in a Nineteenth-Century African Community. Princeton Univ. Press.

Coppens, Y. et al.
1976 Earliest Man and Environments in the Lake Rudolf Basin. Univ. of Chicago Press.

Crazzolara, J. P.
1950 The Lwoo, Part I: Lwoo Migrations. Instituto Missioni Africane, Verona.

Cunnison, I.
1966 Bagarra Arabs. Clarendon Press, Oxford.

Curley, P.
1973 Elders, Shades and Women: Ceremonial Change in Lango, Uganda. Univ. of California Press, Berkeley.

Dahl, G. and A. Hjort
1976 Having Herds: Pastoral Herd Growth and Household Economy. Stockholm Studies in Social Anthropology 2, Department of Social Anthropology, Univ. of Stockholm.

Daniels, R. E.
1975 Pastoralists with Plows: Cultural Continuities Among the Kipsigis of Kenya. Paper presented at the 74th annual meeting of the American Anthropological Association, San Francisco.

Davidson, B.
1969 A History of East and Central Africa to the Late 19th Century. Doubleday, Garden City, New York.

Davis, R. K.
1971 Some Issues in the Evolution, Organization and Operation of Group Ranches in Kenya. East African J. of Rural Development, Vol. 4.

Dawkins, R.
1976 The Selfish Gene. Oxford Univ. Press, New York.

D'Hertefelt, M.
1965 The Rwanda of Rwanda. In J. L. Gibbs (ed.), Peoples of Africa. Holt, Rinehart & Winston, New York.

D'Hertefelt, M., A. Trouwborst, and J. Scherer
1962 Les Anciens Royaumes de la Zone Interlacustre Méridionale [Rwanda, Burundi, Buha]. International African Institute, London.

De Heusch, L.
1966 Le Rwanda et la Civilisation Interlacustre. Université Libre, Brussels.

Delange, J.
1967 The Art and Peoples of Black Africa. Dutton Paperback.

Deng, F. M.
1972 The Dinka of the Sudan. Holt, Rinehart & Winston, New York.

Deshler, W.
1960 Livestock Trypanosomiasis and Human Settlement in Northeastern Uganda. Geographical Review, 50, 541–554.

DeWolfe, J.
1977 Differentiation and Integration in West Kenya [Bukusu of Abaluyia]. Mouton, The Hague.

Donham, D. L.
1977 A Field Theory of Household Production [Malle, southwest Ethiopia]. Paper delivered at annual meeting of American Anthropological Association, Houston.

Doornbas, M. R. and M. F. Lofchie
1971 Ranching and Scheming: A Case Study of the Ankole Ranching Scheme. In M. T. Lofchie (ed.), The State of the Nations: Constraints on Development in Independent Africa. Univ. of California Press, Berkeley.

Douglas, M.
1964 Matriliny and Pawnship in Central Africa. Africa, 34, 301–313.

Driberg, J. H.
1929 The Savage as He Really Is. Routledge, London.

Dumont, L.
1970 Homo Hierarchicus. Weidenfeld & Nicolson, London.
1977 From Mandeville to Marx. Univ. of Chicago Press.
Dunbar, A. R.
1965 A History of Bunyoro-Kitara. Oxford Univ. Press.
Dyson-Hudson, N.
1966 Karimojong Politics. Clarendon Press, Oxford.
Eggan, F.
1955 The Cheyenne and Arapaho Kinship Systems. In Eggan (ed.), Social Anthropology of the North American Tribes. Univ. of Chicago Press.
Ehret, C.
1967 Cattle-Keeping and Milking in Eastern and Southern African History: The Linguistic Evidence. J. of African History, VIII, 1–17.
1971 Southern Nilotic History: Linguistic Approaches to the Study of the Past. Northwestern Univ. Press, Evanston.
1977 Ethiopians and East Africans. East African Pub. House, Nairobi.
Einzig, P.
1966 Primitive Money (2nd ed.). Pergamon Press, New York.
Elam, Y.
1973 The Social and Sexual Roles of Hima Women [Ankole]. Manchester Univ. Press.
Evans-Pritchard, E. E.
1940 The Nuer. Oxford Univ. Press.
1940 The Political System of the Anuak of the Anglo-Egyptian Sudan. London School of Economics.
1948 The Divine Kingship of the Shilluk of the Nilotic Sudan. Cambridge Univ. Press.
1951 Kinship and Marriage among the Nuer. Oxford Univ. Press.
1956 Nuer Religion. Oxford Univ. Press.
Fallers, L. A.
1964 The King's Men [Baganda]. Oxford Univ. Press.
1965 Bantu Bureaucracy [Basoga]. Univ. of Chicago Press.
Fallers, M. C.
1960 The Eastern Lacustrine Bantu [Ganda, Soga]. International African Institute, London.
Feierman, S.
1974 The Shambaa Kingdom. Univ. of Wisconsin Press, Madison.

Feldman, D.
1969   The Economics of Ideology: Some Problems of Achieving Rural Socialism in Tanzania. *In* Colin Ley, Politics and Change in Developing Countries. Cambridge Univ. Press.

Forde, D.
1954   African Worlds, Studies in the Cosmological Ideas and Social Values of African People [Nuer, Abaluyia, Shilluk, Rwanda]. Oxford Univ. Press.

Forde, D. and G. Dieterlen
1965   African Systems of Thought [Sonjo, Borana Galla, Ankole]. Oxford Univ. Press.

Fosbrooke, H. A.
1948   An Administrative Survey of the Masai Social System. Tanganyika Notes and Records, 26, Dec., 1–50.

Fox, R.
1967   Kinship and Marriage. Penguin, Baltimore.

Friedman, J.
1975   Tribe, State and Transformations. *In* M. Bloch (ed.), Marxist Analysis and Social Anthropology. John Wiley and Sons, New York.

Friedman, M.
1962   Capitalism and Freedom. Univ. of Chicago Press.

Friedrich, K.-H.
1968   Coffee–Banana Holdings in Bukoba [Haya]. *In* H. Ruthenberg 1968.

Gamer, R. E.
1976   The Developing Nations. Allyn and Bacon, Boston.

Girling, F. K.
1960   The Acholi of Uganda. Her Majesty's Stationery Office, London.

Glück, J. F.
1973   African Architecture. *In* E. P. Skinner (ed.), Peoples and Cultures of Africa. Doubleday, Garden City, New York.

Gluckman, M.
1971   Marriage Payments and Social Structure Among the Lozi and Zulu. *In* J. Goody (ed.), Kinship. Penguin, Baltimore.

Goldschmidt, W.
1967   Sebei Law. Univ. of California Press, Berkeley.
1969   Kambuya's Cattle [Sebei]. Univ. of California Press, Berkeley.

1972 The Operations of a Sebei Capitalist: A Contribution to Economic Anthropology. Ethnology 11, 187–201.

1976 Culture and Behavior of the Sebei. Univ. of California Press, Berkeley.

Goody, J.

1969 Economy and Feudalism in Africa. Economic History Review 22: 393–405.

1970 Cousin Terms. Southwestern J. of Anthropology, 26, 125–142.

1973 Bridewealth and Dowry in Africa and Eurasia. In J. Goody and S. J. Tambiah, Bridewealth and Dowry. Cambridge Univ. Press.

Gravel, P.

1968 Reniera [Rwanda]. Mouton, The Hague.

Gray, R. F.

n.d. The Mbugwe (MS).

1955 The Mbugwe Tribe: Origin and Development. Tanganyika Notes and Records, no. 38.

1963 The Sonjo of Tanganyika. Oxford Univ. Press.

Griffiths, J. F.

1969 Climate. In W. T. W. Morgan 1969.

Gulliver, P. H.

1951 A Preliminary Survey of the Turkana. Univ. of Cape Town.

1955 The Family Herds, A Study of Two Pastoral Tribes in East Africa, the Jie and Turkana. Routledge & Kegan Paul, London.

1963 Social Control in an African Society [Arusha]. New York Univ. Press.

1968 Age Differentiation. International Encyclopedia of the Social Sciences, 1, 157–162.

1969a Tradition and Transition in East Africa. Univ. of California Press, Berkeley.

1969b The Conservative Commitment in Northern Tanzania: The Arusha and Masai. In Gulliver 1969a.

Gulliver, P. and P. H. Gulliver

1953 The Central Nilo-Hamites [Central Eastern Nilotes: Teso, Kumam, Karamojong, Jie, Dodos, Turkana, Toposa, Donyiro, Jiye, Labwor, Tepes, Nyiakwai, Ngiangeya, Napore, Teuso]. International African Institute, London.

Halland, G.

1977 Pastoral Systems of Production: The Socio-Cultural Context and Some Economic and Ecological Implications. *In* P. O'Keefe and B. Wisner (eds.), Land Use and Development. International African Institute, London.

Hallpike, C. R.
1972   The Konso of Ethiopia. Clarendon Press, Oxford.

Hammersley, A.
1969   Agriculture and Land Tenure in Tanzania. *In* W. T. W. Morgan 1969.

Harris, A.
1958   The Social Organization of the Wataita. Ph.D. dissertation, Cambridge Univ.

Harris, G.
1955   The Ritual System of the Wataita. Ph.D. dissertation, Cambridge Univ.
1962   Taita Bridewealth and Affinal Relationships. *In* M. Fortes (ed.), Marriage in Tribal Societies. Cambridge Univ. Press.

Hartwig, G. W.
1976   The Art of Survival in East Africa: The Kerebe and Long-distance Trade. Africana Publishing Co., New York.

Hedlund, G. B.
1971   The Impact of Group Ranches on a Pastoral Society [Maasai]. Institute for Development Studies, Univ. of Nairobi, Staff Paper 100, June.

Herskovits, M. J.
1926   The Cattle Complex in East Africa. American Anthropologist, Vol. 28, 230-272, 361-388, 494-528, 633-664.

Heyer, J.
1966   Preliminary Results of a Linear Programming Analysis of Peasant Farms in Machakos District, Kenya [Kamba]. East African Institute for Social Research, Conference Paper, Kampala.
1971   A Linear Programming Analysis of Constraints on Peasant Farms in Kenya [Kamba]. Food Research Institute Studies 10 (1), Stanford Univ.

Hill, P.
1972   Rural Hausa. Cambridge Univ. Press.

Hjort, A.
1976   Kenya. *In* A. Rapp, H. LeHóverou, and B. Lundholms (eds.) Can Desert Encroachment be Stopped. NFK, Stockholm.

Hopkins, A.
1973 An Economic History of West Africa. Columbia Univ. Press, New York.

Horowitz, M. M.
1975 Herdsmen and Husbandmen in Niger: Values and Strategies. *In* T. Monod (ed.), Pastoralism in Tropical Africa. Oxford Univ. Press.

Huntingford, G. W. B.
1950 East African Background (second edition). Longmans, London.
1953a The Southern Nilo-Hamites [Nandi, Kipsigis, Dorobo, Elgeyo, Pokot, Barabaig, Iraqw]. International African Institute, London.
1953b The Northern Nilo-Hamites [Bari, Luluba–Lokoyo, Lotuko]. International African Institute, London.
1953 The Nandi of Kenya. Routledge & Kegan Paul, London.
1955 The Galla of Ethiopia; The Kingdom of Kafa and Janjero. International African Institute, London.

Huxley, E.
1949 The Sorcerer's Apprentice. Chatto and Windus, London.

Hyde, R. J. and B. W. Langlands
1974 Patterns of Food Crop Production and Nutrition in Uganda. Department of Geography, Occasional Papers, No. 58, Makerere College, Kampala.

Jacobs, A.
1965 The Traditional Political Organization of the Pastoral Masai. Ph.D. dissertation, Oxford Univ.

Jahnke, H. E.
1974 The Economics of Controlling Tsetse Flies and Cattle Trypanosomiasis in Africa. Institut für Wirtschaftsforschung, Weltforum Verlag, Munich.

Jellicoe, M.
1969 The Turu Resistance Movement. Tanzania Notes and Records.

Johnston, B. F.
1958 The Staple Food Economies of Western Tropical Africa. Stanford Univ. Press, Palo Alto, Calif.

Karp, I.
1978 Fields of Change Among the Iteso of Kenya. Routledge & Kegan Paul, London.

Katate, A. G. and L. Kamugungunu
1977 The Kings of Ankole. East African Literature Bureau, Nairobi.

Katoke, I.
1977   Karagwe Kingdom. East African Publishing House, Nairobi.
Kenyatta, J.
1962   Facing Mt. Kenya [Kikuyu]. Vintage, New York.
Kesby, J.
n.d.   The Rangi (MS).
Kettel, D.
1975   Passing Like Flowers: The Marriage Regulations of the Tugen of Kenya. Univ. Microfilms, Ann Arbor.
Kimambo, I. N.
1969   A Political History of the Pare of Tanzania, c1500–1900. East African Publishing House, Nairobi.
Kimambo, I. N. and A. J. Temu
1977   A History of Tanzania. East African Publishing House, Nairobi.
Kiwanuka, M. S. M.
1971   The Kings of Buganda. East African Publishing House, Nairobi.
Klima, G.
1970   The Barabaig, East African Cattle Herders. Holt, Rinehart & Winston, New York.
Knight, C. G.
1974   Ecology and Change. Academic Press, New York.
Konczacki, Z. A.
1967   Nomadism and Economic Development [Somali]. Canadian J. of African Studies, 63.
La Fontaine, J. S.
1958   The Gisu of Uganda. International African Institute, London.
Lambert, H.
1956   Kikuyu Social and Political Institutions. Oxford Univ. Press.
Lambrecht, F. L.
1964   Aspects of Evolution and Ecology of Tsetse Flies and Trypanosomiasis in Prehistoric African Environment. J. of African History, V., No. 1, 1–23.
Lamphear, J.
1976   The Traditional History of the Jie of Uganda. Oxford Univ. Press.
Laughlin, C. D., Jr.
1972   Economics and Social Organization among the So of North Eastern Uganda. Ph.D. dissertation, Univ. of Oregon.
Laughton, W. H.
1944   The Meru. East African Publishing House, Nairobi.

Leach, E. R.
  1960 The Sinhalese of the Dry Zone of Northern Ceylon. *In* G. P. Murdock, Social Structure in Southeast Asia. Tavistock, London.
  1965 Political Systems of Highland Burma. Beacon Press, Boston (first published 1954).
Leakey, L. S. B.
  1977 The Southern Kikuyu before 1903. Vol. I. Academic Press, London.
Lee, R.
  1969 !Kung Bushman Subsistence: An Input-Output Analysis. *In* D. Damas (ed.), Contributions to Anthropology: Ecological Essays. Queen's Printer, Ottawa.
Legesse, A.
  1973 Gada: Three Approaches to the Study of African Society [Borana Galla]. Free Press, New York.
Lemarchand, R.
  1966 Power and Stratification in Rwanda: A Reconsideration. Cahiers d'Etudes Africaines, 6, 592–610.
Levine, D. N.
  1965 Wax and Gold [Amhara]. Univ. of Chicago Press.
LeVine, R.
  1962 Wealth and Power in Gusiiland. *In* P. Bohannan and G. Dalton, Markets in Africa. Northwestern Univ. Press, Evanston.
Lévi-Strauss, C.
  1963 Structural Anthropology (translated from French, originally published 1958). Basic Books, New York.
  1969 The Elementary Structures of Kinship (translated from French, originally published 1967). Eyre and Spottiswood, London.
Lewis, B. A.
  1972 The Murle. Clarendon Press, Oxford.
Lewis, H.
  1965 A Galla Monarchy [Jimma]. Univ. of Wisconsin Press, Madison.
  1974 Leaders and Followers. Addison-Wesley Module in Anthropology No. 50.
Lewis, I. M.
  1955 People of the Horn of Africa, Somali, Afar and Saho. International African Institute, London.
  1961 A Pastoral Democracy, A Study of Pastoralism and Politics

among the Northern Somali of the Horn of Africa. Oxford Univ. Press.

1973 Modern Political Movements in Somaliland. *In* C. Turnbull, Africa and Change. Knopf, New York.

1975 The Dynamics of Nomadism; Prospects for Sedentarization and Social Change [Somali]. *In* T. Monod, Pastoralism in Tropical Africa. Oxford Univ. Press.

Lienhardt, G.
1961 Divinity and Experience: The Religion of the Dinka. Clarendon Press, Oxford.

Little, P.
1978 The Plantain in East Africa: An Exchange Theory Approach to the Political History of East Africa's Plantain Societies. Presented at annual meeting of the Central States Anthropological Association, Univ. of Notre Dame, March.

Mair, L.
1962 Primitive Government: A Study of Traditional Political Systems in Eastern Africa. Rev. ed., 1977, Indiana Univ. Press, Bloomington.

Malcolm, D. W.
1953 Sukumaland. Oxford Univ. Press.

Maquet, J.
1954 The Kingdom of Ruanda. *In* D. Forde 1954.
1961 The Premise of Inequality in Ruanda. Oxford Univ. Press.
1962 Objectivity in Anthropology. Current Anthropology, 5, 47–56.
1971 Power and Society in Africa. World Univ. Library, London.
1972 Civilizations of Black Africa. Oxford Univ. Press.

Massell, B.
1963 Econometric Variations on a Theme by Schneider [Turu]. Economic Development and Culture Change, XII, 34–41.

Massing, A.
1977 Economic Development in the Kru Culture Area. Ph.D. dissertation, Indiana Univ.

Mauss, M.
1954 The Gift. Free Press, New York.

Mayer, P.
1950 Gusii Bridewealth Law and Custom. Oxford Univ. Press, New York.

Merriam, A. P.
1978 Traditional Music of Black Africa. *In* P. Martin and P. O'Meara (eds.), Africa. Indiana Univ. Press, Bloomington.

Meyn, K.
1970   Beef Production in East Africa. Institut für Wirtschaftsfor-
        schung, Weltforum Verlag, Munich.
Middleton, J.
1960   Lugbara Religion. Oxford Univ. Press.
1965   The Lugbara of Uganda. Holt, Rinehart & Winston, New
        York.
Middleton, J. and G. Kershaw
1965   The Central Tribes of the North-Eastern Bantu [the Kikuyu
        including Embu, Meru, Mbere, Chuka, Mwimbi, Tharaka,
        and the Kamba of Kenya]. International African Institute,
        London.
Middleton, J. and D. Tait
1958   Tribes Without Rulers [Mandari, Dinka, Bwamba, Lugbara].
        Routledge & Kegan Paul, London.
Middleton, J. and E. H. Winter
1963   Witchcraft and Sorcery in East Africa [Nyoro, Kaguru, Man-
        dari, Mbugwe, Nandi, Gisu, Gusii, Lugbara, Amba]. Rout-
        ledge & Kegan Paul, London.
Miracle, M.
1967   Agriculture in the Congo Basin. Univ. of Wisconsin Press,
        Madison.
Moore, S. F. and P. Puritt (eds.)
1977   The Chagga and Meru of Tanzania. International African
        Institute, London.
Morgan, W. T. W.
1969   East Africa: Its People and Resources. Oxford Univ. Press,
        Nairobi.
Murdock, G. P.
1949   Social Structure. Macmillan, Inc., New York.
1959   Africa, Its People and Their Culture History. McGraw-Hill,
        New York.
1967   Ethnographic Atlas: A Summary. Ethnology, VI, 236pp.
Muriuki, G.
1974   A History of the Kikuyu 1500–1900. Oxford Univ. Press,
        Nairobi.
Muthiani, J.
1973   Akamba from Within. Exposition Press, New York.
Mwaniki, H. S. K.
1973   The Living History of Embu and Mbeere. East African Lit-
        erature Bureau, Nairobi.

Nadel, S. F.
  1947   The Nuba. Oxford Univ. Press.
Ndeti, K.
  1972   Elements of Akamba Life. East African Publishing House, Nairobi.
Needham, R.
  1960   The Left Hand of the Mugwe: An Analytical Note on the Structure of Meru Symbolism. Africa, Vol. 30, 20–33.
  1962   Structure and Sentiment. Univ. of Chicago Press.
Newman, J. L.
  1970   The Ecological Basis for Subsistence Change among the Sandawe of Tanzania. National Academy of Science, Washington, D.C.
Nyakatura, J. W.
  1973   Anatomy of an African Kingdom [Nyoro]. Anchor Books, New York.
Oberg, K.
  1940   The Kingdom of Ankole in Uganda. *In* M. Fortes and E. E. Evans-Pritchard, African Political Systems. Oxford Univ. Press.
Ocholla-Ayayo, A. B. C.
  1976   Traditional Ideology and Ethics among the Southern Luo. Scandinavian Institute of African Studies, Uppsala.
O'Conner, A.M.
  1966   An Economic Geography of East Africa. Praeger, New York.
Ogot, B. A.
  1967   History of the Southern Luo. East African Publishing House, Nairobi.
  1967   The Impact of the Nilotes. *In* R. Oliver, The Middle Age of African History. Oxford Univ. Press.
O'Laughlin, B.
  1975   Marxist Approaches in Anthropology. Annual Review of Anthropology, 4, 341–370.
Oliver, R. and A. Atmore
  1967   Africa Since 1800. Cambridge Univ. Press.
Omer-Cooper, J.
  1972   Kingdoms and Villages: A Possible New Perspective in African History. African Social Research, 14, Dec.
Orans, M.
  1966   Surplus. Human Organization, 25, 424–432.

Parkin, D. J.
   1972   Palms, Wine and Witnesses [Giriama]. Chandler Publicity, San Francisco.
Pasternak, B.
   1976   Introduction to Kinship and Social Organization. Prentice-Hall, Englewood Cliffs, N.J.
Payne, W. J. A.
   1970   Cattle Production in the Tropics. Vol. I. Longmans, London.
P'Bitek, O.
   1971   Religion of the Central Luo. East African Literature Bureau, Nairobi.
Peberdy, J. R.
   1969   Rangeland. In W. T. W. Morgan 1969.
Peristiany, J.
   1939   The Social Institutions of the Kipsigis. Routledge, London.
Posnansky, M.
   1969   The Prehistory of East Africa. In B. A. Ogot and J. A. Kiernan 1969.
Pratt, D. J. and M. D. Gwynne (eds.)
   1977   Rangeland Management and Ecology in East Africa. Hodder and Stoughton, London.
Prins, A. H. J.
   1952   The Coastal Tribes of the North-Eastern Bantu [Pokomo, Nyika, Teita]. International African Institute, London.
   1961   The Swahili-Speaking Peoples of Zanzibar and the East African Coast [Arabs, Shirazi, Swahili]. International African Institute, London.
Radcliffe-Brown, A. R.
   1924   The Mother's Brother in South Africa. South African Journal of Science, XXI, 542–555. Republished in Radcliffe-Brown 1952.
   1940   On Joking Relationship. Africa, XIII, 195–210. Republished in Radcliffe-Brown 1952.
   1941   The Study of Kinship. J. of the Royal Anthropological Institute. Republished in Radcliffe-Brown 1952.
   1952   Structure and Function in Primitive Society. Free Press, Glencoe.
Radcliffe-Brown, A. R. and D. Forde
   1950   African Systems of Kinship and Marriage. Oxford Univ. Press.
Rapp, A.
   1976   Sudan. Ecological Bulletin, Stockholm, 24, Chap. 8.5, 156–164.

Raum, O. F.
1940 Chagga Childhood. Oxford Univ. Press.
Reche, O.
1914 Zur Ethnographie des abflusslosen Gebiets [Turu, Iramba, etc.]. Hamburg Institute, Hamburg.
Reining, P.
1967 The Haya. The Agrarian System of a Sedentary People. Ph.D. dissertation, Univ. of Chicago.
1972 Haya Kinship Terminology: An Explanation and Some Comparisons. *In* P. Reining (ed.), Kinship Studies in the Morgan Centennial Year. Anthropological Society of Washington, Washington, D.C.
Richards, A. I.
1940 The Political System of the Bemba Tribe—North-Eastern Rhodesia. *In* M. Fortes and E. E. Evans-Pritchard, African Political Systems. Oxford Univ. Press.
Richards, A. I. (ed.)
1959 East African Chiefs [Ganda, Soga, Nyoro, Toro, Nyankole, Haya, Zinza, Ha, Sukuma, Gisu, Kiga, Alur, Lugbara]. Praeger, New York.
Rigby, P.
1966 Dual Symbolic Classification Among the Gogo of Central Tanzania. Africa, XXXVI, 1–17.
1968 Pastoralism and Prejudice: Ideology and Rural Development in East Africa. Nkanga, 4, Makerere Institute of Social Research.
1969 Cattle and Kinship Among the Gogo. Cornell Univ. Press, Ithaca.
1977 Local Participation in National Politics: Ugogo, Tanzania. Africa, 47, 1, 89–107.
Roscoe, J.
1911 The Baganda. An Account of Their Nature, Customs and Beliefs. Macmillan, London.
1915 The Northeastern Bantu. Cambridge Univ. Press.
Rounce, N. V.
1949 The Agriculture of the Cultivation Steppe. Longmans, Cape Town.
Ruthenberg, H.
1968 Smallholder Farming and Smallholder Development in Tanzania. Weltforum Verlag, Munich.
Saberwal, S.
1972 Embu of Kenya, Hraflex Books, New Haven.

282   Bibliography

Sahlins, M.
  1963   Poor Man, Rich Man, Big Man, Chief; Political Types in
         Melanesia and Polynesia. Comparative Studies in Society and
         History. 5, 285–303.
  1968   Tribesmen. Prentice-Hall; Englewood Cliffs, N.J.
  1972   Stone Age Economics. Aldine, Chicago.
Salim, A. I.
  1973   Swahili-Speaking People of Kenya's Coast 1895–1965. East
         African Publishing House, Nairobi.
Salisbury, R.
  1962   From Stone to Steel. Melbourne Univ. Press.
Sangree, W.
  1966   Age, Prayer and Politics in Tiriki, Kenya. Oxford Univ. Press.
Särbo, G. M.
  1977   Nomads on the Scheme—A Study of Irrigation Agriculture
         and Pastoralism in Eastern Sudan [Shukriya]. In P. O'Keefe
         and B. Wisner, Land Use and Development. International
         African Institute, London.
Scherer, J. H.
  1965   Marriage and Bride-Wealth in the Highlands of Buha [Tan-
         ganyika]. V. R. B. Kleine, Gronningen, Holland.
Schneider, H. K.
  1953   The Pokot (Suk) of Kenya with Special Reference to the
         Role of Livestock in their Subsistence Economy. Univ. Mi-
         crofilms, Ann Arbor.
  1964a East African Aboriginal Economics. In M. J. Herskovits and
         M. Harwitz, Economic Development in Africa. Northwestern
         Univ. Press, Evanston.
  1964b A Model of African Indigenous Economy and Society. Com-
         parative Studies in Society and History, VII, 37–55.
  1966   Turu Esthetic Concepts. American Anthropologist, 68, 156–
         160.
  1969   A Statistical Study of Brideprice in Africa. Paper delivered
         at annual meeting of American Anthropological Association,
         New Orleans.
  1970   The Wahi Wanyaturu: Economics in an African Society.
         Aldine, Chicago.
  1974   Economic Man. Free Press, New York.
Shack, W. A.
  1966   The Gurage: A People of the Ensete Culture. Oxford Univ.
         Press.

Shorter, A.
 1972   Chiefship in Western Tanzania. Oxford Univ. Press.
 1973   Interlacustrine Chieftainship in Embryo? A Discussion of
         Traditional Political Institutions in Western Tanzania. Tan-
         zania Notes and Records, 72, 37–50.
 1974   East African Societies. Routledge & Kegan Paul, London.
 1977   Nyungu-ya-Mawe. East African Publishing House, Nairobi.
Smith, C. A.
 1976   Exchange Systems and the Spatial Distribution of Elites: The
         Organization of Stratification in Agrarian Societies. *In* C. A.
         Smith (ed.), Regional Analysis Vol. II. Academic Press, New
         York.
Southall, A. W.
 c1953   Alur Society. W. Heffer and Sons, Ltd., London.
 1970   Rank and Stratification Among the Alur and Other Nilotic
         Peoples. *In* A. Tuden and L. Plotnicov, Social Stratification
         in Africa. Free Press, New York.
Southwald, M.
 1965   The Ganda of Uganda. *In* J. L. Gibbs, Jr. (ed.), Peoples of
         Africa. Free Press, New York.
Spencer, P.
 1965   The Samburu. Routledge & Kegan Paul, London.
 1973   Nomads in Alliance: Symbiosis and Growth among the Ren-
         dille and Samburu. Oxford Univ. Press.
 1974   Drought and the Commitment to Growth. African Affairs,
         73, No. 293, 419–427.
Spooner, B.
 1973   The Cultural Ecology of Pastoral Nomads. Addison-Wesley
         Module in Anthropology No. 45.
Stahl, K. M.
 1964   History of the Chagga People of Kilimanjaro. Mouton, The
         Hague.
Stauder, J.
 1971   The Majangir. Cambridge Univ. Press.
Stevenson, R. F.
 1968   Population and Political System in Tropical Africa. Colum-
         bia Univ. Press, New York.
Sündstrom, L.
 1975   The Exchange Economy of Pre-Colonial Africa. St. Martin's
         Press, New York.

284 Bibliography

Sutton, J. E. G.
  1969 The Settlement of East Africa. In Ogot and Kiernan 1969.
  1973 The Archaeology of the Western Highlands of Kenya. British
        Institute in Eastern Africa, Nairobi.
Talbot, L. M.
  1972 Ecological Consequences of Rangeland Development in
        Masailand, East Africa. In M. Farvar and J. Mitton, The
        Careless Technology. Natural History Press, Garden City,
        New York.
Taylor, B. K.
  1962 The Western Lacustrine Bantu [Nyoro, Toro, Nyankore,
        Kiga, Haya, Zinza, Amba, Konja]. International African In-
        stitute, London.
Tempels, P.
  1959 Bantu Philosophy. Présence Africaine, Paris.
Thomas, E. M.
  1965 Warrior Herdsmen [Dodoth]. Random House, New York.
Trigger, B. G.
  1969 The Personality of the Sudan. In D. F. McCall et al. (eds.),
        Eastern African History, Vol. III. Boston Univ., Papers on
        Africa.
Turner, V.
  1969 The Ritual Process. Aldine, Chicago.
Turton, D. and C. Ruggles
  1978 Agreeing to Disagree: On the Measurement of Duration in
        a Southwest Ethiopian Community [Mursi]. Current An-
        thropology, September.
Uchendu, V. C. and K. R. M. Anthony
  1975 Agricultural Change in Teso District, Uganda. East African
        Literature Bureau, Nairobi.
Van Heeken, P. M. and H. U. E. Thoden van Velsen
  1972 Land Scarcity and Rural Inequality in Tanzania. Mouton,
        The Hague.
Vincent, J.
  1971 African Elite: The Big Men of a Small Town [Gondo,
        Uganda]. Columbia Univ. Press, New York.
Von Sick, E.
  1916 Die Waniaturu (Walimi). Baessler-Archiv, 1–42.
Wagner, G.
  1954 The Abaluyia of Kavirondo. In D. Forde 1954.
  1956 The Bantu of North Kavirondo. Oxford Univ. Press.

Were, G. S.
  1967 A History of the Abaluyia of Western Kenya. East African
         Publishing House, Nairobi.
Whisson, M.
  1964 Change and Challenge [Luo]. Christian Council of Kenya.
Willis, R. G.
  1966 The Fipa and Related Peoples of South-West Tanzania and
         North-East Zambia. International African Institute, London.
Wilson, G. M.
  1961 Luo Customary Laws and Marriage Laws, Customs. Govern-
         ment Printer, Nairobi.
Winans, E. V.
  1962 Shambala. Univ. of California Press, Berkeley.
Winter, E.
  1955 Bwamba Economy. East African Institute of Social Research,
         Kampala.
  1956 Bwamba. Heffer, Cambridge.
  1962 Livestock Markets among the Iraqw of Northern Tanganyika.
         In P. Bohannan and G. Dalton, Markets in Africa. North-
         western U. Press, Evanston.
  1966 Territorial Groupings and Religion among the Iraqw. In
         Anthropological Approaches to the Study of Religion. Tavi-
         stock, London.
Wittfogel, K. A.
  1957 Oriental Despotism, A Comparative Study of Total Power.
         Yale Univ. Press, New Haven.
Woodburn, J.
  1970 Hunters and Gatherers: The Material Culture of the No-
         madic Hadza. British Museum, London.
Wrigley, C. C.
  1964 The Changing Economic Structure of Buganda. In L. A. Fal-
         lers 1964.
Young, R. and H. Fosbrooke
  1960 Smoke in the Hills, Political Tension in the Morogoro Dis-
         trict of Tanganyika [Luguru]. Northwestern Univ. Press,
         Evanston.

Index

Abaluyia, 30, 50–51, 96, 257
Abyssinians, 80
Acholi, 31, 98–99, 107, 163, 233
Adams, R., 213–214, 215
Afro-Asiatic peoples, 12, 14–15, 19, 26, 29, 36, 52. *See also* Cushitic peoples
Age organization, 154, 157–158, 164, 182–192, 202, 211
Agricultural Zone, 8, 40, 69, 81, 104
Agriculture, 11, 80–81, 193; crop varieties, 21, 69–72, 76–78, 80; swidden, 73, 76, 80, 84, 104. *See also* Grain, production of
Alliance theory, 123–136, 148
Alur, 2, 31, 147; political organization, 154, 156, 163, 164, 167, 179–180
Amba, 180
Amhara, 36, 39, 52, 165
Ankole, 31, 42, 124, 179, 180; ranching, 249, 251, 252
Anuak, 163, 164
Arabs, 93, 147–148; trade, 36, 96, 98, 165, 172, 232–237, 258
Architecture, 47
Art, 20, 56–59
Arusha (Arush), 64, 96–97, 190, 196, 201, 207, 244–245. *See also* Maasai
Aussa, Sultanate of, 165
Avunculocal residence, 22–23, 24, 114–115

Bachwezi kingdom, 31, 162, 163, 171
Baganda, 5, 45, 177–178, 240. *See also* Buganda
Bagarra, 93, 147–148
Bajun, 111
Bakonjo revolt, 258
Bananas, 29, 30, 37, 39, 64, 69–73, 75, 78, 81, 244, 245; false (ensete), 80; and states, 177–178, 180, 232

Bantu peoples, 12, 14, 29–30, 31, 36, 47, 124, 143, 150, 208, 232; political organization, 23, 156–157, 158–159, 162–163, 164, 166–168, 171, 173, 180; philosophy and religion, 49–50, 52
Barabaig, 5–6, 14, 15, 22, 23, 24, 30, 82, 87, 97, 101
Bari, 58, 206–207
Barley, 80
Barth, F., 105–106, 221–222
Belgian colonial rule, 238, 259
Bemba, 117, 158–159, 193
Bena, 30, 47
Binary classification, 54–56, 255
Boas, F., 2, 15–17
Bodi, 34
Bondei revolt, 258
Boni, 111
Borana Galla, 42, 43, 64, 86, 87, 165; age organization, 157, 184–186, 188–189. *See also* Galla
Boserup, E., 75, 76
Boulding, K., 219–220, 229
Brideprice and bridewealth, 3, 76, 82–83, 98, 102, 104, 116–117, 119–122, 126, 146, 149, 200, 203, 204, 242–243, 244
Brideservice, 193
British colonial policy, 238–239, 241, 243, 251
Buganda, 8, 124, 159, 162–163, 172, 181, 238, 241; political organization, 167, 175, 177, 180; and bananas, 177–178, 180, 232; trade, 233, 236–237. *See also* Baganda
Buha, 179. *See also* Ha
Bungu, 30
Bunyankole, 31, 179. *See also* Ankole
Bunyoro, kingdom of, 2, 8, 31, 34, 159, 175, 233. *See also* Nyoro

286